# The Movement and Technology Balance

*To those who matter most . . . your love, support, and encouragement means everything.*

—Traci Lengel

*For Hannah, who is my answered prayer. Your sweet soul is an example to me. I love you more than you will ever know.*

—Jenna Evans

# The Movement and Technology Balance

## Classroom Strategies
## for Student Success

**Traci Lengel and Jenna Evans**

*Foreword by Eric Jensen*

FOR INFORMATION:

Corwin

A SAGE Company

2455 Teller Road

Thousand Oaks, California 91320

(800) 233-9936

www.corwin.com

SAGE Publications Ltd.

1 Oliver's Yard

55 City Road

London EC1Y 1SP

United Kingdom

SAGE Publications India Pvt. Ltd.

B 1/I 1 Mohan Cooperative Industrial Area

Mathura Road, New Delhi 110 044

India

SAGE Publications Asia-Pacific Pte. Ltd.

18 Cross Street #10-10/11/12

China Square Central

Singapore 048423

Program Director:  Jessica Allan

Content Development Editor:  Lucas Schleicher

Senior Editorial Assistant:  Mia Rodriguez

Production Editor:  Tori Mirsadjadi

Copy Editor:  Erin Livingston

Typesetter:  C&M Digitals (P) Ltd.

Proofreader:  Barbara Coster

Indexer:  Jeanne R. Busemeyer

Cover Designer:  Janet Kiesel

Marketing Manager:  Deena Meyer

Copyright © 2020 by Traci Lengel and Jenna Evans

All rights reserved. Except as permitted by U.S. copyright law, no part of this work may be reproduced or distributed in any form or by any means, or stored in a database or retrieval system, without permission in writing from the publisher.

When forms and sample documents appearing in this work are intended for reproduction, they will be marked as such. Reproduction of their use is authorized for educational use by educators, local school sites, and/or noncommercial or nonprofit entities that have purchased the book.

All third-party trademarks referenced or depicted herein are included solely for the purpose of illustration and are the property of their respective owners. Reference to these trademarks in no way indicates any relationship with, or endorsement by, the trademark owner.

Printed in the United States of America

Library of Congress Cataloging-in-Publication Data

Names: Lengel, Traci, author. | Evans, Jenna, author.

Title: The movement and technology balance : classroom strategies for student success / Traci Lengel and Jenna Evans.

Description: Thousand Oaks, California : Corwin, [2019] | Includes bibliographical references.

Identifiers: LCCN 2019004502 | ISBN 9781544350431 (pbk. : alk. paper)

Subjects: LCSH: Movement education. | Education—Effect of technological innovations on. | Academic achievement.

Classification: LCC GV452 .L463 2019 | DDC 372.86/8—dc23

LC record available at https://lccn.loc.gov/2019004502

This book is printed on acid-free paper.

Certified Chain of Custody
Promoting Sustainable Forestry
www.sfiprogram.org
SFI-01268

SFI label applies to text stock

19 20 21 22 23 10 9 8 7 6 5 4 3 2 1

DISCLAIMER: This book may direct you to access third-party content via web links, QR codes, or other scannable technologies, which are provided for your reference by the author(s). Corwin makes no guarantee that such third-party content will be available for your use and encourages you to review the terms and conditions of such third-party content. Corwin takes no responsibility and assumes no liability for your use of any third-party content, nor does Corwin approve, sponsor, endorse, verify, or certify such third-party content.

# CONTENTS

# FOREWORD

Have you struggled with the misuse or overuse of technology in your classroom? Have you wrestled with your students' lack of movement and engagement? If so, you may have a solution in your hands right now.

As an evidence-based author, I have written over 30 books on student learning, and the majority of them share this message at least once: "Get students engaged! Move their bodies!" But how do you actually do that while at the same time teaching students who seem to like their devices more than movement, their peers, and even themselves?

The answer: Listen to these pros. The authors of *The Movement and Technology Balance* have artfully crafted the *what*, *how*, and *why* in each chapter. That's what I love most about this book: While you can feel the enthusiasm of the authors, the *why* you might care and the *how* to take action are clearly evident in every chapter.

Traci and Jenna thoughtfully walk you through the most commonly held assumptions about technology. You'll get deep, personal questions and practical suggestions that will save you from one to three hours a day. That's the kind of real-world impact I like!

Just as importantly, you'll get movement strategies, mindsets, and tools that you can use with little or no practice. You'll also discover the evidence that blows away every single excuse *not* to incorporate daily movement with your students.

Reading this book is vital. It's more than just research and practical applications. It is your resource for rethinking sloppy habits, making better curriculum and engagement decisions, and becoming a far better educator.

We all know that technology is not going away. We also know that physical activity is more than a good idea; it is a core part of health, brain function, and vitality. If you've ever wondered, "How on earth am I ever going to do my job, juggling engagement with technology?" the solution is between these pages. Jump in and start reading!

Eric Jensen, PhD

Educational consultant and author of the bestselling books
*Brain-Based Learning, Teaching with the Brain in Mind* and
*Poor Students, Rich Teaching*

# ACKNOWLEDGMENTS

## A Sincere Thank You to the Following People

Jessica Allan for believing in us right from the beginning. We can't thank you enough!

Eric Jensen for his positive energy and professional leadership and for writing the foreword.

Rose Minniti, Mike Kuczala, and Jean Blaydes Moize for their professionalism, support, and encouragement.

Mia Rodriguez and Lucas Schleicher for creating a welcoming "team approach."

All the supporters of ActivEDge.

Ed Pinney and the Kidsfit team for believing in us and helping us to grow.

Our loving families for their endless support, dedication, and commitment.

Our dear friends for their never-ending encouragement and loyalty.

Nicole Januik, Kristen Spratford, Sarah Young, Melissa Lavell, Amy Crowe, and Mindi Andreski for always cheering us on.

Mike Kuczala for allowing us to incorporate some teaching activities from *The Kinesthetic Classroom*.

Tara Murphy and Dorca Serrano for their editing and feedback.

Our spirited elementary students, who have helped to shape, develop, and strengthen our teaching philosophies.

Our innovative colleagues for their brilliance, talents, and collaboration.

Our open-minded graduate/undergraduate students who share their strengths and experiences while pushing themselves to grow and improve.

## Publisher's Acknowledgments

Corwin gratefully acknowledges the contributions of the following reviewers:

Gayla LeMay
Teacher
Waycross Middle School
Waycross, GA

Dr. Debbie Smith
Elementary Numeracy Coach
Beaufort Elementary
Beaufort, SC

Denise Traniello
High School Teacher
O'Bryant School of Math & Science
Boston, MA

# ABOUT THE AUTHORS

**Traci Lengel** is a health and physical education teacher in the Pocono Mountain school district. With more than twenty-six years of experience, Traci's knowledge in movement education, kinesthetic furniture, motor development, lifelong fitness/wellness, health education, movement/technology balance, curriculum design, and educational/content publication has contributed to the success of her insightful programs and consultations. Additionally, Traci is an adjunct professor at La Salle University in Pennsylvania and The College of New Jersey. In conjunction with these positions, she is a designer/coauthor of three graduate courses. These highly esteemed graduate courses, titled "Wellness: Creating Health and Balance in the Classroom," "The Kinesthetic Classroom: Teaching and Learning through Movement," and "The Kinesthetic Classroom II: Moving across the Curriculum," have had a profound effect on the personal and professional lives of thousands of educators. Furthermore, Traci is coauthor of the book *The Kinesthetic Classroom: Teaching and Learning through Movement*, which was published in 2010 and is a best-selling educational publication. Her most recent publications are *Ready, Set, Go: The Kinesthetic Classroom 2.0* in 2017 and *Classrooms on the Move: Using Kinesthetic Furniture to Create a New Age of Learning* in 2018.

As co-owner of her own educational consulting company ActivEDge, Traci is a consistent leader in her field. She also balances an additional career position with the company Kidsfit. This corporation manufactures and sells kinesthetic furniture while providing educational experiences for instructional usage and application for these innovative designs. These careers allow her to show others how to utilize active teaching methods in a variety of settings to enhance educational achievement and peak performance of learners of all ages and abilities. Traci travels extensively to support and promote her passion for improving the health and well-being of children all over the world while bringing learning to life.

Known for her enthusiasm, innovation, work ethic, and passion, Traci devotes much of her time to both her personal and professional successes. With her motivational teaching methodology, she presents and facilitates professional development trainings and workshops. Traci provides keynote presentations for active education along with meaningful programs in the areas of movement/technology balance, wellness, stress management, and teaching/learning through movement in a kinesthetic classroom. Her ultimate professional challenge is to inspire educators at all levels to incorporate movement into their daily teaching. Traci's greatest joy is the unconditional love and support she shares with her family and friends. She is kindhearted and committed to bringing fun and laughter to education and the people who share her journey. Traci is persistent and dedicated and leaves a lasting impression. She can be reached at theactivedge@gmail.com.

**Jenna Evans** is a teacher in the Pocono Mountain school district with over seventeen years of experience in the classroom. Jenna has extensive knowledge of best practices in early childhood education, and she prides herself on delivering innovative, developmentally appropriate instruction that reaches all learners. Jenna is a leader in her profession, having served on a variety of committees that support positive schoolwide behavior programs, Read Across America, technology growth and integration, and specialized school events. In addition, she serves on a collaborative writing team that continuously assesses and rewrites the kindergarten English Language Arts (ELA) curriculum to ensure that her school district is providing rigorous instruction that supports all of the PA Core Standards. Jenna is the coauthor of the book *Classrooms on the Move: Using Kinesthetic Furniture to Create a New Age of Learning.*

Jenna received her bachelor's degree in early childhood education from East Stroudsburg University and her master's degree in classroom technology from Wilkes University. She is the co-owner of the educational consulting company ActivEDge and is passionate about integrating kinesthetic education into the classroom. Jenna has formed an instantaneous bond with learning environments that balance movement, technology, and innovative teaching methodologies to optimize student performance while educating the child as a whole. In combination with her teaching career, Jenna also dedicates her professional energy toward private consulting and freelance writing for specialized publications and graduate/undergraduate course designs in the following areas: curriculum development, movement education, applied educational technology, differentiated instruction, and classroom management.

Jenna's experience in technology integration and design, accompanied with her growing passion for kinesthetic education, ignites her desire to find a delicate balance between the two in her own classroom while encouraging other teachers to consider doing the same. As she welcomes continued progress in her current occupation, Jenna is also excited about postsecondary opportunities to develop the future of her profession. When not advocating for positive change in schools, Jenna devotes her time to her family. As a loving wife and a mother to both a son and daughter, she enjoys spending her days in the organized chaos of raising children. She sneaks in date nights with her husband whenever she can, and together, they enjoy movies, day trips, and quiet time at home. Jenna dedicates her efforts to her personal priorities and her professional goals without fail as she strives to continually grow and strengthen her aspirations.

# INTRODUCTION

*Balance in education is like balance in life . . .*

*You gotta have it!*

**Traci Lengel**

Imagine a world where technology consumes every fiber of our existence, where learning, socializing, and personal growth are linked and dependent upon screens and digital advancements. Are you able to see that we are already headed in this direction with minimal hesitation or reflection of potential dangers? *The Movement and Technology Balance: Classroom Strategies for Student Success* places education in the driver's seat to redirecting this detrimental, singular path by uniting movement and technology to optimize learning while educating the child as a whole. The greatest philosophers of all time heavily advocate the importance of gaining and maintaining balance in life. Balance is often viewed as a critical component for personal and professional success, good health, and overall happiness. This life concept should be equally supported in educational curriculums, goals, and standard practices.

*The Movement and Technology Balance* is a resource that provides all teachers (in every grade level and content area), administrators, and educational leaders/affiliates with ample evidence and practical applications on how to define, promote, and implement this innovative methodology. The concepts and activities found herein outline a unique balance that incorporates movement and technology strategies to enhance the cognitive, physical, social, and mental/emotional well-being of students to prepare them for life's challenges and opportunities. Society is engrossed in technology and addictions are intensifying. The movement and technology (MT) balance can help education redirect this course while creating a healthier, more productive alternative. In Chapters 1–3, detailed, thought-provoking research and ideas are presented to encourage the reader to stop and take a closer look at current societal and educational trends regarding movement and technology, along with the roles that each play in the lives of our younger generation. Teachers, curriculum developers, administrators, and parents alike are urged to embrace and develop the MT balance as a necessity for building a brighter, health-conscious, and well-rounded learner.

Chapter 4 describes the concept of using the MOST method in the 21st-century classroom by <u>m</u>oving students <u>o</u>ften with a <u>s</u>teady flow of <u>t</u>echnology as a best practice model. Movement and technology usage and comfort levels are explored to allow readers to identify their own strengths and weaknesses from their individual, personal perspective. Additionally, in this chapter, the acronym STRIDES is defined and described as a means for bridging the gap between movement and technology to uncover an effective balance that enhances learning potential and student success. STRIDES is as follows:

**S**—Structuring and Managing

**T**—Transforming with A.A.A.

**R**—Refining Movement and Technology

**I**—Interconnecting Communities

**D**—Defining the Balance

**E**—Employing SMART Activities

**S**—Supporting a United Approach

This structure assists the educator (MTE) by providing a step-by-step approach to either increase/decrease kinesthetic activities or technology usage with the objective of discovering the MT balance.

Becoming an MT educator (MTE) is a journey that does not and should not take place with haste. It is a process that requires practice, trial and error, knowledge, and experience. Chapters 5–11 are devoted to breaking down each step of STRIDES to guide the reader on this educational endeavor. Structuring and managing the MT classroom is a concern for many teachers, especially when it comes to physically moving students around expensive technological equipment/devices. Chapter 5 addresses these issues by discussing classroom designs, space fluidity, and management strategies. In Chapter 6, readers are given the opportunity to analyze their personal and professional outlooks on movement and technology while setting goals to uncover their own MT balance. Once specific goals are established, an abundance of functional, hands-on classroom application strategies can be shared to make these ambitions a reality. These suggestions are often the most valued by educators who are open to growth and change and want to provide the best possible learning environment for their students. For this reason, Chapters 7–10 are detailed with a wide variety of useful, viable activities that can be incorporated into any academic setting to increase student achievement while offering a fun, vibrant learning environment for all.

The final chapter of this book emphasizes the significance of fostering a united approach that includes schools, homes, and communities to truly establish and grow the MT balance philosophy. The reality is that change will not come easily, and working in isolation will only take us so far. With educational pioneers at the forefront, we must bond together as a society to establish an all-inclusive, comprehensive attitude that helps our younger generation find this balance in their lives. Technology is here to stay; therefore, we must welcome it with a practical plan that benefits and simplifies our lives but doesn't include overuse. Physical activity and increased movement are critical to our overall health and well-being. When these two concepts are united in a balanced manner, they create an intelligent, capable individual and society that is ready for just about anything!

# AN UNDENIABLE SHIFT

## MOVEMENT AND TECHNOLOGY: THE ADVERSARIAL RELATIONSHIP

### Moving in Opposition

It's quite paradoxical that in our past, our societal needs included maximum movement with minimal technology, yet today's public demands are almost in complete opposition as technology is expanding and movement is diminishing. This technological transition is laced with immeasurable benefits! However, the educational direction that ultimately results from this adversarial movement/technology relationship is limiting the academic achievement of today's learners while deteriorating their health and well-being. The concept of a blended teaching and learning approach that defines the balance between utilizing kinesthetic teaching methodologies and technological resources to optimize student learning and success is long overdue. Merging these two concepts promotes a classroom environment that meets content standards effectively, increases standardized test scores, and enriches the learning process while preparing students for future challenges. In addition, this teaching philosophy educates the learner as a whole: encouraging social, physical, mental/emotional, and cognitive growth. Preparing students for life's future tasks and trials goes beyond grades and test scores. This blended teaching style provides a comprehensive means for improving academic success while enhancing the overall life skills of the learner.

As a society, we have idly observed the health, fitness, and physical activity levels of our children rapidly decrease as technology has taken the spotlight in our educational practices and designs. We have observed a shift toward the need for technology engulfing nearly every aspect of our learning and being. As we deepen our knowledge about the capabilities of this era, it is easy to get swept away by its vast advantages, uses, and rewards. In many aspects, technology has simply made things easier for us as human beings and as learners. Having access to unlimited resources at the tap of a finger makes it easy to see how our society continues to develop and increase the demands for technology uses with aggressive efforts for future growth and expansion. However, as educators in a technologically run society, it seems as though we are not pausing enough to see the entire picture of how this is affecting our students. We are failing to see all the consequences, especially the negative ones. We need to take the time to evaluate the delivery of our lessons and question whether we are moving in the direction that supports best practices for optimal learning in all situations and conditions. Perhaps most importantly, we need to consider whether or not we are educating our youth to be healthy, intelligent, well-rounded humanitarians who will lead our country with grace and success and for the good of all.

## A Time for Concern

There is an abundance of quotes that define the importance of having balance in one's life. Many people are familiar with the common saying, "everything in moderation." What about balance and moderation in the classroom? These concepts should also exist in teaching and learning. As educational leaders, we tend to overuse technology and underuse kinesthetic teaching strategies to optimize learner success. We fail to consistently deliver curriculums with multiple teaching techniques to meet the needs of a variety of learning preferences. In your own classroom, would you say that you engage students physically to improve their learning state for greater cognitive output? Often, students sit for too long as educators deliver content through traditional means and digital resources. What are your concerns when you look at your current students and the ways in which you've seen children changing through your years of service?

The reality is that children and adolescents devote much of their time, at both school and home, to technology and digital resources. In later chapters, statistics and detailed information will be shared that illustrate the significance of this, along with the damaging effects it is having on our youth. The younger generation is spending too much time watching television, playing video games, texting, and interacting on social media. At a quick glance, these outlets may seem harmless. However, as digital addictions grow, children and adolescents are becoming sedentary people with an increasing collection of physical, social, and mental/emotional health problems. The time for concern is now! As educators, we've made a commitment to care for the well-being of the whole child, and the overall wellness of our students cannot be ignored. Educational facilities are encouraged to look for active means to reverse these damaging trends. Implementing more movement and kinesthetic teaching methodologies into schools and classrooms is a step in the right direction to combat these technological dependencies. Action must be immediate, persistent, effective, and ongoing.

# A SOCIETY ON THE MOVE

## A Past Perspective

Later in this chapter, as we dive deeper into the history of movement, we will clearly see that we were consistently a society of movers. The reasons for physical activity and the levels of intensity evolved over time to fit our societal, cultural, and personal needs. When you recall your own childhood, would you describe yourself as active? In the past, children played outside with their peers for extensive hours. This sense of free play was enjoyed and valued. Physical activity was viewed as an important part of making childhood memories. These experiences played a role in helping youngsters become the people they are today. Life skills were developed during peer encounters and free play, while movement and physical activity were highly esteemed throughout history. We were a society that moved for our livelihood, work, play, fitness, health, and enjoyment. It was essential, desired, and expected. Most viewed physical activity as a standard, and minimal thought was put into its process. We just did it and it was a part of who we were.

When most teachers reflect on their own childhood education, they typically recall minimal movement throughout the school day with the exception of recess and physical education classes. However, these same people will also say they were physically active outside of school hours. It was common for children and adolescents to play outside until it was dark and a family member ordered them back to the home for the evening. In this example, the sedentary nature of the school day had a minimal effect on the health and well-being of this generation because of the active lifestyles in the home environment. Children often played with neighbors as they organized and managed their own games and activities without parental assistance. The historical viewpoint in regard to movement is strong and constant. Although needs and interests changed throughout the years, we were steadily viewed as a society of movers.

## A Present and Future Perception

Is our younger generation still considered to be a society of movers? At one point in history, we moved all day long for survival. Eventually, we developed into a culture that sat during the school day but was physically active in the evenings. What about today? Many would agree that we have now produced a generation that is not only sedentary during the school day but throughout the evening as well. If you can recognize this transition, you will find it difficult to consider us a youthful society that leads physically active lives. This perspective is not meant to discount the percentage of our children and adolescents who engage in sports and clubs that include exercise and movement. However, when we look at the statistics forthcoming, there is evidence of a recognizable decrease in the amount of physical movement of the current generation in comparison to their predecessors.

This decrease in movement and active lifestyles is affecting the future health and well-being of our youth. Students' values are changing. Many believe that education is influencing this downward spiral. If we step back and look at the big picture of where technology is taking us, it's frightening. The more technology increases, the more the movement and physical activity of human beings decreases. We must learn to profit from technology without allowing it to consume our existence. If we don't take action to reverse this direction, the potential results are disturbing. Why aren't more people in education and in the world combining efforts to *unite* movement and technology instead of having them move in opposition of one another? The potential outlook for a society that doesn't value movement is grim. We are not physically designed to live sedentary lives; we were created as "movers." We must find our way back to the basics.

# THE DECLINE OF MOVEMENT >

## A Timeline of Change

The evolution of movement can be visually represented by the *greater than* symbol (>). This character illustrates the power of movement in the past (the infinite, wide end), along with its decline and future possibilities (the pointed end) as we look ahead. Reviewing this timeline may give you a different perspective on how our society has deteriorated concerning physical activity over time. As we look at Figure 1.1, we see a progressive timeline that shows a shift in our needs, values, and viewpoints regarding the necessity of movement in our culture. Throughout primal times, people used movement for survival as they escaped physically life-threatening situations. Physical activity was needed to feed the family and to keep everyone safe and out of harm's way. Basic movements were also vital during the Neolithic times, as farming and labor provided a standard way of life. This lifestyle resulted in strong bodies that could withstand many extensive hours of physical demands. As we moved to ancient times, men had to prepare for war through the use of physical training that improved their strength, speed, and power. These developments demonstrate that from 10,000 BC to 4,000 BC, physical activity was a requirement to sustain our very existence.

Movement was valued and frequent for basic survival and daily activities for many generations. The Renaissance marks a significant change in the importance of the body. Health and physical education were introduced to our schools, as anatomy and biology interests increased. Our society recognized the importance of intentional, purposeful exercise. People began to notice their body as they made time to strengthen it in an effort to improve their appearance, health, well-being, and fitness levels. The 18th and 19th centuries indicate an increase in exercise in the home environment. During the Industrial Revolution, people began to have more inactive occupations that restricted the amount of physical activity they received during work hours. This led to an increase in exercise regimens that took place around an individual's employment schedule.

The 20th century is considered the birth of the modern fitness industry. Organized sports and a focus on fitness expanded as physical activity maintained its worth. Today, in the 21st century, fitness and technology unite forces. Although this unification brings many advantages, this period also illustrates a critical alteration in the way our society views movement and physical activity. Once given high value and importance, exercise is now seen as a chore. People lead busy lives, yet

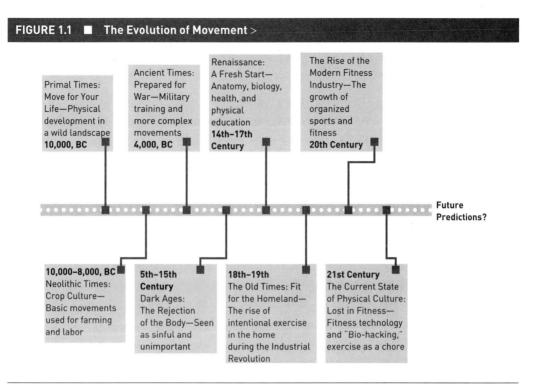

**FIGURE 1.1  ■  The Evolution of Movement >**

Source: Adapted from https://www.artofmanliness.com/articles/the-historyof-physical-fitness/ by Erwan Le Corre. Retrieved December 13, 2018.

they are sedentary. Work and family responsibilities are time consuming and overwhelming. Where physical activity and exercise were once perceived as our go-to outlet, we now use technological resources and options for relaxation and pleasure. This is true for adults, adolescents, and children alike. This transferal of priorities comes with heavy consequences that question the role that movement plays in our future—if it even has a role.

## The Impact on Learning

How has the evolution of movement impacted our schools and teachers? What role does movement and physical activity play in your own life? Maintaining a physically active lifestyle is important for everyone. We should be committed to including intentional movement in our daily regimen to maintain our individual health and well-being. Most Americans are so overwhelmed with abundant responsibilities and demands that exercise simply takes a back seat in their daily routines. The reality is that our health should always be our number-one priority, as it affects everything about us, including our parenting, relationships, and teaching. We cannot be elite in our careers if we are not taking the time to be the best version of ourselves. This development would include a consistent exercise plan that improves our body, mind, and spirit. This topic will be addressed in Chapter 6. Additionally, this dedication will have a positive effect on our thinking, energy, and stamina so that we can meet life's challenges head-on with success and triumph, both in our home and classroom.

Students are affected by inactive lifestyles; this often shows in their learning. Our younger generation's expectations for their education and their teachers have changed. Unfortunately, many schools are taking minimal measures to ensure that movement continues to evolve as a high priority in the lives of their students. The sedentary lifestyle of students is damaging their health, energy, work ethic, and endurance. Many students are becoming unmotivated to move; they resist it as if it were a punishment. For the first time in history, there is now talk of designing organized recess protocols because students simply do not have the skills to play by themselves or with one another. The social abilities of today's children and adolescents are diminishing, and they are often unable to use their imaginations, creative thinking, and problem-solving strategies. This is a concern! Technology overuse is playing a part in these alarms, but the ultimate culprit is the direction and choices we are making as a society and as educational leaders. Supporting the balance between active teaching methodologies and technological resources in educational environments is an assertive means for safeguarding the evolution of movement as a societal priority. Evidence confirms that finding this balance is no longer an option: It is an obligation.

# THE DIGITAL AGE

## A Past Perception

The digital age is commonly known as the *information age*; it is a period in human history characterized by a shift from traditional industry to an economy based on information technology. This era is associated with the Digital Revolution, recognized as a time when industry creates a knowledge-based society encircled by a high-tech global economy. As technology was introduced into our society, many of us did not predict its potential power and immense capabilities. During their arrival, devices had one function. We wrote papers, played video games, listened to music, and used cell phones in conjunction with our traditional means of communication and supplementary enjoyments. Technology lived alongside our customary lifestyles and moved parallel with our behaviors, habits, and simple ways of life. Progress was steady but largely linear, which made life still feel uncomplicated at the time. As we slowly evolved into the predigital age, products became digitized, photos became bits, and knowledge moved to Wikipedia. This was only the beginning of a conversion that would eventually consume our existence.

Can you recall the onset of the digital age and the first technological device you used or owned? How did it simplify or complicate your life? How did it change your teaching or learning? Computers and laptops have had a direct impact on education. Typing and editing became a breeze once you mastered the keyboard and all its functions. Research and information gathering was also faster and more accessible. Some schools had the initial funding to make immediate purchases, where others lagged behind. However, everyone was headed toward acquiring as much technology as the budgets would allow. Comparable to societal reactions and responses to the increase in technology, the initial impact in schools was also slow and steady. This allowed for minimal changes in the day-to-day teaching and learning process. Technology was viewed as a positive contribution to education and its practices.

## A Present and Future Perception

Mid- and post–digital-age viewpoints deliver a much different perspective of the role that technology plays in our current and future lives. We have entered an age in which digital devices have been accepted into the mainstream and are fully immersed into our society. We must learn to appreciate the pros that these advances provide us yet see the areas of concern that result. Much of the younger generation has become dependent on technology for socializing and gaming enjoyment. Many people of all ages might be addicted to their device(s). This is a concerning and frightening notion. Taking precautions to ensure that you do not become one of these people is essential to sustaining a healthy balance in your life. Implementing strategies in your classroom or educational environment to reverse this current dependency is equally important.

Continuing the growth pattern of our current technology usage will affect our future generations. No one will think of being digital in this age because it will be a vast, silent element that outlines the essence of our being. The Internet and cell phones will be background utilities and only noticeable when they are not in our presence. Technologies will be instinctively used by babies as they grow alongside one another. A society that fully emerges and isolates itself in technology will have an uninviting social agenda. Human connection and interaction will be redefined with a complete overhaul of new expectations and behaviors. Teaching and learning will be transformed. Questioning the need for educators may even take place as robots and online education develop and expand. Perhaps the most blurred line will become that of what is real or virtual. It's critical to bear in mind that the future can be changed, as nothing is definite. We can learn to acquire the benefits of technology while refusing its demand, so it does not consume our children's lives as well as our own. There is a line we must discover and identify before we can truly ensure that the proper steps will be taken to defend against this all-consuming direction. Balancing movement and technology in the classroom will help us to define and intentionally navigate this line for appropriate redirection.

Some educators are not using technology in their classroom because they have rejected this teaching methodology. This book will ask all teachers and school leaders to reconsider this way of thinking as well. Technology will play a significant role in the future of education. We must embrace this notion with the same energy that we have for kinesthetic strategies. The goal is for movement and technology to work together in unison to optimize learning. Each teaching and learning technique will have its advantages and disadvantages, but merging their strengths will create a powerhouse teaching tool that will peak performance and learning potential. Students will become well-rounded learners prepared to tackle future challenges and tasks with a healthy body and mind.

# THE RISE OF TECHNOLOGY <

## A Timeline of Change

The evolution of influential technology is represented by the *less than* symbol (<). This character illustrates the initial impact of technology in the past (the pointed end) along with its growth and future possibilities (the infinite, wide end) as we look ahead. In Figure 1.2, an undisputable timeline of growth is represented with technology inventions, advances, and devices. Computers, video games, laptops, and cell phones were the first to arrive on the market. At first, these products came with a hefty price tag, limiting sales to those who had the financial means to purchase them. Eventually, prices were lowered, and more people were able to afford these creations. In 1990, the World Wide Web was developed and global communications and networking became readily accessible.

The early 1990s brought about PlayStation, Yahoo, and smartphones. Many believe that PlayStation redefined gaming as sales skyrocketed and numbers climbed. Cell phones became multifunctioning devices, and people began to use them as personal planners. Technology was becoming as much a part of social fabric as it was in the world of business. From 1995 to 1997, Amazon, eBay, Hotmail, Java, WebTV, Google, and blogging hit the scene. Technology seemed to be growing at an unstoppable rate. Online shopping was a novelty that provided a desired convenience to the overworked consumer who had limited time.

From 2000 to 2006, noticeable attention was directed toward social media outlets such as Myspace, Skype, Facebook, and Twitter. It seemed as though there was a need for social networking opportunities, and technology was ready to respond. Communication was being revised. Face-to-face conversations were decreasing and online chatting, texting, and tweeting were becoming the norm. Gaming inventions were also escalating as PlayStation2, Xbox, Xbox 360, and PlayStation 3 were advancing and increasing persistently. We were quickly becoming a society consumed with technological uses and advancements. Before we knew what had happened, much of our society became engrossed in digital devices. Today, our devices frequently serve as a distraction as we attempt to focus on "old-fashioned"

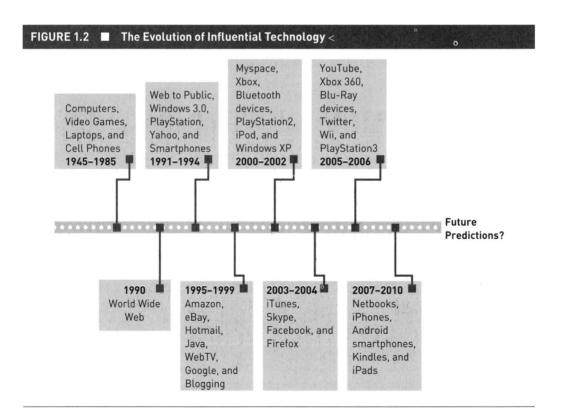

**FIGURE 1.2 ■ The Evolution of Influential Technology**

notions such as verbal communication, listening, and physical activity. Out with the old and in with the new. But what if the new is detrimental to the health, overall happiness, and survival of the people it serves?

## The Impact on Learning

The evolution of technology has and will continue to impact our schools, teachers, and students. In Chapter 6, we will evaluate the role it plays in your own life. We will ask if you are addicted to your cell phone, television, texting, gaming, or Facebook. You will be encouraged to consider how much time you spend using technology and whether you place limits on yourself. Technological advancements have brought convenience, entertainment, and opportunities for socialization to us with the click of a button—but at what cost? Some people are always viewing special moments in life through a lens on their phone, camera, or iPad. Sure, there is something to be said about capturing a significant event in a picture or video. However, some would argue that viewing an entire concert through a lens really isn't worth it. It is questionable whether we are enjoying the production to its fullest extent. The beauty of the sounds being sung might not be heard, and our attention might instead be on whether or not the camera is focused and centered. Are you one of these people? If you realize that you are addicted to technology, you may be able to see how this can affect your teaching and maybe even your content delivery. In this book, you will be encouraged to evaluate your own life choices in regard to your digital usage. It will be difficult for you to reverse the current direction of our society if you are also following a destructive path and are not willing to change. Life is meant to be about growth, change, and redirection. Sometimes, the redirection takes us back to a time in life when our values were more in line with a happier, healthier individual or to a childhood filled with great memories of play, physical activity, and face-to-face time with friends. There is also something to be said about looking for balance in life (and in classrooms) while providing the effort to sustain it.

Consider how students have been affected by technology and how their learning, attention, or focuses have been influenced. Their priorities and interests have shifted as a result of digital advancement, and schools should take action to ensure that technology plays a significant role in learning but is not overused. Schools will need to provide support to students who suffer from addictions related to their devices or depression that is connected to social media. Excessive technology dependency is a serious concern in our current culture. We must evaluate our choices, priorities, and behaviors to determine if we are acting in our best interest. As an educator, you are the leader of your classroom or school and can determine how it functions and proceeds. You can deliver your content in a manner that fits learners' needs yet stretches them outside their comfort level to build stronger humanitarians. Without question, technology has its value. However, it can—and is—being overused in many instances.

Schools will be urged to incorporate policies and limits on cell phone usage, if these are not already in place. If students are using their phones throughout their class for personal means, even though they are instructed not to, this is an educational concern. Cellular usage is a difficult gray area. We want children to have phones for safety and educational purposes, but addiction can consume their thoughts and distract them from the very purpose you intended them to have. Education and self-management on healthy digital usage needs to be a top priority in classrooms and home environments. We must look for learning, social, and entertainment outlets for our youngsters that do not include technology. Physical activity, exercise, and active teaching techniques should be first on our list. These experiences will allow for social, physical, mental/emotional, and cognitive development that many children are presently lacking.

# A CHANGE OF COURSE

## From "Sitness" Back to Fitness

Jean Moize, cocreator of Action Based Learning and expert in the field of kinesthetic teaching, has spent her career examining the benefits of movement on the learning process and the deterioration of physical activity in our society. She describes our culture as engaging in "sitness" as opposed to fitness as we have done in the past (ACHPER National, 2011). Are we currently breeding a generation that sits for most of their waking hours? Many people would agree with Moize in that our younger generation is leading inactive lifestyles. How we address these concerns is a fundamental matter for educators. In Chapter 2, we will explore the power of movement in our classrooms and our society. There is extensive research that links fitness to academic achievement and performance. This information is supportive and convincing in that education must embrace active teaching methodologies in an effort to revert our society back to one that produces physically active children that are fit and healthy.

Ponder how children spend their time after school hours. Are they outside playing sports and physical games with their peers, as many of their parents did when they were children? Many youngsters are watching television, playing video games, and interacting on social media for countless hours. Therefore, a large percentage of our children are participating in activities that result in sitting and stationary movements. These choices have a negative impact on the health and fitness levels of our youngsters. Parents are frustrated and, in many instances, do not know how to motivate their children to become active and curious movers. A pattern has developed, and now we can create strategies that reverse this direction to bring our children from "sitness" back to fitness.

Does it surprise you that research provides evidence that physically fit students perform better academically? Teachers are often able to make the connection among the physical, mental/emotional, and cognitive benefits that will naturally result from engaging in regular physical activity. As discussed previously in this chapter, we used to be a society of movers. This basic human need is still within our children. Behaviors and habits can be reformed through purposeful, effective agendas. However, we can no longer sit back and be bystanders in this societal shift. We must become agents of change.

## Agents of Change

Educators make ideal candidates to be agents of change. Teachers are not able to control the experiences their students face in their home environments, but the classroom is a different story. It's easy to fall into a routine of teaching the same lesson without alteration over and over from year to year. Society is always evolving; hence, education should be doing the same. Agents of change are always a step ahead of what learners require and desire for motivation, success, and growth. This is an important consideration in all learning environments. Constant reflection and redirection are two key components of staying ahead of the changing times. We must contemplate movement and technology's purposes in education. If you are committed to this new direction, celebrate your determined nature as you provide an innovative perspective for creating this balance in your classroom. Search for opportunities to help students grow as people, not only as learners.

Since you are reading this book, chances are that you are already an agent of change. It goes without saying that many of us find transformations difficult, especially in circumstances where we have been doing the same or similar things consistently for an extended period of time. This is the case for countless educators and leaders in our learning environments. The more our comfort builds, the more complacent we tend to become. There is nothing wrong with feeling a little uneasy about change; however, the way you handle those feelings defines who you are as an educator. Embrace change, whether it be increasing movement or decreasing technology (or maybe even the opposite, when you believe it's in the best interest of your students). Turn your feelings of fear into thoughts of challenge and excitement! When we tackle challenges and move at a pace that is right for us, we gain insight and energy to advance forward. There is something exhilarating about being an agent of change, especially when research and common sense are behind your actions.

# WHAT DOES THIS MEAN TO ME?

### K–12 Teachers

1. Consider your students' experiences with the decline of movement and increase in technology in their lives. Define your role in this shift.

2. Reflect on your recent lesson plans. Take note of the amount of both movement and technology in each lesson.

### Administration

1. Engage in thoughtful dialogue with your faculty about the decline of movement and the rise of technology in schools. Define the school's role in this shift.

2. Consider what a typical classroom environment looks like in your school. Take note of what you see students doing to engage with the lesson.

### Educational Leaders/Affiliates

1. Reflect on the decline of movement and the rise of technology on society as a whole. Define education's active role as we look toward our future.

2. Review current core curriculum standards and the roles that movement and technology play within them. Take note of the balance (or lack thereof) between the two.

# CHAPTER SUMMARY

- A blended teaching and learning approach regarding movement and technology optimizes student learning and success, promotes a classroom environment that meets content standards effectively, increases standardized test scores, and enriches the learning process while preparing students for future challenges.

- Human beings are historically considered to have been a society of movers. Today's younger generation is sedentary and unmotivated to move. This decrease in movement and active lifestyles is concerning for the health and well-being of our youth.

- The decline of movement (>) represents the cultural shift from movement being a necessary requirement to sustain our very existence to something considered a chore in our modern, sedentary world.

- The digital age introduced innovative and engaging technological advances that changed the face of our society, economy, and educational practices.

- The rise of technology (<) represents the impact that the digital age has left on society. Today, our devices frequently serve as a distraction in all aspects of our modern life (communication, education, physical activity levels, etc.).

- Today's students are engaged in a highly digital and sedentary classroom that mimics this societal shift. These choices have a negative impact on the health and fitness levels of our youngsters.

- Education and self-management on healthy digital usage needs to be a top priority in classrooms. Educators make ideal agents of change by restoring the balance of movement and technology that their students face in the classroom!

# 2

# THE POWER OF MOVEMENT

## WANTING PAST VALUES BACK

### Wellness: The Downward Dive

What is happening to the overall wellness of our society? If you were asked to predict statistics regarding obesity, nutrition, physical inactivity, and causes of death or illness, what would you say? The reality is that our civilization has taken a downward dive when it comes to our overall public health and well-being. It is imperative for our society to bring the value of physically active lifestyles back to the forefront. As a culture and as educational advisers, we must take these disturbing statistics seriously as we unite and construct active plans to battle these formidable extremes. Ponder this data with worry and allow it to serve as motivation for you in becoming a pioneer who combats these trends with energy, confidence, and conviction. The figures that follow (reviewed in 2017 by the U.S. Department of Health and Human Services) are alarming and demand our direct attention and action:

- More than 80% of adults do not meet the guidelines for aerobic and muscular-strengthening activities, and more than 80% of adolescents do not get enough aerobic physical activity to meet the guidelines for youth.

- Twenty-eight percent of Americans (80.2 million people) age six and older are physically inactive.

- Reports project that by 2030, half of adults (115 million) in the United States will be obese.

- Overweight adolescents have a 70% chance of becoming overweight or obese adults.

- Prevalence of obesity from the early 1970s to 2007/2008 has doubled for ages 2–5, quadrupled for ages 6–11, tripled for ages 12–19, and doubled for adults.

- Obesity-related illness, including chronic disease, disability, and death, is estimated to carry an annual cost of $190.2 billion.

The bottom line is that we are not making wise choices when it comes to our behaviors, routines, and habits in order to maintain good health. We've gone from a society of movers to one that is obsessed with technology usage, social seclusion, poor nutritional selections, and inactivity. It is devastating to think that we might be headed for extinction. This descending plunge can be redirected with purposeful intention that starts in our educational environments. If we look at Figure 2.1, there is clear evidence that as technology usage rates have risen, so have obesity levels. We will explore technology overload in Chapter 3, but the evidence sufficiently supports a required need for a cultural transformation. Excessive digital usage is damaging our minds, bodies, and well-being; educators are encouraged to be the trailblazers in this revolution. As school systems play a significant role in shaping our youth, balancing movement and technology in the classroom is a starting point that must be applied immediately. We owe it to ourselves, our future, and our existence.

## An Unmotivated Society, an Unmotivated Student

As an educator, have you seen a change in your students' work ethic over your years of service? Are students sedentary? Do they resist physical movement and active involvement in class activities? Many teachers have spoken out regarding this concern. It seems that many learners expect instant gratification and continual praise, with minimal effort. Many believe this to be a current trend in our society. It is common to hear this era referenced as the "Age of Entitlement." This label is related to millennials/postmillennials and suggests that members of this generation have an overinflated sense of entitlement and lack the work ethic to achieve their goals. Do you witness this in your classroom and school environment? Teachers often feel that there has been a decrease in students' energy levels. This change has a direct effect on day-to-day teaching challenges.

Researchers believe that this notion starts at birth. Throughout their growing years, babies and infants are told how special they are; now they believe this to be true, even when their actions and decisions are less than favorable. These youngsters have a sense of expectation, feeling they should be treated with individual attention and exclusive focus. They have a driving concentration for self-fulfillment, while strong work ethics and self-sacrifice are qualities that are lost as a result. There has been a noticeable decrease in motivation with our younger generation as well. As technology dependencies increase, delaying adulthood, financial responsibilities,

**FIGURE 2.1** ■ Technology Usage vs. Obesity Rates

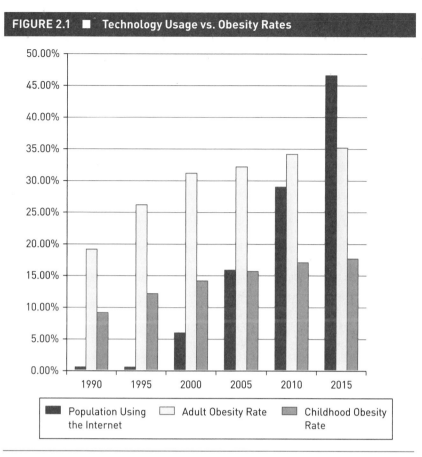

*Note:* All percentages are approximate, based on varying data

*Sources:* http://internetworldstats.com/emarketing.htm

http://stateofobesity.org/childhood-obesity-trends/

http://stateofobesity.org/adult-obesity/

and a casual approach to life seem to increase. Many people feel this generation is physically lazier than the ones before it. New research appears to prove that this stereotype is true. Technology and the decisions we make regarding it may be the primal cause of this unmotivated society. Changes in parenting styles, educational expectations, and the choices we are making as human beings with both ourselves and our youngsters are also contributing to this descent. Combining movement and digital progressions in the classroom with equality can help to bring the value of physical activity back to our society. This will aid in strengthening the work ethic and energy levels of our youth.

## New Normal

Describe a typical day of a young child or teenager in our society. These descriptions may vary greatly, depending on which individual you are considering. However, what if we defined the average day of the majority of our youth? You would more than likely describe an overuse of technology. Hopefully, you would also label a group of active movers. More often than not, our images will tend to include a collection of inactivity and sedentary children and adolescents. There is a new normal in our culture in which children are spending more time inside their homes as opposed to outside enjoying nature. Digital usage has become a main source for socializing. Binge-watching television and reality TV has replaced family time, where everyone viewed popular shows in order to enjoy common time together.

Is there a new normal in school environments as well? Some educators feel that we have transformed from a culture that educated the child as a whole to one that is preoccupied with making the grade. Standardized tests also play a part in how we design our curriculums. As teachers feel pressure to move at a certain pace through their content, even when students are not mastering the material, stress levels rise and demands increase. Are these current tendencies best practice for optimal learning and success? Educational facilities are playing a significant role in defining this new normal. Our goal must be to keep the positive qualities of this generation while redirecting their undesirable traits. Implementing kinesthetic teaching strategies is one serious tactic that can help get our society back on track while producing children who are active movers.

## Turning Point or Point of No Return

The *greater than* symbol (>) is used in this book to represent the decline of movement in today's society. Experts have reported that we may be raising the first generation of children that may not outlive their parents. This statistic is shocking and alarming! Researchers have declared that we are fighting a war against the increase of childhood obesity, and many are convinced we are losing drastically. Yet, minimal educational countermeasures have been taken to combat these devastating concerns. Health challenges are increasing and physical activity and fitness levels are plummeting. Have we reached a point of no return?

We must redefine our perspective on movement and physical activity. Fitness has typically been linked to sports, physical performance, coordination, and what someone looks like. The time to change this way of thinking has come. Moving forward, physical fitness will be connected to health (brain and body equally), feeling good about oneself, and improving academic performance in the classroom. Everyone has the ability to be physically fit at a level that fits each individual. Fitness is not for the elite athlete and has nothing to do with talent and/or skill. Instead, it's about *you* and becoming the strongest version of yourself possible. The game is not over; we can still turn things around! Teachers, administrators, parents, community supporters, school board members, and other agents of change who are reading this book are ready to rally! The health and well-being of our youth has already fallen too far. We are prepared to unite and plan for a big comeback. Directing this rally will be you, an educational leader, who will show equality for active learning strategies and technology uses. Chances are, you have already started your role in this comeback and you purchased this publication to strengthen your edge. Making the commitment to change the future direction for the health and well-being of your students is the first step. We have reached the turning point!

# MOVEMENT MATTERS

The timeline presented in Chapter 1 provided evidence that we were an active society throughout much of history. We went from a culture that had to move for survival to a civilization that is inactive and sedentary. It is crucial to the future health and success of our nation that we begin to make a shift by reverting back to some of our past practices regarding movement. Increasing physical activity and fitness levels in today's youth is a serious challenge that we must face with a united approach. Movement matters in a classroom setting to improve academic achievement, and kinesthetic teaching methodologies can help make this happen! Comfort levels regarding movement are so unique to an individual's personality that some students are hesitant to engage in various forms of physical activity. However, the more we move learners, the better our chances are for increasing these comfort levels. Exposing students to positive movement experiences can help elevate their confidence while minimizing resistance. The more we move, the better we feel and perform. So, let's move more!

Movement also matters in a classroom environment because as human beings, we have many needs aside from food, water, and shelter. Kinesthetic teaching methodologies can help meet these needs. Tony Robbins, a well-known American author, philanthropist, entrepreneur, and life coach, references "6 Core Human Needs" (Jane, 2013). Utilizing active learning strategies can help meet these core human needs:

1.  **Certainty/Comfort:** Feeling in control and having basic comfort is very important to us as human beings. When using kinesthetic strategies, the learner has control of his or her body, and successful movement can provide a feeling of confidence and comfort.

2.  **Uncertainty/Variety:** Teachers have an abundance of choices when considering movement activities for a classroom setting. This allows for an extensive range of preferences, mixtures, and selections.

3.  **Significance:** We all want to feel important and/or special. Using active learning activities creatively in a classroom environment can do that when educators follow the recommendations found herein.

4.  **Love and connection:** Kinesthetic environments help build a community connection within a school setting. These bonds are meaningful and can aid in establishing a rewarding learning setting that is kind, respectful, and interconnected.

5.  **Growth:** Growing as individuals and contributing to others will naturally occur in a community learning environment. It is simply the nature of a connected atmosphere.

6.  **Contribution:** Giving/contributing to others or perhaps sharing with others is important for individual growth and will be essential in organizing efficient kinesthetic learning environments.

# THE BRAIN–BODY CONNECTION

The brain is responsible for both cognitive functions and physical actions. Brain health is vital for all beings and is critical in the learning process. The mind and body are interconnected and can affect one another in a variety of ways, both positively and negatively. For example, if we feel nervous, we may get nauseous or our palms may start to sweat. Or if we exercise regularly, we may sleep better and think more clearly. The mind and body are always working together to either hinder our performance or to bring out our best. Consistently, physical activity is related to a healthier body as well as a healthier mind (Hillman, Erickson, & Kramer, 2008). Therefore, it stands to reason that the benefits of implementing kinesthetic teaching methodologies would have a positive effect on boosting brain function and memory.

Balancing movement and technology in the classroom will reinforce the brain–body connection. This combined effort can energize the body while providing the brain with the novelty it desires. Throughout this book, you will receive numerous ideas on how to make this happen with ease and practicality. Physical activity serves the body and the brain simultaneously; however, technology will do the same if it is delivered properly. Teachers will be encouraged to see beyond the initial design of a product or practice. We will examine methods to engage the brain and body for a united effort that enhances students' learning potential. Together, these powerful teaching tools will be joined to maximize learners' success.

# THE SUPPORTIVE RESEARCH

## Increasing Physical Activity Improves Academic Performance

*Physical activity* involves low-intensity, submaximal movements that expend energy. Using kinesthetic teaching strategies in a classroom environment will significantly increase students' physical activity levels while supporting an increase in academic success. In education, there is a constant focus on improving academic performance and test scores, and technology is at the forefront of this process. Administrators, curriculum developers, and teachers examine past practices to discover what will work best in the 21st-century classroom to optimize learning. This search is an effort to reveal techniques that heighten success and productivity. Teachers and researchers alike are using a variety of physical activities while delivering instruction to increase academic scores. Creating and implementing lessons that use active learning can increase both physical activity and academic success. Here are some motivating examples of research that supports implementing active teaching methodologies to improve academic achievement.

## The Effects of Increasing Physical Activity on Academic Achievement

| Study | Findings | Reference |
| --- | --- | --- |
| Approximately 499 second and third graders in the Netherlands were studied over a two-year period. Half received traditional lessons, half received lessons supplemented with movement. | The results showed an increase in speed and general mathematics and spelling scores for the students that engaged in the physical activity after two years. Building movement and exercise into lessons helped the students get better grades. | Mullender-Wijnsma, Hartman, de Greeff, Bosker, Doolaard, & Visscher, 2015 |
| The University of Kansas studied the link between physical activity, academic achievement, and cognitive function. | Standardized test scores improved 6% when brief bouts of physical activity were added to academic lessons (75 minutes/week over three years). | Donnelly & Lambourne, 2011 |
| Action Based Learning used specific movements to link physical skills and brain development in an elementary school in Pennsylvania. | Results indicated improved performance in math and reading in Grades K–2. Conclusions were made that movement builds the framework for learning and proper development. | Blaydes Madigan & Hess, 2004 |
| A Canadian study investigated 287 fourth and fifth graders to find the link between physical activity and standardized test scores in children who were performing below grade level. | Students who received the increase in physical activity were more likely to improve their standardized test scores when compared to the students who maintained their daily routines. | Ahamed, Macdonald, Reed, Naylor, Liu-Ambrose, & McKay, 2007 |
| A South Carolina study examined physical activity effects on classroom lessons and students' achievement in Grades 3–6 by adding exercise equipment in conjunction with teaching content. | Standardized test scores were compared from the years before and after the program was established. The percentage of students reaching their goals was 55% before the start of the program and 68.5% after the program was initiated. | American Academy of Pediatrics, 2011 |
| A Denmark study examined the effects of first graders learning math while engaging in full-body movements. | Math performance improved. Students benefited from individualized mathematical learning and movements. | Beck, Lind, Geersten, Ritz, Lundbye-Jensen, & Wienecke, 2016 |
| The connections between physical activity, attention, and academic achievements were researched in children. | A positive correlation was made after 20 minutes on a treadmill. Children responded faster and with greater accuracy to cognitive challenges after physical activity. | Budde, Voelcker-Rehage, Pietrabyk Kendziorra, Ribeiro, & Tidow, 2008; Ellemberg & St-Louis-Deschenes, 2010; Hillman, Buck, Themanson, Pontifex, & Castelli, 2009 |
| "Take 10" was a ten-year study of a classroom-based physical activity program. | Results showed that students had higher physical activity levels, reduced time off-task, and improved reading, math, spelling, and composite scores. | Kibbe et al., 2011 |

*(Continued)*

**(Continued)**

| Study | Findings | Reference |
| --- | --- | --- |
| A meta-analysis review based on a random-effects model studied 579 participants ages 3–25. | Results showed small to medium effects from exercise on certain aspects of cognitive performance in individuals with autism spectrum disorder and attention deficit hyperactivity disorder. | Tan, Pooley, & Speelman, 2016 |

## Fitness Levels Affect Academic Achievement

If we are more active with our bodies, it stands to reason that we will perform with greater success in many areas, including cognitive function and execution. As a result, we will become the best version of ourselves as learners. For decades, the term "dumb jock" suggested just the opposite. Physical attainment and cognitive excellence were seen as conflicting abilities. Students with higher intelligence were expected to master their intellectual gains. Athletes were seen as skilled competitors; making the grade was only necessary to allow them to continue or extend their athletic careers. Thanks to current research, we now understand that on average, students who maintain standard physical fitness levels tend to receive higher grade point averages and elevated scores on their standardized tests when compared to students who are not physically fit. These findings do not suggest that students with low fitness levels aren't highly intelligent or can't produce premium grades with superior standardized test scores. However, the correlation between fitness levels and academic achievement is consistent and deserves notable attention. The findings described in the following table show a clear, positive link among fitness, academic performance, and standardized test scores.

**The Effects of Fitness Levels on Academic Achievement**

| Study | Findings | Reference |
| --- | --- | --- |
| Michigan State University examined 312 public school students in Grades 6–8. Physical assessments (shuttle runs, curl-ups, push-ups) were compared to academic achievement, along with standardized test scores in four core classes over a one-year period. | Students with the highest fitness levels performed better on the standardized exam and earned higher grades. | Coe, Pivarnik, Womack, Reeves, & Malina 2012 |
| In 2004–2005, a group of students in Grades 4–8 were studied on their ability to pass a number of fitness tests. | The results indicated that standardized test scores in math and English were higher for students that were able to pass those tests. | Wiley-Blackwell, 2009 |

| Study | Findings | Reference |
| --- | --- | --- |
| A study on children was conducted to analyze the relationship between exercise and cognitive functions. | Conclusions were made that exercise enhances mental function, cognitive development, and brain health. | Davis et al., 2011 |
| A 14-study meta-analytic review looked at the connection between physical activity and academics. | Summaries concluded that the more physically active students are, the better they do academically. The brain works at an optimal capacity as nerve cells strengthen their connectivity and multiply. After thirty minutes on a treadmill, students were able to solve problems 10% more efficiently. | Mercola, 2012 |
| Thirty-eight children were grouped based on their performance on a field test of aerobic capacity. | The study concluded that fitness is associated with better cognitive performance on an executive control task through increased cognitive control. | Hillman et al., 2009 |
| Naperville, Illinois, studied the effects of physical fitness and academic achievement on high school students by offering an early morning exercise program. | Participating students significantly increased both their math and reading standardized test scores. | Ratey, 2008 |
| Two thousand California students who were considered to be outside their "healthy fitness zone" were analyzed. | These students scored lower on their standardized tests than those who had higher fitness levels. | Adams, 2013 |
| A 13-week study in Georgia observed the effects of an exercise program on overweight 7- to 11-year-old students. | Results showed better performance in planning, organizing, and standardized math tests in the group that received the exercise than the 60 students who did not. | Adams, 2013 |
| The University of Southern Mississippi studied the relationship between standardized test scores in language arts and math and fitness levels. | A positive relationship was reported. | Blom, Alvarez, Zhang, & Kolbo, 2011 |
| A study in Charlotte–Mecklenburg Schools compared the school's fitness standards to math and reading scores. | A positive correlation found notable growth in math and reading for students who met the standards. | Wooten Green, 2016 |
| A longitudinal study analyzed students who are physically fit to students who are not. | Results indicated academic disparities in both language arts and math and reported that physical fitness is a better indicator of academic achievement than obesity (as measured by body mass index). Academic disparities seem to start before fifth grade physical fitness testing begins. | London & Castrechini, 2011 |

## Enhanced Brain Function and Memory

When movement is used in an academic environment, it can enhance a student's episodic learning and memory. During a learning episode, the brain takes a mental picture of the surroundings and circumstances it is in. This can play a significant role in memory recall. Technology does not always provide a clear, detailed picture in the brain because human connections are typically not involved in the process. A vibrant mental image can be beneficial in helping to move information from short-term memory to long-term memory. One concern for educators today is the constant need for reteaching content that students should have already mastered. If students are not interested in the information being taught, or the content is not delivered in a meaningful manner, it is difficult for learning to take place. Technology is strong in this aspect when it delivers information with bright colors, animation, and flashes of novel characters. Utilizing active learning strategies can have a similar benefit. It can help to enhance brain function and memory in order to hold students' interest when content is given and tasks are being completed. The points made in the following table show a positive connection among physical activity, healthy brain function, and memory.

### The Effects of Physical Activity on Brain Function and Memory

| Study | Findings | Reference |
|---|---|---|
| A study compared 11- and 12-year-old students who were active in a physical education setting to their peers who sat for the same amount of time. | A positive relationship between physical activity and immediate and delayed memory was found. Students in the physical education lessons showed better recall and delayed recall on a memory task with vocabulary words. Results proclaimed that physically fit children demonstrate brain efficiency and use more working memory to complete given tasks. | Castelli, Glowacki, Barcelona, Calvert, & Hwang, 2015 |
| Studies analyzed the effects of physical activity for American children on mental functioning. | They concluded that physical activity should promote fitness as well as social, emotional, and intellectual development. Exercise enhanced children's mental functioning, especially executive functioning. | Tomporowski, Lambourne, & Okumura, 2011 |
| Studies analyzed effects of aerobic fitness on brain regions. | Aerobic fitness was associated with greater white matter integrity in children, which optimizes functional connectivity and communication between brain regions. Children with lower fitness levels showed greater fractional anisotropy in the corpus callosum, corona radiate, and superior longitudinal fasciculus. | Chaddock-Heymen et al., 2014 |

| Study | Findings | Reference |
|---|---|---|
| The Institute of Medicine studied the activity levels of children. | Children who were more active than their peers had faster cognitive processing speeds, performed better on standardized tests, and had better attention rates. | Adams, 2013 |
| Research was conducted to show the correlation between exercise and the brain. | Conclusions were made that exercise improves the ability of different parts of the brain to work together. Aerobic and resistance training help to maintain cognitive and brain health by improving focus and one's ability to coordinate multiple tasks. | Mercola, 2012 |
| A meta-analysis review was conducted on the effects of physical activity and physical fitness on children's achievement and cognitive outcomes. | A positive correlation among physical activity, fitness, and memory was found. | Fedewa & Ahn, 2011 |
| The Committee on Physical Activity and Physical Education in the School Environment: Food and Nutrition Board studied physical activity and brain health. | Cognitive functions related to memory and attention, which facilitate learning, were enhanced by physical activity and high levels of aerobic fitness. Single bouts of physical activity, as well as long-term participation in physical activity, improved brain health and cognitive function. | The Committee on Physical Activity and Physical Education in the School Environment: Food and Nutrition Board, 2013 |
| Studies monitored the simple reaction and choice response times in 7- to 10-year-old boys. | Boys who participated in aerobic activity for 30 minutes showed significant improvement in both tasks over boys who watched television for 30 minutes. | Ellemberg & St-Louis-Deschenes, 2010 |

## Fueling the Body and Brain for Optimal Learning

The brain requires water, sleep, oxygen, blood flow, and proper nutrients for an optimal learning state. If the brain does not have a healthy status, how can we ask students to perform at peak levels? The next important question is, "Which of these components can school settings actually control, monitor, and/or change?" Traditional technology usage does not deliver all these benefits. Additionally, many students attend school without receiving a restful night of sleep, nor do they have access to proper nutrition. These are crucial factors and, in most cases, out of the schools' hands. Students of all ages have nodded off at their desks because their bodies and brains were simply demanding sleep. The delivery of a physically active academic lesson can help a sleepy child maintain some attention and state of alertness during instruction and while completing tasks. Ideal cognitive processing may not be a realistic expectation in this sleep-deprived state, but active learning can surely help make a difference.

Oxygen is essential for learning, yet 90% of the oxygen in our body/brain is stale unless we breathe deeply or exercise (Moize & Hess, 2017). Can you predict what fuels the brain and has been referred to by Dr. John Ratey (2008) as "Miracle-Gro" for the brain? If you answered "exercise," you would be correct! Physical activity and exercise grow new brain cells (neurogenesis) in the learning and memory centers of the brain. Additionally, movement activates the BDNF (brain-derived neurotropic factor), which is a protein in humans that nourishes and protects the neural pathways for learning. Experts have suggested that student engagement increases 10% to 12% more during class simply by standing (Blaydes Madigan, 2009; Moize & Hess, 2017). When we sit for a certain amount of time, blood begins to pool in the feet and gluteus maximus, which is not beneficial for the body or the brain. Exercise provides protective effects to the brain through the production of nerve-protecting compounds, decreased cardiovascular disease, improved development, and survival of neurons (Mercola, 2012). When kinesthetic strategies are added to the classroom, students will be less likely to fall asleep and the brain can get the oxygen, blood flow, and nutrients it needs for optimal learning performance.

## Improving Concentration While Refocusing the Brain

Most educators would admit that they have seen a significant decrease in children's attention spans over the years. Developmental studies have found a positive link between physical activity and performance on concentration tests. Using movement in a learning environment helps improve focus and awareness for many learners. Active student engagement provides an alert state that holds students' attention. As a result, educators can continue to teach with traditional methodologies for a slightly extended period of time while getting desirable results. Physical activity can also be used as a break from academics, and research has shown this to have a positive effect on attention spans as well (Bartholomew & Jowers, 2011; Grieco, Jowers, & Bartholomew, 2009). When students remain seated during instruction or when utilizing technology for extended periods of time, it is beneficial to allow them the opportunity to move their body as it feels comfortable and/or is necessary for them. Studies have shown that immediately after engaging in physical activity, children are better able to concentrate on classroom tasks, which can improve learning (Castelli et al., 2015). Kinesthetic teaching methodologies are realistic solutions that can help redirect wandering minds while improving students' time on task.

## Increasing Motivation While Differentiating

Motivation for learning is one of the most important factors for student achievement and success. Educational progress will be significantly limited if students are not motivated to learn (Basch, 2010). Active learning balanced with digital resources is a fun combination that can be individualized and can help provide this necessary influence. Physical activity and technology are both easy to differentiate in order to meet students' needs, interests, and attractions. Adapting movements or physical activities often happens naturally. A student may need to move slower, choose a different position, or adjust their body to perform the task or skill. Many students are able to do this with little or no assistance from the teacher, all while receiving the benefits from the physical activity in the process. Implementing movement in the classroom may bring feelings of pride, accomplishment, and success. These feelings can easily produce intrinsic motivation along with a desire to move more. Kinesthetic teaching and learning in the classroom can provide motivation for additional reasons as well. These activities can be individualized, attainable, creative, relaxing, energizing, and unique. In turn, learning motivation will increase and continue as students feel confident and stimulated to learn at the same time.

## Increasing Attendance
## While Decreasing Behavioral Challenges

When students enjoy school and they are healthy, attendance can increase as behavioral challenges decrease. Multiple studies and research confirm that there is a clear connection between health, learning, attendance, and selected behaviors. Some students just need to move. Employing active learning strategies provides an outlet. When teachers increase physical activity and movement in schools, students' overall health, well-being, and energy levels will benefit. This may also lead to an increase in attendance because students will have the stamina to meet the physical demands of the school day. Below are some findings that support this link.

### The Effects of Physical Activity on Student Behavior

| Study | Findings | Reference |
|---|---|---|
| Research was done on the effects of regular physical activity and academic performance. | Research showed that using physical activity as a break from academic classwork throughout the school day can significantly increase on-task behavior. | Trost & van der Mars, 2009 |
| New York examined the effects of health-related fitness on school attendance. | An inverse relationship showed a change in fitness levels to days absent for both genders, with a slightly stronger effect for girls and youth in high poverty areas. Improvements in fitness could have a significant impact on child attendance over time, and recommendations were made that fitness interventions should be examined as a means for improving attendance. | D'Agostino, 2016 |
| A school in Mississippi examined the relationships among health-related fitness, academic achievement, and selected behaviors in both elementary and middle school students. | A positive correlation between fitness and standardized test scores in math and language arts was reported, along with a negative relationship for school absences. These findings should be considered when developing educational policies. | Blom et al., 2011 |
| A meta-analysis review of 59 studies was conducted. | It summarized that students who are physically active tend to have better attendance, grades, cognitive functioning, and classroom behaviors. | Fedewa & Ahn, 2011 |

### Engaging the Senses and
### Increasing Student Engagement

Sight, hearing, and touch—all elements potentially used in kinesthetic experiences and technologies—contribute most to our learning (Sousa, 2017). The more senses that are used in the learning process, the more likely the information will be retained and recalled at a later date. Traditional classrooms are consumed with writing, listening, reading, and seatwork—some with high digital usage, some without. These established skills are still valued in a learning environment, especially when partnered with technology. However, limiting the length of time students need to hold their attention to these tasks is an important consideration in all classrooms and school environments. Kinesthetic teaching techniques engage the learner and can be applied alongside traditional teaching methodologies, similarly to technology use. Increasing student engagement during instruction and delivering a multisensory experience by balancing movement and technology is an approach that will help teachers enhance student learning and peak performance.

# COMMON SENSE:
# AS STRONG AS THE RESEARCH

This chapter offers extensive research that supports the concept of using academic teaching methodologies to help students increase their academic success, brain function, health, and well-being. These studies are current, thorough, and plentiful. It is important to recognize the significance of the consistent evidence that validates the benefits of implementing lessons with kinesthetic learning and movement. However, what role does common sense play? Is it feasible to trust that when students are actively engaged in educational environments, they will perform better academically? Does it make sense that increasing oxygen, blood flow, and nutrients to the brain will enhance cognitive output? Is it logical to believe that having students move throughout the school day will develop their health, fitness, and overall well-being? Yes! What about the studies that have connected movement and physical activity to an increase in attendance and a decrease in behavioral challenges? Is it believable that healthier students will attend school more frequently? Can utilizing movement daily help to meet this objective? Can you agree that students who are physically active and enjoying their school day will behave better? The answer to all these questions is a resounding *yes*! The overflow of research presented in this chapter has colossal value; however, so does common sense. The bottom line is that when it comes to developing and enriching 21st-century learners, active learning simply fits our needs! As time passes, this chapter will fade and you may only recall the big picture that the evidence provides: Active teaching strategies create a new era of learning while magnifying student success. Nevertheless, reasonable summations of the advantages of physical activity and movement are timeless. It is plausible to predict that growing research on the power of movement in classroom settings will continue and expand while strengthening the support behind this cause. However, it is equally valuable to know that common sense justifies the research regarding this convincing teaching tool.

# WHAT DOES THIS MEAN TO ME?

### K–12 Teachers

1. Implement brain breaks and brain boosts when transitioning between subjects or daily activities and routines.

2. Incorporate age-appropriate exercises or kinesthetic review games that energize the brain and body while improving the learning state.

### Administration

1. Encourage teachers to utilize daily movement in all lessons and classroom environments.

2. Provide your faculty with professional development opportunities on kinesthetic teaching and learning.

### Educational Leaders/Affiliates

1. Support and develop curriculums that include kinesthetic applications that meet academic standards.

2. Provide research and create policies backing the implementation of kinesthetic education in all learning environments.

# CHAPTER SUMMARY

- We've gone from a society of movers to one that is obsessed with technology usage, social seclusion, poor nutritional selections, and inactivity.

- Technology usage has replaced traditional socialization and family time as the new normal.

- Utilizing active learning strategies can help to meet the following core human needs: certainty/comfort, uncertainty/variety, significance, love and connection, growth, and contribution.

- Balancing movement and technology in the classroom is a teaching method that reinforces the brain–body connection and improves cognitive function and academic performance.

- Current research shows that on average, students who maintain standard physical fitness levels tend to receive higher grade point averages and elevated scores on their standardized tests when compared to students who are not physically fit.

- Using movement to balance the long stretches of sitting that technology can cause will support an optimal learning state for the brain.

- Active learning, balanced with digital resources, is a fun combination that can be individualized to increase attendance and improve student motivation.

- Limiting the length of time students need to hold their attention to traditional and technological tasks is an important consideration in all classrooms and school environments.

# 3

# THE TECHNOLOGY MACHINE

## TECHNOLOGY OVERLOAD

You've probably witnessed the explosion of technology in your own life as well as in the lives of the adults and children around you. We live in a digital world. Technology drives our lives. It plays an important role in many aspects of communication, information access, business and finances, education, and medicine, to name a few. Innovative ideas have produced modern-day gadgets and gizmos that many people would say they can't live without. There is no argument that fast-changing technology has made way for advancements in society that were once unimaginable but have now simplified a multitude of tasks in our daily lives.

Americans of all ages are using technology for an alarming number of hours per day. Cell phones, tablets, and portable gaming devices have enabled us to consume digital media on the go. A report by Common Sense Media ("Landmark Report," 2015) indicates that teens are spending more than one third of their day using technology for entertainment such as music, social media, and gaming. When you add in the time students are using technology in school and for academic purposes, children and teens are experiencing a technology overload!

## The Physical Breakdown

The reality of the digital age is that this abundance of technology is taking a toll on our physical health. Children and adults alike are prone to an alarming number of ailments that affect our everyday wellness and can leave us with chronic problems. The risks that occur with too much technology usage adversely affect the entire body, including our brain, sensory organs, spine, and overall health. According to the American Optometric Association (AOA) (2015), screen time can cause digital eye strain, which results in burning, itchy, tired eyes; headaches; fatigue; blurred vision; and double vision. We blink two thirds less than we normally do when we are using a screen, which dries out the eyes and can increase the need for artificial tears (Barker, 2018). In addition, digital screens can

> give off high-energy, short-wavelength, blue and violet light, which may affect vision and even prematurely age the eyes. Early research shows that overexposure to blue light could contribute to eye strain and discomfort and may lead to serious conditions in later life such as age-related macular degeneration (AMD), which can cause blindness. (AOA, 2015)

This increased exposure to blue light is causing much alarm for the general eye health of our youth. And as students are increasingly using cell phones, tablets, Chromebooks, and laptops, this exposure is increasing dramatically both in and out of school.

With the introduction of streaming music sites such as Spotify, Apple Music, and Pandora, as well as instant access to movies and TV through sites such as Netflix and Amazon, our love affair with earbuds and headphones has exploded. Consumers want to take their music and movies with them everywhere they go. We demand quality listening devices that provide concert- or theater-level sound that drowns out all background noise; however, any device that produces more than 85 decibels of sound can cause hearing loss. "According to research conducted by the National Institute for Occupational Safety and Health, earphones inserted into the ear produce sound levels that can exceed 120 dB, which is comparable to a plane leaving the runway" (Thompson, 2017). This is alarming for our youth, considering the amount of time students are using headphones both in and out of the classroom. From cell phones on the school bus to software programs in the computer lab, today's student is exposed to a variety of immersive, loud noises that can cause hearing loss; 12.5% of kids between the ages of 6 and 19 have hearing loss as a result of listening to loud music, particularly through earbuds at unsafe volumes (Packer, 2015). Untreated hearing loss can negatively affect a student's academic progress, ability to perform tasks, and entry into the workforce. Additionally, the Centers for Disease Control and Prevention (CDC) state that children with hearing loss can have difficulty communicating and developing important language and social skills (2018).

Continuous usage of devices that require us to look down at 30- to 60-degree angles—such as cell phones, tablets, and laptops—causes neck strain. The weight of the human head tilted to those degrees places forty to sixty pounds of force on the neck and spine, resulting in headaches, pinched nerves, arthritis, bone spurs, muscular deformation, disc degeneration, and nerve complications (Jolly, 2018). Teens and preteens are spending an enormous amount of time with cell phones in hand. HealthCorps (2016) reports that the number of 16- to 18-year-olds reporting neck pain is increasing and that these teens have decreased flexibility, worse posture, and decreased neck muscle strength. Teens with neck pain are at an increased risk for developing chronic inflammation. This technology-driven neck pain has been given the nickname "tech neck" and has the potential for developing into ongoing neck and shoulder pain, headaches, and pain radiating down the arms (Sinicropi, 2016.)

Technology changes have brought about a profound alteration in the eating and activity habits of Americans. This increase in digital media usage has resulted in a nation that is larger than ever, and sadly, our students are not excluded from the effects. In the war against childhood obesity, screen time is one of our greatest enemies. With obesity being the most challenging health epidemic in the nation, the relationship between excessive technology use and obesity has been extensively researched. Since the 1980s, studies have been done to correlate the number of hours a child spends watching television to obesity and body mass index (BMI). The 21st-century child now has television, websites, streaming media, and social media competing for their undivided attention. Children who engage with more screen media also consume fewer fruits and vegetables; eat more calorie-rich snacks, drinks, and fast foods; and have a higher total calorie intake. Combined with a decrease in physical activity and reduced sleep, screen time makes weight management a challenge (Robinson et al., 2017). Our future generation is at risk for a variety of health complications and psychological concerns that include but are not limited to type 2 diabetes, high blood pressure, liver disease, sleep and eating disorders, respiratory problems, depression, low self-esteem, difficulties with peer relationships, increased stress and anxiety, learning disabilities, and behavioral challenges (Childhood Obesity Foundation, 2015). We now have a nation of youth who may not outlive their parents. It is imperative that we seriously consider the role that the technology overload plays in this scary statistic.

## The Cognitive Crash

While there's no denying that technology has its positive effects on cognition—such as increased task analyzation ability, multiple sources to gather information, and better spatial awareness—excessive technology usage by millennials is physically changing the brain's gray matter and resulting in potentially permanent changes in brain function (Weng et al., 2013). Gray matter controls functions such as memory, muscle control, emotion, speech, decision making, self-control, and sensory perception. This cognitive crash is becoming more apparent with children born after the year 2000, who have embraced technology from infancy, some of whom could effectively manipulate a tablet screen before their first birthday. Consider this: On any given day, 29% of babies under the age of 1 year engage in about 90 minutes of screen time a day (Rideout, 2011) and up to more than four hours per day in the preschool years (Tandon, Zhou, Lozano, & Christakis, 2011). Without a doubt, our younger generation is living in a world that's drastically different from 20 years ago. It isn't surprising that this obsession with screen time is physically and psychologically changing the minds of children. In fact, Dr. Larry Rosen, a leading research psychologist, has coined the phrase *iDisorder* as

> changes to your brain's ability to process information and your ability to relate to the world due to your daily use of media and technology

resulting in signs and symptoms of psychological disorders—such as stress, sleeplessness, and a compulsive need to check in with all of your technology. (Rosen, 2012)

Rosen also states that daily exposure to the blue light emitted from devices is leaving plaques on the brain of children—plaques that are similarly found in Alzheimer's patients (National Geographic, 2018).

It is widely known that today's youth are obsessed with their devices, particularly smartphones. Many children and teens have a super computer in their pocket that makes the world accessible to them 24/7. According to one report (Nielsen, 2017), 26% of American children get their first smartphone at age 8, while nearly 45% have one between the ages of 10 and 12. And while this technology may make it convenient to entertain kids on the go, excessive mobile technology has a negative impact on focus and cognitive function. Children may be less able to focus (or maintain focus) on tasks due to the constant desire to check their devices. Technology is overstimulating our brains and cutting out our creativity by depriving our brains of much-needed downtime (Richtel, 2010). Rosen states that technology "stifles your ability to live within boredom" (National Geographic, 2018) by eliminating the creativity that comes from daydreaming and relaxing. Today's child is less likely to engage in free play and more likely to crave the constant stimulation that electronics provide. This need for stimulation, combined with the lack of imaginative play and self-soothing activities, produces kids who may be misdiagnosed with conditions that require the use of medication. Our ability to shut down has been compromised and children exhibit signs of insomnia, restlessness, and neurotic behavior. According to Dunkley (2012), the two most diagnosed disorders in pediatrics are childhood bipolar disorder and attention deficit hyperactivity disorder (ADHD). Dunkley notes that the unnaturally stimulating nature of an electronic screen affects both our physical and mental health, a condition she calls *electronic screen syndrome*. Nowadays, situations that once would be considered "distraction-free zones," such as school, church, or meetings at the office, are easily interrupted by the technology that hides in our pockets. These constant distractions are negatively affecting our cognitive control (the ability for our mind to override our impulses and help us make logical decisions). When faced with tasks that require our undivided attention, we need to choose our actions based on the goal at hand. Adolescents already have an immature system to regulate risky behavior; expecting them to override their impulses can often be unrealistic.

Adolescents and teens engage in several types of media at the same time throughout their day. It's not uncommon to see a teen gaming online while video chatting with their friends, streaming music, and receiving snaps and texts on their phone all at the same time! But our brains are not built for media multitasking. In fact, what we have here is a distracted brain. Our brains are limited in their ability to pay attention. When it comes to technology, we aren't actually multitasking; instead, we are switching back and forth from one activity to another (Gazzaley & Rosen, 2016). We are not selectively processing information based on priorities or goals; rather, we are jumping erratically back and forth from one activity to the next. This also encourages students to engage their attention in the activity that they find most interesting rather than most relevant, causing constant disruption. The distracted brain results in work that may be completed faster but at the cost of more stress and pressure, higher frustration, and increased effort (Gazzaley & Rosen, 2016).

## The Mental/Emotional Roller Coaster

Today's youth are using their devices most often to connect with their peers and social platforms. The digital age has created a world of interconnectedness for children, a place where news travels fast and someone is always watching. While the positive effects of this can be a sense of online community and belonging, there is another side that fosters a sense of competition, fear, and inadequacy. Consider the following studies:

- A study at the University of Pittsburgh found a correlation between social media and negative body image. Kids who spent more time on social media had between 2.2 and 2.6 times the risk of eating and body image concerns compared to their peers who spent less time on social media.

- A separate study from the University of Pittsburgh School of Medicine showed that more time on social media increases the likelihood of sleep problems and symptoms of depression.

- The UCLA Brain Mapping Center studied 13- to 18-year-olds and found that receiving a high number of likes on photos showed increased activity in the reward center of the brain (Hurley, 2018).

Adolescents and teens are living in a world where they are constantly on display in order to achieve social acceptance. The selfie-taking, Snapchatting, Instagraming world they live in is all about image and how many likes you can get. This social media madness results in a life riddled with anxiety and low self-esteem. The Royal Society for Public Health surveyed 14- to 24-year-olds about social media, and the results showed that all platforms led to increased feelings of depression, anxiety, poor body image, and loneliness (Ehmke, 2018). Teenagers are admitting to feeling depressed, hopeless, and considering suicide. Twenge (2017) and her colleagues conducted research that found a sudden increase in teens' symptoms of depression, suicide risk factors, and suicide rates in 2012—around the same time that smartphones became popular. Twenge's research found that teens who spend five or more hours per day on their devices are 71% more likely to have risk factors for suicide. Kids are watching the "highlight reel" of their peers' lives and comparing their own life to the perfectionist angle the camera shows. The perspective of only seeing the good parts that others are willing to share makes teens feel inadequate and self-conscious about their imperfect lives. Bad news travels so fast within the social circles that there is little room for error because saying or doing one wrong thing can leave a lasting scar and be digitally replayed over and over for years to come. It's a scary world to grow up in not only physically but emotionally.

Another factor in the mental/emotional roller coaster is the need for instant gratification. As younger generations become more accustomed to the immediate response and instant gratification that technology provides, we will become a nation of impatient humans who feel entitled to instant fulfillment. Even as adults, we demonstrate this impatience: Think about your reaction the last time the Internet froze or a webpage wouldn't load. What fuels our love affair with streaming music and movies? How many people do you know that pay a significant yearly fee to an online retailer in order to get free two-day shipping any time they buy something? Even amusement parks will let you buy "skip the line" passes to avoid having to wait. But this impatience has an impact on our youth that can be devastating in the workforce. Graduates who have gotten used to immediate feedback in every aspect of their lives now have to enter the workforce or climb the corporate ladder that is riddled with failures, setbacks, and slow growth. How will they handle it? Are we preparing our future leaders to live in the real world, where change rarely happens overnight? What's worse is that this desire for instant gratification can actually be physically addicting. "About 60% of 18- to 34-year-old respondents to a Pew Research Center survey said they sleep next to their cell phones so they don't miss calls, texts or updates during the night" (Alsop, 2014). Instant gratification fuels our innate human pleasure principle and triggers a very real psychological response. We start to believe that we should instantly get a job, instantly fall in love, and instantly have success in life, and we end up with feelings of depression, rejection, and failure when we don't get it.

## The New Civil/Social Connection

The current generation is growing up socially and emotionally in a world driven by technology and screen time. The amount of time children and adults alike spend using electronic devices takes away from the traditional interactions that past generations once knew. Figure 3.1 shows us the growth in household Internet access from 1997 through 2015. Today, more than 77% of the nation uses the Internet in their homes. In fact, only 11% of U.S. adults do not use the Internet at all (Anderson, Perrin, & Jiang, 2018). Children's access to electronic devices has grown tremendously, and they engage with screens almost all day long. It's safe to say that families are not interacting and communicating with one another nearly as often as they were 20 years ago. And it's not only families; children aren't physically engaging with one another anymore. Technology has created an avenue for kids to stay in contact without ever having to see or speak to one another. In 2016, teenagers said they spend less than two hours a week socializing with friends outside of school, only one third of the time GenX students spent at parties in 1987 (Twenge, 2017). In 2010, teens between the ages of 12 to 17 reported using text messages more than any other form of communication, including face-to-face interaction (Lenhart et al., 2010). These days, many teens use Snapchat as their primary form of communication, citing several reasons for the app's main appeal: the informality, the choice to use photos or text to communicate, and the ability to view friends' stories (or not) with no obligation to reply (Godlewski, 2016).

All of this digital communication leads to young children who aren't benefitting from the emotional cues, nonverbal cues, body language, and facial expressions that social interactions provide. Children who engage with one another in real life acquire the skills needed to form positive relationships and participate effectively in social situations. It helps them read the emotional context clues of the situation and make decisions to act accordingly. It allows them to develop their skills in the art of conversation making. "Teaching the younger generation the finer points of interpersonal skills is key to their long-term success. No matter how advanced technology becomes, landing a scholarship, job interview or fiancé will still require some form of verbal communication" (Fine 2017).

The demise of emotional recognition contributes to the rising trend of poor decisions adolescents and teens make when engaging with each other online. Approximately 39% of teens admit that they have posted something online that they regret and 25% have shared a profile with a false identity ("Is Social Networking Changing Childhood?," 2009). Social media sites and online gaming

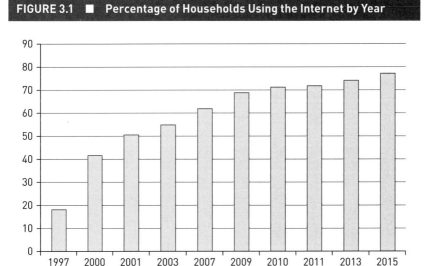

**FIGURE 3.1   ■   Percentage of Households Using the Internet by Year**

Source: *Computer and Internet Use in the United States: Population Characteristics*, Thom File. Issued May 2013: https://www.census.gov/prod/2013pubs/p20-569.pdf.

profiles allow children to create alter egos or fictional identities to foster a level of anonymity that they feel protected by. It also provides a false sense of invincibility and distance that they believe will prevent them from being held accountable for their online actions. About 32% of teenagers who use the Internet say they have been targets of threatening messages, have had their private e-mails or text messages forwarded without consent, have had an embarrassing picture posted without permission, have had rumors about them spread online, or have experienced other forms of cyberbullying, with girls more likely to experience it than boys (Lenhart, 2007). The Internet has provided children with a platform to say whatever they want whenever they want without having to physically face the consequences of their words. It used to be that you could actually see the hurt in someone's eyes when you were caught name-calling on the playground. Now you can close your eyes to it while the cyber world shuffles it around from person to person, destroying the target of your words with every click and forward.

# LEARNER BENEFITS

## Community Connections

Technology has been labeled as harmful to the development of social skills for obvious reasons: Students are texting instead of talking, and social media websites cannot compare to face-to-face communication. However, the benefits that digital resources have brought to social skills (in and out of school settings) should also not be ignored. Now, students can stay connected to anyone, any time, in any location, broadening the concept of community relations. That's a pretty powerful benefit. Social media platforms provide students who feel socially awkward with a place to fit in and perhaps excel. Written communication can take away from the stresses that eye contact and verbal communication sometimes bring. In a sense, technology can be used to expand communication skills and build learner comfort, which is a notable benefit and can increase academic success.

How does technology affect a sense of community in a classroom setting? This will depend on the teacher. Digital resources can and should be used to build a community atmosphere. In order for this to occur, technological applications, consumptions, and deliveries cannot always take place with students working in isolation. Teachers must allow students to work together with partners or teams to magnify the advantages that technology provides. Combing class or whole-group projects with technology is also an effective strategy that can be used to strengthen a community connection. In Chapter 8, tech community connectors will be explored. Utilizing technology through interactive means is a strong approach for creating a cohesive community in any and all learning environments.

## Personalized Technology

You may think with all the negative effects that technology has had on our students' lives that we'd be against its current role in education and its upward usage trend. However, that is not the case. The value of technology in the classroom cannot be denied, and we're not alone in our thinking. According to a CDW-G national survey, 86% of teachers agree that classroom computers improve student performance (Starr, 2003). The widespread inclusion of various forms of technology in the school setting has changed the way teachers teach and, thereby, the way students learn. From tablets to laptops to interactive whiteboards, technology in the classroom provides an endless variety of methods that teachers can use to personalize the learner's experience.

Using technology to drive student learning involves creating student-centered lessons in which the technology supports the instruction rather than having the technology influence the lesson. Technology allows teachers to design instruction that caters to the interests, personalities, cultural differences, and languages of their students rather than delivering traditional one-size-fits-all lessons. By developing strong insights into their students' strengths, weaknesses, and learning styles, teachers can carefully choose the appropriate strategy to implement varied lessons that use technology to meet each student's individual needs. Content is delivered through a variety of media, students are engaged in several forms of instructional practice, and teachers can gather immediate formative data on student progress. Often, using technology allows students a sense of choice over their own learning, as curriculum objectives can typically be met in a variety of ways. For example, a traditional book report could now be formatted as a slide show, a video response, a blog or vlog, or a collaborative shared document. The differentiation that comes from using technology in the classroom can create a truly personalized educational experience for the learner.

## Flexible Pacing

The abundance of computers in today's classrooms lends itself perfectly to a new way of thinking about education: flexible pacing. No longer do students need to move through the curriculum at a predetermined rate, scope, and sequence. Flexible pacing allows students to engage in content through websites or software platforms at their own pace. Teachers are present to answer questions, guide and assist students as needed, and monitor progress. They are able to add to and modify the content each student sees online based on the needs of those students. Teachers can motivate their students by including content that is tailored to the students' interests and can make accommodations or revisions at any time, depending on the students' feedback and responses. Goals are set for individual student progress as opposed to expectations geared toward grade level or content standards. At any given time, a classroom could potentially have 25 students working on 25 different lessons, each student working on the lesson that he or she needs the most. Students who are ready to move forward are not held up by the students who need more review time, and students who are struggling with a concept do not get swept ahead before demonstrating mastery. Flexible pacing through technology fosters a classroom where teachers have the ability to meet every student exactly where they are.

## Remediation and Enrichment

It is critical for teachers who are using technology with their students to be intentionally responsive to student content outcomes, both positive and negative, in order to deliver instruction that is appropriate for the learner. The U. S. has been struggling for years to find a solution that closes the educational gap between students. Although there is no one solution to the complexity of varied student achievement, technology can play a positive role in helping teachers design instruction to remediate struggling students. At the elementary level, a variety of software programs are available in both reading and math for students to gain additional practice on skills. Educational websites and apps are loaded with skill-building games for learners as young as preschool age. At the secondary level, schools are providing online courses and resources that are available 24/7 for students to access any time they need additional instruction or material. Schools are using technology to implement systematic, research-based progress monitoring systems in order to identify students in need. In addition, there is no shortage of online programs teachers can use to gather student responses quickly and efficiently, allowing teachers to have access to formative assessments that measure and track individual student performance and to differentiate instruction accordingly.

Today's technology provides unique opportunities for enrichment in the classroom. The use of social media platforms, apps, and websites allow students to collaborate, and audio/visual media can instantly grab students' attention and encourage them to take their learning beyond standard classroom instruction. Students can explore concepts in depth through podcasts, design software, and videos. Students can engage in open dialogue about a topic, debate with one another, and collaborate on writing assignments through the use of social media or Google classrooms. Students can take charge of their own learning, solving complex problems at home through WebQuests or independent investigations of a concept. Technology provides a way for students to explore the world without ever leaving their seat, gives them access to the great wonders of the world and images and videos of faraway places, and offers opportunities to make global connections with students in other countries. The use of technology can provide students with opportunities for learning that extend far beyond the walls of the classroom.

## Personal Comfort

The digital lifestyle is an ingrained part of the 21st-century learner. Today's student is not only comfortable with using technology; they are uncomfortable without it! Technology is entwined in every aspect of our young generations' lives, and using technology in the classroom is a considerable factor in the comfort level of the modern learner. Students are looking for a classroom that is relevant and meaningful to them. Teachers who encourage students to use modern technology in the learning process are making a connection to the students' digital identities. Using platforms such as Twitter, Facebook, and Google Classroom to engage students in discussion encourages all students to be a part of the dialogue and enhances student collaboration with one another. Students already feel comfortable speaking through text and are more likely to participate and engage in the discussion this way. Allowing students to use mobile devices appropriately throughout instruction can give them access to up-to-date and relevant information that is pertinent to classroom discussions or can assist them in solving problems. Students are given a variety of ways to demonstrate their learning through different media and can complete assignments through digital avenues that they are already accustomed to using. Creating lessons that apply learning through technology helps students relate the classroom content to their current lives and future careers. Channeling technology in ways that enhance student learning, rather than distracting from it, fosters a classroom environment in which students feel respected and comfortable!

# CURRENT EDUCATIONAL TRENDS AND LEARNER OPTIONS

As educational practices change, students are engaged in new learning opportunities in their online and digital classroom environments. Teachers are better able to develop more personalized instruction, while students are offered more options for collaboration and engagement. The educational trends of technology in the classroom are facilitating fresh and interactive learning environments that provide benefits for teacher and student alike. Let's take a look at a few of the innovative ways in which technology has influenced instruction.

## Delivering Instruction

Best practice in instructional delivery has long been a topic of debate among educators. From historically lecture-based content delivery to more modern small-group and differentiated instruction methods, teachers have explored a variety of ways to get information and content to their students. Technology has opened up a whole new avenue of doors for delivering instruction and has widened our global reach. What once was unimaginable in the classroom has now been made possible through technology. Technology-assisted or technology-supported instruction can tailor instructional delivery to meet the needs of a diverse group of learners. This is meant to supplement direct teacher instruction and doesn't simply rely solely on student-to-tech interaction. A classroom with a good movement and technology (MT) balance that employs this type of delivery may use and include interactive whiteboards, video conferencing, digital learning programs and materials, virtual travel, online informational or text-based resources, computer software programs, and digital communication. In the MT classroom, instructional delivery combines tech tools with traditional content delivery to create the best learning environment possible for the 21st-century student. Research has shown that struggling readers who use individual computer programs that match and support the curriculum, in combination with traditional instruction, show great improvement in their reading skills (Cheung & Slavin, 2012). Additionally, this positive correlation is also evident in math when students are continuously engaged in a technology-rich environment (Cheung & Slavin, 2013). Students are using these tech tools daily to make connections with the curriculum and the teacher's direct instruction to build a deeper understanding of the content.

## Consuming Instruction

The cookie-cutter method of consuming instruction does not work for today's digital learner. As the evolution of technology continues, students are consuming more and more content digitally. Siri and Alexa answer their beck and call. Media giants such as Apple and Netflix provide endless bingeable content. Apps prevent boredom, and social media platforms provide socialization. Marketing expert Heidi Cohen (2017) explains that there are five types of media consumption that today's generation engages in: focused (fully engaged with one device), dual (engaged with multiple devices at the same time), information snacking (consuming small bits of media to fill time, such as checking e-mail or reading the news), time-shifted content (saving or storing media to use later), and content binging (consuming large portions of content in one sitting). Today's youth is comfortable with consuming information from a variety of modern formats. This is the generation in which newspapers, cable and local television, and libraries are becoming obsolete. This digital lifestyle translates into the academic setting as well. Students are craving a variety of ways to get information, and traditional textbooks and workbook pages are becoming a thing of the past. With curriculum becoming so packed, there are more things to cover in less time, and it's inevitable that students have to consume at least some of their instruction independently. Using technology to assist with this provides a variety of ways for students to get what they need outside of explicit teacher instruction. Examples of digital means in which students may consume instruction include webpages, online simulators, online and digital books, podcasts, YouTube channels, gaming platforms, and WebQuests.

## Applying Instruction

Increasing rigor in instruction is all the buzz today. Educators are looking for ways to improve the cognitive depth that their students demonstrate. The idea is that students truly have attained mastery when they can apply their learning, synthesize information, and transfer information from one context to another. Technology in the classroom assists students in gathering the information they need for deeper understanding and provides avenues for them to demonstrate their learning. By presenting interactive experiences and assignments, teachers can provide students with unique opportunities to learn by doing. It's important that teachers are using technology to bring real-world problems into the classroom for students to explore and connect with. This application of learned content helps students transfer what is happening in the classroom to real-world skills needed in the 21st century. Students are using problem-solving skills not only to find a solution to the task; they are discovering their own strengths and weaknesses and challenging themselves to persevere through problems. With an increased focus on college and career readiness among graduates, the value of this cannot be overlooked. Students can apply instruction through technological means such as collaborative work/group assignments, using software programs for design or creation, interactive discussions through online forums or social media sites, online multimedia projects, student-created websites, and online journal entries.

# FUTURE EXPECTATIONS

## 1:1 Computing

With all the benefits of using technology in the classroom, it is no wonder that it can be considered the future of education. Schools across the country are making a big push to get technology into the hands of their students. Having computers or tablets for every single learner so that they can access digital media and online content to enhance the learning process is referred to as *1:1 computing*. The prevalence of 1:1 computing in classrooms around the U. S. is rising every year. Schools are hoping to increase student achievement and build 21st-century skills at the same time. A report from Front Row Education shows that more than 50% of teachers now have a 1:1 student-to-device ratio (EdTech Staff, 2017.) The goal is that the increased technology in the classroom will assist teachers in creating the more personalized learner experience we discussed earlier in this chapter. Students will be able to access content tailored to their instructional level while having the resources needed to complete complex and rigorous assignments. Ideally, student-centered, project-based learning would increase without sacrificing the individual attention the teacher can provide.

## College and Career Ready in the 21st Century

College and career readiness has been on the forefront of educational discussion since the introduction of Common Core standards in 2009. Being ready for a career means that high school graduates have the skills needed to succeed in the workforce or college studies. But exactly what role does technology play in that? Students who are college and career ready are those that have experienced personalized, rigorous, and differentiated schooling—an experience that we've already noted can be provided by using technology in the classroom. David Goodrum, director of academic technology and information services at Oregon State University, states that "a 21st century view of learner success requires students to not only be thoughtful consumers of digital content, but effective and collaborative creators of digital media, demonstrating competencies and communicating ideas through dynamic storytelling, data visualization and content curation" (Kelly, 2018). We are looking for students who can strategize solutions for real-world problems, partner with others to develop unique ideas and bring them to fruition, and use digital resources to shape the outcome. In an article by Piliouras et al. (2014), the authors state that "technology proficiency confers a competitive edge to students competing on a global stage" and "can help students develop soft skills—such as helping others, teamwork, collaboration, and group research." Using technology to support academic instruction provides meaningful experiences that help students develop into thoughtful, intentional decision makers who can successfully work in a collaborative environment. Open-ended projects that use technology enhance creativity and encourage out-of-the-box thinking to prepare students for life experiences in the 21st century.

# BEST PRACTICE IN QUESTION

## Cautionary Thoughts

As technology changes, there is no doubt that the way we teach and learn can and will change, too. We can't—and shouldn't—detach ourselves from the ever-changing technology machine or the digital influences in our lives. We must proceed with caution, though, in allowing technology to consume our educational system. With every new trend in education comes the potential for underlying problems. Where is the line between enough technology and too much? How can you ensure authentic and original work in online collaborative communities? What are the long-term health risks from overusing technological devices? Does technology make students lazy? As educators, it is our responsibility to remove the obstacles that prevent our students from reaching their greatest potential. That means creating classrooms that provide an eclectic approach to designing and delivering instruction. The education system needs to adapt to new methods of teaching while being mindful of the research that supports a variety of methodologies. The most innovative way to improve student performance is to use multiple modalities of instruction and keep the varied learning intelligences of the student in mind. Using technology to support those efforts is wise, but it must be done carefully and intentionally.

## A Desire for Change

The best practice in education is to use what we know from research to drive our decisions in the classroom. That being said, we can't deny the research presented both here and in Chapter 2 that supports the importance of balancing both movement and technology. The physical, social, and emotional effects of increasing technology are alarming. The physical, social, and emotional effects of increasing movement are encouraging! We must unite the two in order to create a 21st-century classroom that has the best interests of the whole child at heart—a balanced classroom in which students can satisfy their body's need for movement and their brain's desire for novelty, one in which the digital devices that provide students with comfort and security are balanced with activities that build interpersonal skills and stretch students outside their comfort zone. Teachers who desire positive change for their students and our future leaders need to promote health and wellness while embracing technology and its advantages. The 21st-century classroom is not a place where all traditional teaching is exempt. It is a community of learners that recognizes the importance of multiple facets of the educational system and balances them wisely. The time for change is now. It is important to recognize the benefits of implementing lessons with both kinesthetic learning and technological resources and searching out ways for movement and technology to complement—not compete with—each other in the classroom.

# WHAT DOES THIS MEAN TO ME?

### K–12 Teachers

1. Take continuing education courses and technology trainings to stay current and up-to-date. Consider being on a technology committee at your school so your voice can be heard.

2. Utilize technology programs and devices as standard practice in classroom teachings, routines, and procedures, but be aware of overuse.

### Administration

1. Allocate funding toward increasing technology resources in your school.

2. Offer yearly trainings and workshops to keep your faculty up-to-date with new technology uses and programs.

### Educational Leaders/Affiliates

1. Build awareness and concern regarding technology addictions and overuse.

2. Support and create technology subsidies for schools with low financial funding.

# CHAPTER SUMMARY

- Fast-changing technology has made way for advancements in society that were once unimaginable but have now simplified a multitude of tasks in our daily lives.

- The digital age doesn't come without risks, and it is taking a toll on our physical, mental/emotional, and social well-being.

- Excessive technology use is linked to visual problems, hearing loss, neck strain, and obesity.

- Cognitive ability is negatively affected by too much technology: Focus overload, overstimulation, and distractibility are common.

- Children and teens are facing a variety of mental/emotional issues from the effects of social media and technology usage, including depression, isolation, decreased self-esteem, and the inability to recognize emotions in others.

- Using technology appropriately in the classroom has a variety of positive effects on education and learners.

- Students who engage with technology within the classroom receive a more personalized experience and content that meets their individual needs.

- Technology is an important tool for effective content delivery and application and can have a lasting impact on college and career readiness.

- It is important to recognize both the positive and negative effects of using technology and to make wise decisions about using it in the classroom.

- The 21st-century classroom should be a place where technology is embraced yet balanced with the need for other research-based methodologies, such as kinesthetic learning.

# 4

# MAKING THE MOST OF IT

## A BALANCING ACT

How do we define the balance between movement and technology in an academic environment, and will all classroom teachers' sense of balance look the same? *Balance* is defined as different elements that are equally proportioned. In other words, movement and technology will play an equal role in the learning process in our classroom settings to enhance student achievement. In most cases, this is not considered common practice nor is it defined by schools as necessary protocol—at least, not yet. The concept of a balancing act between movement and technology is a novel phenomenon that is only now starting to get attention. Although technology usage has become a standard in our daily lives, many teachers have not yet implemented all its benefits into their classroom environments. Similarly, many teachers are fearful of active teaching and learning strategies and are not incorporating these methodologies into their classrooms either. While recognizing that 85% of students are predominately kinesthetic learners, teachers should be using these active techniques on a regular basis. However, this is typically not the case. This publication promotes the idea that both movement and technological methodologies should be used daily in classrooms to produce optimal learning results.

The time has come for schools as well as our society to identify the terms of this balancing act that must exist between movement and technology. In Chapter 2, you examined the powerful benefits of implementing movement into the learning process to increase academic achievement. After viewing this abundant research, the concrete evidence shows us that kinesthetic teaching methods belong in classroom environments as standard practice. Additionally, the role that digital overuse plays in our existence cannot be disputed. Therefore, when moving forward in education, we must combine these dynamic teaching and learning tools on a routine basis to allow our students to benefit from both methodologies equally for the greatest impact. Teachers have different strengths, experiences, and knowledge that will play a part in how they operate their classrooms and the strategies they utilize. A challenge that lies in defining this balancing act is the different categories and types of educators that must be identified and addressed. They are as follows:

- **Movement/Active educators:** These teachers are already using active learning strategies in their classroom environment to enhance the learning process. However, there is a wide range of how much and how often educators are teaching kinesthetically or using physical activity to improve performance. Some teachers are using these activities every 15–20 minutes, while others are using them once a week or even less frequently.

- **Tech teachers:** These educators are utilizing technological teaching and learning methodologies on a regular basis. The range of usage can be wide here as well. While some teachers use technology throughout the week here and there, other educators use these tactics throughout the entire school day for a multitude of reasons.

- **Newcomers:** These teachers have not yet committed to being a movement educator or a tech teacher. Perhaps these educators are holding on to the value of traditional teaching benefits or they haven't received the support they need to make these changes in their lessons at this point. It is also possible that these educators are stuck in their routines. Having taught a certain way for an extended period of time can make it difficult to adjust and modify teaching practices, even in situations where an educator knows this is necessary.

The reality is that when you measure the advantages of movement and technology (MT) in learning environments, both practices should receive equal rights, time, attention, and usage. Schools and teachers are in the business of improving students' academic success, and these two avenues must be equally balanced for the best results. In this book, the goal is to develop what will be referred to as *MT educators* (*MTEs*). These teachers are either in the process of or have mastered the balancing act between movement and technology in their learning environment. MTEs are utilizing combined strategies to get the best of both of these methods. This concept will also be called the *MT balance* or the *movement and technology balance*; other similar language may also be used to identify this philosophy.

Balancing movement and technology will allow students to be actively engaged throughout the school day while also being exposed to the technological advancements that currently rule our society. MTEs create the ideal win–win scenario. Students will thrive in these settings as the whole child is developed and their physical, mental/emotional, social, and cognitive growth increases. This balancing act will probably look a little different from classroom to classroom. MT teachers, by nature, will view practices and procedures based on their comfort levels and personalities. These will have a direct effect on the way teachers conduct their MT classrooms. It is essential for all educators to attempt to define and create a balanced learning environment in which movement and technology operate as a united effort to enhance learning. This is not only important for a successful academic performance but also for well-rounded students who will be prepared for future challenges.

## Move Students Often With a Steady Flow of Technology

In Chapter 1, the greater-than sign (>) was used to describe how movement has declined over the course of history. This symbol demonstrated how we have gone from a society of movers to one that is sedentary and inactive. We are hopeful that we have currently reached a turning point as opposed to a point of no return. In Chapter 2, the concept of WANTing some of our past values back was explored. These morals and standards are desirable and should be a part of our future direction so that we can once again become a society of movers. The less-than sign (<) was used in Chapter 1 to represent the rise of technology over time. This symbol shows the minimal role that technology played in our past, along with its vast usage in the present and potential future. In Figure 4.1, we show the overlapping of these symbols with the word *MOST* emphasized as a means for finding the balance between movement and technology in the modern-day classroom.

**FIGURE 4.1    ■    Making the MOST of It!**

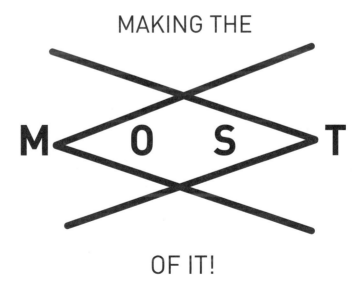

The 21st-Century Classroom:

Move Students Often with a Steady Flow of Technology

*MOST* stands for *__move__ students __often__ with a __s__teady flow of __t__echnology*. This refers to utilizing both movement and technology daily in learning environments as standard protocol. Teachers are encouraged to move students often so that blood flow, oxygen, attention, and focus can be increased and heightened. Technology should also be used steadily throughout the class period to keep up with current trends while preparing students for college and future demands. This combination provides an enticing learning environment for even the most reluctant learner. MTEs will have lively lessons that are active, modern, and desirable for a wide range of learners. These blended classrooms will continue to use traditional teaching and learning methodologies while including twists and turns along the way by incorporating MT tactics. Adding kinesthetic activities will surely engage students while demanding their attention and allowing them to interact with their peers. Technology will keep things bright and inviting while appealing to the novelty-seeking brain. Each lesson will present a unique challenge to educators: Some standards will lend themselves more naturally to kinesthetic learning while others are more linked to technology. The fundamental goal is for teachers to seek a sense of balance with all their lessons as best they can. This balancing act must be viewed on a sliding spectrum. The balance may not be completely straight down the middle with every lesson. On one day, a standard might be reached with a time-consuming kinesthetic activity while technology plays a small part in the learning. The next day, the roles may be reversed. This will happen as we grow and find the balance between movement and technology on a day-to-day basis. The most important thing to keep in mind is that educators will use both strategies regularly while continually looking for the balance between the two. This will take time and energy as teachers experiment to uncover best practices for advanced results.

## Where Are You Now

The first step in becoming an MTE is to define where you currently are in this process. Chances are, you will be stronger or more comfortable with either movement or technology. Would you describe yourself as a movement educator, a tech teacher, or a newcomer? If you consider yourself to be an MTE, be prepared to be a leader to your peers as you continue to grow and help them along their journey.

### Movement

Let's focus on movement first. Look at Figure 4.2 and identify where you are on the spectrum regarding your usage of movement within the classroom. (View Chapter 7 for appropriate examples of how movement can be used effectively to improve academic achievement.)

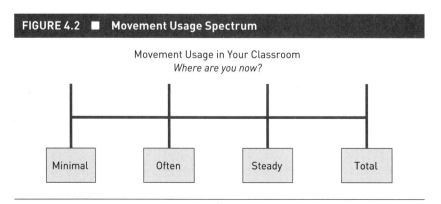

FIGURE 4.2 ■ Movement Usage Spectrum

Movement Usage in Your Classroom
*Where are you now?*

Minimal    Often    Steady    Total

The levels of usage are described as follows:

- **Minimal:** rarely utilize movement in your classroom to optimize learning (having students physically transition from one place to another is not considered a suitable example of movement within the classroom)

- **Often:** utilize movement from time to time to optimize learning

- **Steady:** utilize movement regularly while actively engaging students in a variety of ways to optimize learning

- **Total:** utilize a variety of movement activities and kinesthetic lessons as a daily practice to reach academic standards

Look at Figure 4.3 and identify your comfort level with using movement in your learning environment.

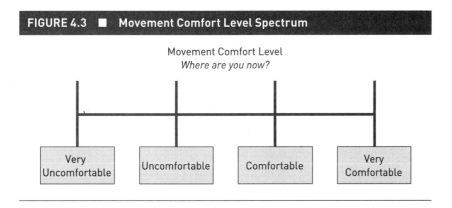

**FIGURE 4.3 ■ Movement Comfort Level Spectrum**

After categorizing your usage and comfort levels related to movement in your learning environment, please answer the following questions:

- Do you think your use of movement in the classroom provides students with a balanced learning approach?

- Do you need to add more movement activities to your teaching methodologies? Why or why not?

- Why do you currently use a lot of movement in your classroom setting or why haven't you done this already?

- What are some examples of movement activities you use in the teaching and learning process? (Specific examples are given in Chapter 7.)

## Technology

Now, let's focus on technology. Look at Figure 4.4 and identify where you are on the spectrum regarding your usage.

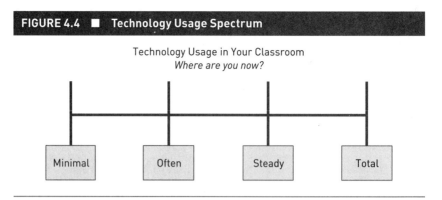

**FIGURE 4.4 ■ Technology Usage Spectrum**

Technology Usage in Your Classroom
*Where are you now?*

Minimal  Often  Steady  Total

The levels of usage are described as follows:

- **Minimal:** rarely utilize technology in your classroom to optimize learning
- **Often:** utilize technology from time to time to optimize learning
- **Steady:** utilize technology on a regular basis and for different purposes to optimize learning
- **Total:** utilize technology as a daily practice and with a variety of approaches to reach academic standards

Look at Figure 4.5 and identify your comfort level with using technology in your learning environment. (Specific examples are given in Chapter 7.)

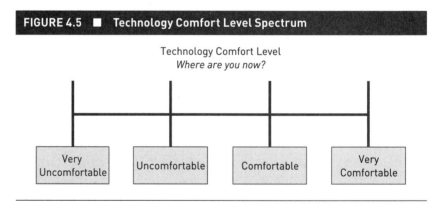

**FIGURE 4.5 ■ Technology Comfort Level Spectrum**

Technology Comfort Level
*Where are you now?*

Very Uncomfortable  Uncomfortable  Comfortable  Very Comfortable

After categorizing your usage and comfort levels related to technology in your learning environment, please answer the following questions:

- Do you think your use of technology in the classroom provides students with a balanced learning approach?
- Do you need to add more technology to your teaching methodologies? Why or why not?

- Why do you currently use a lot of technology in your classroom setting or why haven't you?

- What are some examples of how you use technology in the teaching and learning process?

## Goals

Once you have identified where you stand regarding MT use and comfort levels, it is time to define your goals for growth and improvement. Changing and developing a new teaching philosophy for educators should never be expected to happen overnight or with the snap of a finger. Instead, this process should be based on a continuum of what you believe to be a realistic approach for yourself. Your personality, experiences, knowledge, and education will all need to be considered when determining your goals. You may need to focus your attention on adding more technology if you are currently a movement educator or on adding more movement if you are a tech teacher. Or you may be a newcomer that needs to direct equal attention to increasing both movement and technology in your classroom. Remember, the ultimate goal of an MTE is to use both strategies equally and daily. Therefore, in every lesson, you want to be using some form of movement and technology to elevate the learning environment for all students. You may find yourself constantly challenged to define this balance while incorporating both teaching techniques equally; however, over time, you will sharpen this skill and your abilities. We will analyze your goals and define your starting point in more detail in Chapter 6.

It's important to realize that you should not be expected to reach these goals on your own. School districts and administrative leaders are encouraged to provide faculty support by offering professional development trainings and workshops that are informative, practical, and hands on. This teaching philosophy cannot mature properly without a united approach between teachers and administrative leaders. It is recommended that schools work hand in hand to promote this endeavor. Educators should also search for graduate courses that specialize in this topic to help them advance their knowledge. Teachers are urged to learn from one another as they capitalize on each other's strengths. Look for opportunities to present and share ideas with your colleagues. For example, if you grasp the concept of being a movement educator more easily, search for a tech teacher who can help you grow in that area. We can't be experts in everything, but we can learn from others the strengths we lack as we continually sharpen our own skills. To truly excel as MTEs, we will need to learn to do just that. Our goals can be aggressive or slow moving, but we must combine our efforts as we move forward. MT teachers are the leaders of today and tomorrow as they take the younger generation in a direction that strengthens education like never before. Set goals for yourself, continue to grow as an MTE, and become part of redefining education in a way that makes sense and can stand the test of changing times. MT environments are comprehensive classrooms built for learners of any age.

# BLENDED TEACHING AND LEARNING

*Blended teaching and learning* often refers to combining traditional classroom methods with digital media. MTEs define this concept as a balanced merging of movement, technology, and traditional teaching methodologies in a learning environment to increase academic achievement. This blended educational approach considers the mind–body connection while delivering an all-inclusive model that meets the entire needs of the learner. The mind and body are always working together; it only makes sense to produce a blended teaching approach that takes this notion into consideration. Imagine developing the body without strengthening the mind. Even the latest exercise programs have made the connection that fitness and physical activity are no longer solely related to developing a stronger, healthier body. The brain will equally benefit.

When we sustain a blended teaching and learning approach in the 21st-century classroom, we are upholding a higher standard of what best practice in a learning environment should look like. For centuries, we have identified different types of learning intelligences that exist in our society. All students have different learning strengths and weaknesses. Ideally, content should be delivered with a wide variety of approaches to meet the needs of these different intelligences. But this does not happen consistently in our classrooms. Educators who are using blended methods for content delivery are always looking for unique ways to enhance their subject matter. Having students sit all day while receiving traditional teaching methods and increasing screen time is not going to get the higher cognitive output we are searching for. The MTE will implement blended teaching strategies that incorporate a multitude of techniques to actively engage students in the learning process. This is the true intention of a blended teaching and learning educational philosophy. Balancing movement, technology, and traditional teaching methods will create an ideal blended academic experience.

# BRAIN-BASED LEARNING

*Brain-based learning* refers to teaching methods, lesson designs, and academic programs that are supported by the latest scientific research about how the brain learns. This theory suggests that we can accelerate the learning process if educators base *how* and *what* they teach on neuroscience as opposed to past practices and learning traditions. Cognitive science has shown us that the brain can physically change and adapt as it learns; this is referred to as *neuroplasticity*. Brain-based learning affects cognitive functioning and working intelligence, giving teachers something to consider when designing their lessons and educational experiences for their classroom environments. Eric Jensen, an expert in the field of brain-based education, explains that brain/mind scientific discoveries can be applied to classroom practices and designs. On his website (http://www.jensenlearning.com), you can find a list of examples of research that has had important implications for learning, memory, schools, and trainings. A few examples that connect directly to the MT balance are the social brain (how interactions and social status impacts stress levels), the moving brain (how movement influences learning), the emotional brain (the impact of threats on hormones, memory, cells, and genes), the computational brain (the role of feedback in forming neural networks), and the connected brain (how our brain is body and body is brain).

## Perfectly Aligned

Some educators question the validity behind neuroscience and the role of brain-based principles in determining educational directions for best practice. Others believe that the research is consistent and speaks for itself while providing a solid framework for considering effective teaching strategies. Brain research doesn't really "prove" anything, but it can support the value of a particular teaching approach, tool, or technique. How does balancing movement and technology in the classroom stack up to the twelve brain/mind learning principles developed by Renata and Geoffrey Caine (Caine, Caine, McClintic, & Klimek, 2009)? Their principles are as follows:

1. The brain is a complex adaptive system; balancing movement and technology will provide a multifaceted learning experience.

2. The brain is a social brain; movement activities often include partner and small-group activities.

3. The search for meaning is innate; exposing students to the MT balance will encourage them to explore the significance and value of their experiences.

4. The search for meaning occurs through patterning; both movement and technology will aid in this pursuit.

5. Emotions are critical to patterning; movement typically escalates emotions.

6. Every brain simultaneously perceives and creates parts and wholes; the MT balance will provide opportunities that enhance both perceptions.

7. Learning involves both focused attention and peripheral attention; movement and technology can stimulate both.

8. Learning always involves conscious and unconscious processes, which will be fueled by movement and technology in isolation and in unison.

9. We have at least two ways of organizing memory; a variety of MT programs can help with this process.

10. Learning is developmental and so are numerous physical movements.

11. Complex learning is enhanced by challenge and inhibited by threat; the MT balance can provide exciting opportunities through nonintimidating means.

12. Every brain is uniquely organized; both movement and technology can reinforce this logical structure.

Considering the connection between these brain principles and the MT balance, it appears as though they are a perfect match! Utilizing a blended teaching and learning approach that unites movement, technology, and traditional teaching techniques gives the brain what it needs for higher-order thinking to take place. MTEs will provide a novel learning environment that attracts the brain and motivates the student to learn. As we continue to study the brain while seeking guidelines for best teaching practices, it stands to reason that MTEs will offer lesson designs that meet the criteria for what students want and need from a neural standpoint. The MT balancing act will quickly become a staple in the modern-day classroom to obtain peak performance and cognitive output.

# CORE HUMAN NEEDS

## Perfectly Aligned

In Chapter 2, Tony Robbins defined the "6 core human needs" (Jane, 2013) as certainty/comfort, uncertainty/variety, significance, love and connection, growth, and contribution. Would utilizing the MT balance provide an environment that meets these basic needs? As previously suggested, movement in the classroom can do just that. However, it will be difficult for teachers to meet these needs if they continue to overuse technology in their classroom environment. Love and connection will be challenging to foster when screen times are at an all-time high. Students will have minimal opportunities to contribute to their peers and feel growth or emotional development if they are working independently on their digital devices. Tech teachers may struggle to meet these six needs when technological uses operate in isolation. This comprehensive philosophy not only gives the brain what it wants and needs, but it also feeds the emotional well-being of our learners. This advantage will play a significant role in helping children feel accepted and supported in their classroom setting, making academic challenges less intimidating. As a result, students will grow as people—not only as learners—in a warm, cohesive environment.

# BRIDGING THE GAP WITH STRIDES

STRIDES (Figure 4.6) is the acronym used in this book to assist teachers in bridging the educational gap between movement and technology. Currently seen as moving in opposition to one another, the goal of STRIDES is to inspire educators to balance movement and technology to increase academic performance while having these methodologies move in the same direction. This way of thinking creates a superior learning environment for all students. Educators that embrace STRIDES will be on the right track to becoming MTEs. Defining this balance is a difficult task due to the extensive variables that all teachers and administrators will encounter. STRIDES can play a significant role in guiding schools through this process. View STRIDES as a stepping-stone to bridging this gap, as each phase of the process improves teaching practices and procedures. With each step that is taken, teachers and administrators will strengthen education and their learning environments while increasing the successes of their students. STRIDES plays a meaningful role in educating students as both humanitarians and high-level learners.

Implementing movement and technology in the classroom can be intimidating for many educators. It is rare to find a teacher who excels equally in both of these areas. If you consider a health and physical education teacher as an example, many of them are often comfortable with movement in the gymnasium but not in the health classroom. An educator who can blend, balance, and unite movement,

**FIGURE 4.6   ■   STRIDES**

## BRIDGING THE GAP WITH

**S**tructuring and Managing

**T**ransforming with A.A.A.

**R**efining Movement and Technology

**I**nterconnecting Communities

**D**efining the Balance

**E**mploying SMART Activities

**S**upporting a United Approach

### STRENGTHENING EDUCATION
### STEP BY STEP

A.A.A. (awareness, attention, action)
SMART (stress management and relaxation techniques)

technology, and traditional teaching methods is currently ahead of the times. As educators work their way through STRIDES and implement its concepts, teachers will master this philosophy little by little. Realistic goals must be set with doable and sensible timelines. Teachers will increase their ability to use the MOST method in their classroom. MTEs may find some sections of STRIDES more comfortable to incorporate and address as a result of their own personalities and interests. On the other hand, other components may be outside of a teacher's comfort zone and will require patience and endurance along this exciting journey. STRIDES is meant to be a method schools continually build upon as MTEs grow through their trial-and-error processes. Each letter of STRIDES is defined and described in Figure 4.6 to introduce this educational philosophy. Moving forward, each component of STRIDES will have an application chapter to guide educators through this teaching and learning approach at a workable pace. This progressive style is fun, thought provoking, and stimulating for the teacher and student alike.

## Structuring and Managing

Structuring the classroom environment is an important first step in becoming an MTE. Balancing movement and technology in an academic environment means that you will have potentially expensive digital equipment coexisting with physical activity in a limited space. The classroom environment must be designed so that students can move safely while technological devices are kept out of harm's way. Additionally, this component of STRIDES addresses classroom management techniques, which are a constant challenge in most learning environments. Structuring and managing an MT environment is explored in detail in Chapter 5. Space fluidity and classroom designs will be introduced for your consideration. Planning, preparation, safety, and management strategies will also be an important part of that chapter. Prior to fully becoming an MTE, you will need to make some decisions about your classroom setup and function so the environment will be secure and you can get the best use of your space. Also, students will need to be clearly informed of class expectations and procedures prior to uniting movement and technology in a designated area.

## Transforming With A.A.A.

This component of STRIDES is equally important for the teacher and the student. Transforming with A.A.A. will be explained in Chapter 6 as digital responsibility and personal/professional intentions are identified. *A.A.A.* stands for *awareness*, *attention*, and *action*. In this chapter, the reader will be given the opportunity to describe their beliefs about the role of movement and technology in their own lives as well as in their classroom. Strategies for having students tackle these same questions and concerns will also be suggested. Change in our own lives or in our classrooms cannot happen until we have an awareness of where we are and a vision of where we want to be. Furthermore, these adjustments may be difficult and take time. Our images must be followed by direct attention and action to make these desired transformations. Teachers and students will be encouraged to develop a passion for balancing movement and technology in school and in their personal lives. Our values tend to be visible in our decisions; therefore, they must be aligned with one another whether we are at home or at school.

## Refining Movement and Technology

The benefits of both movement and technology in the learning process were examined in Chapters 2 and 3. The evidence is extensive and supports the suggestion that movement and technology should occur regularly and even daily in all academic environments. In Chapter 7, the ABCDs of movement and technology for *ALL* will be defined. Practical activities for gaining the advantages of physical activity, movement, and technology will be shared and described in detail. *ALL* stands for *academic achievement*, *learner attention and focus*, and the *learner as a whole*. Consistent, abundant use of movement and technology in the classroom must be planned, be intentional, and have purpose. This component of STRIDES is significant to the MTE; students will receive a wide array of MT activities and deliveries depending on the learner's needs or the teacher's goals. Utilizing active learning strategies and technology effectively and efficiently in classroom settings is critical to maintaining this balancing act. Some strategies will be as quick as two to three minutes, while others will require more time. The main objective is to increase academic success and learning potential through a variety of means and approaches. An additional bonus is that the classroom environment becomes a fun, lively place to learn and grow.

## Interconnecting Communities

Social skills are diminishing as a result of technology overuse. Interconnecting communities, presented in Chapter 8, is an area of STRIDES in which suggestions for combatting this concern are made. Schools can no longer sit by while students' listening and communication abilities deteriorate. This chapter will examine the current social trends stemming from excessive technology, along with the societal/educational concerns that result. The concept of interconnecting communities focuses on how the social/emotional well-being of the student affects the learning process. If a student does not feel a connection to the learning environment, the opportunity for peak performance is minimized and perhaps lost. Students can still achieve and produce in nonsocial academic settings; however, will they be well-rounded and achieve their best outcomes? A sense of belonging is a basic human need that only interconnected classrooms can fill. Applicable activities will be suggested for this component of STRIDES as a means for rebuilding communication skills, class unity, and cohesive learning.

## Defining the Balance

This is a critical component of STRIDES. In Chapter 9, a variety of approaches and methods for maintaining the balancing act between movement and technology will be detailed. The essence of blended teaching and learning strategies will be shared as specific examples. The ABCDs of MT will be broken down and specifically organized for thoughtful application and reflection. Movement examples will be linked to technology while digital uses will be coupled with movement activities. The unification process of movement and technology will be addressed with topics such as academic content, kinesthetic furniture, gaming, projects, testing, homework, and virtual education. The future implications of uniting movement and technology are innovative and exciting and reach as far as the mind can imagine. Defining the balance between movement and technology is the component of STRIDES that will be built upon as we grow and develop our thinking as MTEs. This chapter is only the beginning of a new era of learning.

## Employing SMART Activities

Mental/emotional challenges of the younger generation are on the rise. Students' lives can be stressful and complicated. This anxiety has a direct effect on the learning process and students' ability to achieve at optimal levels. In Chapter 10, relaxation techniques will be introduced and explained. Combining these stress management techniques with movement and technology are beneficial to improving students' learning potential. *SMART* stands for *stress management and relaxation techniques*. Too much screen time can be very harmful to the mental/emotional state of our learners, yet this is often a classroom and societal norm. Taking time to ensure students are in a good mental/emotional state is essential to the learning process. A supplementary benefit of these activities is that they often require minimal time and lead to great results. Teaching students how to be mindful while managing their distracted brain is critical to learning in the modern-day classroom.

## Supporting a United Approach

Educational channels must take the initiative to bridge the gap between movement and technology. However, ultimately, there must be a united approach among schools, homes, and communities for total success. In Chapter 11, the importance of this unified effort will be outlined, and suggestions will be offered on how to progress through this process. Summaries of the power of and the need for the STRIDES philosophy will be revisited, and readers will be motivated to commit to this endeavor. Supporting a united approach is a must-have in order for STRIDES to truly shift the current educational trends that determine our classroom practices. Content delivery and educational outcomes must consider the whole child during the school day as well as outside of the school environment. It is irresponsible to only make changes in what happens at school, even though this is where most of our control lies. Although it is difficult to change the home and community outlooks, there needs to be a solid effort to redirect our priorities in all areas of our children's lives. We cannot bring past values of good health, well-rounded social skills, and physically active beings back to our culture if we focus on school time alone. We must push for and encourage a universal change in our thinking and behaviors in homes and communities as well. This combined effort is the only way to truly ensure growth and transformation to a modernistic and improved means for learning and living.

## EDUCATION'S RESPONSIBILITY

STRIDES cannot become a standard in the 21st-century classroom without educational leaders taking on this responsibility. The reality is that this balancing act is as important in our society as it is in our schools. As technology rules our lives, it is slowly destroying the very qualities that make us a great nation. We are interacting with each other less and less; we coexist parallel to one another as opposed to sharing connected lives. We are linked through digital means instead of face-to-face laughter, communication, and social learning. We are on a slippery slope to raising a generation of children who will increase their screen time and decrease their human interactions. The consequences that could result from this direction are frightening to ponder. It is education's responsibility to say enough is enough! We need to embrace the positive strengths of our progressive society but also refuse to let go of the past values that helped us care and support one another as human beings. Educators must show society how to embrace this redirection as they implement STRIDES and make the most of their academic environments. This book provides a guideline to help all school leaders along this ambitious path. Teachers, principals, curriculum developers, and collegiate administrators have the means for defining a new standard of what's acceptable and desired in our learning and way of life. We must embrace this shift in thinking immediately, before it is too late.

## A NEW BRAIN, A NEW LEARNER— A REASONABLE PERSPECTIVE

Chapter 3 examined the pros and cons of technology in our schools and society. Chapter 2 asked you to consider how your students are different today as compared to previous years in your career. If we disregard the research for a minute and focus only on rational thinking, it is logical to see how effective the MT balance can be in any and all learning environments. We are working with a new brain that has different requirements for peak performance. Of course, there will be challenges along the way, but stop and imagine how powerful this balancing act can be to today's learner. Students will be actively engaged for most of their class time. Technology will be used steadily so that students receive continual exposure to its strengths. The setting will have an upbeat vibe as students hustle and bustle around the classroom to meet their academic standards. Students will be attentive and focused as boredom ceases to exist. Instructional delivery will be ever-changing, keeping students on their toes as they wonder what will happen next. Educators will use the MOST method, and a new era of learning will be created. STRIDES will lead the way to increasing academic achievement, and education will treat students as people by developing their overall well-being. Schools are working with a new type of learner; implementing STRIDES will meet their desired needs. This is a reasonable perspective!

# WHAT DOES THIS MEAN TO ME?

### K–12 Teachers

1. Identify whether you are mostly an active educator, tech teacher, newcomer, or MTE. For one week, place your focus on increasing either movement or technology in your classroom. Direct your energy to the other concept the following week.

2. In Week 3, balance movement and technology in your classroom, even if this means you are using basic, well-known breaks, exercises, videos, or a whiteboard.

### Administration

1. Complete an analysis on STRIDES as it directly relates to your school or district and label the areas that need improvement as well as your strengths.

2. Consult with your faculty to see if they are in agreement with your findings. Lead your team by setting small, realistic goals for each or some of the sections of STRIDES. Continue to build on this plan while taking your faculty's readiness into consideration.

### Educational Leaders/Affiliates

1. Employ and explore potential hires that are knowledgeable and experienced with the concepts of the MT balance.

2. Develop guidelines that require schools to use the MOST method in the 21st-century classroom while focusing on the health and well-being of the younger generation.

# CHAPTER SUMMARY

- The concept of a balancing act between movement and technology in learning environments is a novel phenomenon that is only now starting to get attention. Requirements for balancing movement and technology in the 21st-century classroom will soon be an educational standard.

- MT methodologies should be used daily in the learning process to produce optimal results.

- MTEs are either in the process of mastering or have already mastered the balancing act between movement and technology in their learning environment. These teachers utilize combined strategies to get the best of each of these methods. This concept will also be called *the MT balance* and *the movement and technology balance*; other similar language may be used to identify this philosophy.

- It is essential for educators to attempt to define and create balanced learning environments in which movement and technology operate together to enhance learning.

- Figure 4.1 shows the overlapping of the greater-than and less-than symbols with the word *MOST* emphasized as a means for finding the balance between movement

and technology in today's classroom. *MOST* stands for **m**ove students **o**ften with a **s**teady flow of **t**echnology.

- School districts and administrative leaders are encouraged to provide faculty support by offering professional development trainings and workshops that are informative, practical, and hands on. This teaching philosophy cannot mature properly without a united approach between teachers and administrative leaders.

- MTEs define *blended teaching* as a balanced merging of movement, technology, and traditional teaching methodologies in a learning environment to increase academic achievement.

- MT environments are perfectly aligned with brain-based learning and meeting core human needs.

- STRIDES is the acronym used in this book to assist teachers in bridging the educational gap between movement and technology. STRIDES stands for **s**tructuring and managing, **t**ransforming with A.A.A., **r**efining movement and technology, **i**nterconnecting communities, **d**efining the balance, **e**mploying SMART activities, and **s**upporting a united approach.

# 5

# STRUCTURING AND MANAGING

## SPACE FLUIDITY

### Thinking Ahead

Balancing movement and technology (MT) in any academic environment requires strategic planning and thinking ahead. It is important for movement and technology educators (MTEs) to create a classroom space conducive to movement while being careful of the expensive technology within it, all while working within a limited classroom size. Students must be able to move freely and efficiently around the room, with safety for other people and equipment at the forefront. Classroom setup is going to be an important factor in finding success in balancing movement and technology. A chaotic classroom will raise a variety of safety concerns and can be discouraging as you take on this new initiative. You will need to make some decisions up front about your classroom setup in order to make the best use of your space. Keep in mind that you are merely thinking ahead for now; you can (and most likely will) make changes as you gain experience as an MTE. Start by imagining what you want this innovative environment to look like. When you close your eyes, what do you see? Where are the students working, and what are they working on? How are they moving? What types of technology are they engaging with? It's important to recognize that sometimes students will be using movement, sometimes they will be using technology, and sometimes they will be using both at the same time. Think about the order and flow of the classroom. Some teachers may consider the need for a specific direction of movement and will place tape along the floors for students to follow. Other teachers may decide that the desks are too close together for movement and will place the desks in a horseshoe to open up more space. Each classroom is different in terms of size and shape, and you'll need to consider what will work best for you in your specific situation. Consider the fluidity of the environment you'll be creating and exactly how you intend to balance movement and technology. Make a list of the goals you want to achieve in your MT space and anything you'd like to try to reach those goals. Determine the nonnegotiable locations you need within your classroom as well as anything new you'd like to add to support movement and technology. Remember, the way the classroom space is set up gives students a powerful insight into what's important to the teacher.

## Trial and Error

Some of the best lessons we learn in education come from our failures. The lesson plans that bombed, the project that didn't quite work out, or the good ideas that turned into chaos often teach us more about ourselves and our students than the best-laid plans. In order to be successful educators, we must embrace our failures and use them to bounce back with a better and clearer vision. When structuring your MT classroom, there is going to be a period of trial and error. Regardless of how much planning you do for setting up the physical space, the reality of students actually *using* that space may be very different from the ideas in your head. There are going to be many variables that can affect the success of your physical setup, such as the students' personalities, the instructional needs, and assessment windows, to name a few. Learning what doesn't work in the MT classroom will be as important as learning what does work! Cut yourself a little slack and be ready for quick-thinking modifications when things aren't working out. No matter how you set up the classroom, you can always make changes! Most furniture in your space isn't permanently fixed to the floor, so don't be afraid to move things around. You may even want to consider several options for the space and give each option a trial period with the students to see which one you like best. What works today may not work a month from now and can even change from school year to school year. Be flexible, be ready to learn on the go, and embrace the trial-and-error process. Winston Churchill said, "Success consists of going from failure to failure without loss of enthusiasm." Think of it this way: If you're never failing at anything, then you're never trying anything new!

## CLASSROOM DESIGNS

We're going to explore some suggested designs for creating a fluid and safe MT space. Keep in mind that these are simply models that you may choose to use when starting out, and that at any given time, students may be using movement, technology, or both simultaneously. Remember the vision you have for what a balanced

MT space looks like. Then consider the grade level you teach, the types of technological devices you have, and the assortment of furniture you use (or want to use). The size of your physical space as well as your class sizes will also influence your decisions here. The goal is to create a classroom in which you and your students feel comfortable and can meet the objectives while using both movement and technology safely and seamlessly.

## Perimeter

A perimeter design simply involves setting up desks and seating around the outside perimeter of the classroom, creating a large, open center space. This arrangement, as shown in Figure 5.1, is best in classrooms that do not have an overabundance of furniture and have a relatively simple shape. The perimeter design creates two clear areas that provide great flexibility for the MTE. This basic, open-concept layout creates a space where both movement and technology can be used with ease. It's a great place for beginning MTEs to start their journey.

**FIGURE 5.1 ■ Perimeter**

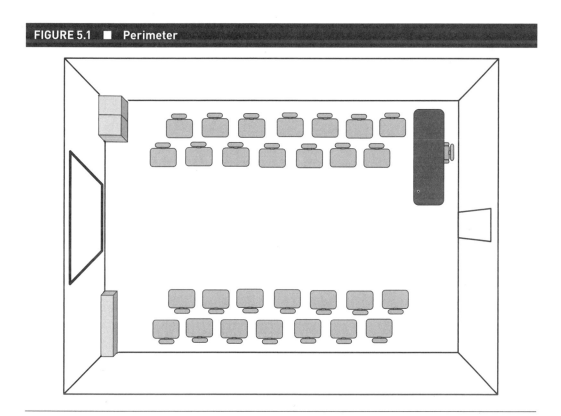

## Unified Teams

Creating a classroom of unified teams is as straightforward as grouping together small sets of students to establish cooperative pods. In this scenario, small groups of 3–5 students would be placed at the center of the room, generating teams of students who could easily work together (see Figure 5.2). Meanwhile, the outside perimeter is kept clear for movement activities that happen around the teams. This setup allows students to easily share technology and work cooperatively in the seating areas while providing enough safe space outside of the pods for engaging in kinesthetic learning. It will be important to consider the types of seating you have (which can vary greatly from grade level to grade level) and your class size, as these will impact the ease of using the unified teams arrangement.

**FIGURE 5.2 ■ Unified Teams**

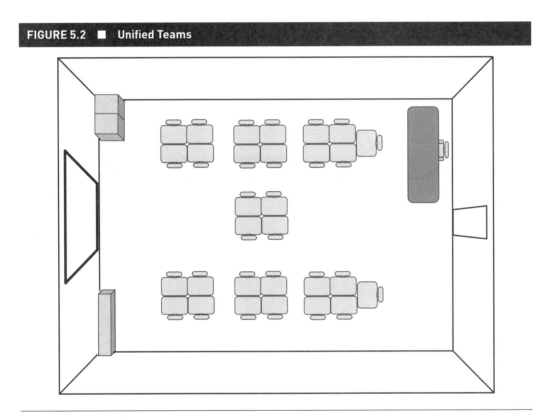

## Centers

Creating centers in the classroom is a valuable and highly regarded teaching strategy. Centers have many benefits, including ease of differentiation, the ability to offer student choice, equity in classroom amenities, and increased student engagement. Utilizing centers is a great way to ensure that students are given plenty of opportunity to use both kinesthetic activities and technological devices to enhance their learning. One advantage to creating a centers-based classroom is the variety of designs for those centers. MTEs have a multitude of options for centers, from stationary centers that are set up at specific areas of the room to flexible centers that can be transported back to the seating area in classrooms that are tight on space (see Figure 5.3). Learning centers work well in both the elementary and secondary classrooms, making this a great choice for an effective MT space.

**FIGURE 5.3 ■ Centers**

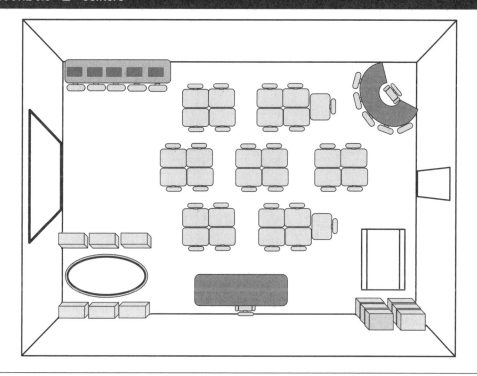

## U-Shape

Organizing furniture in a U-shaped design is similar to the perimeter setup in that it creates ample open space in the center of the room. What the U-shaped design provides that the perimeter setup may not is a clear visual viewpoint (see Figures 5.4a and 5.4b). This is particularly important when an interactive whiteboard is present in the room. Students can easily see and access the whiteboard from the seating arrangement, while movement activities are safely completed in the middle or even out around the seated areas. The drawback to U-shaped seating is that it can be difficult to create in small classrooms. However, teachers with adequate space will find this design a great choice for balancing MT lessons.

## Corners

Creating corners is a unique concept that refers to sectioning off one or more corners (or small areas) of your classroom for specific purposes (see Figure 5.5). In the MT classroom, teachers can create areas specifically for movement or technology and will need to define exactly how those spaces will be used. Routines will be put in place for students to transition to and from the corners, and the teacher will need a clear vision for how those corners support the learning objectives for each lesson. The possibilities for this exclusive space in a classroom are fun and creative and will be motivational for students to earn and/or enjoy.

**FIGURE 5.4A ■ U-Shape**

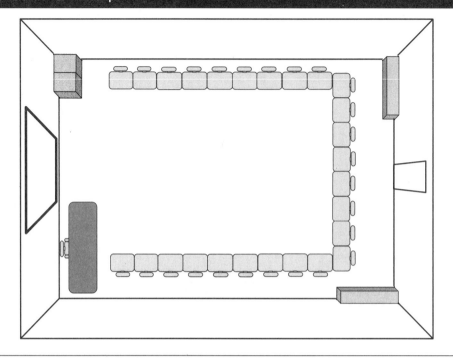

**FIGURE 5.4B ■ U-Shape**

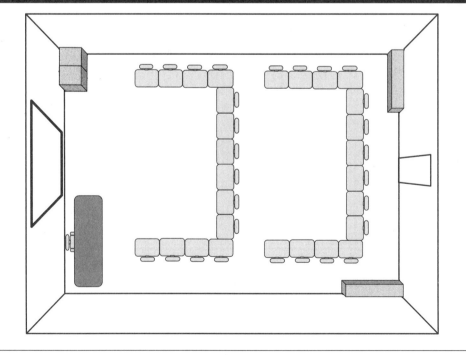

**FIGURE 5.5   ■   Corners**

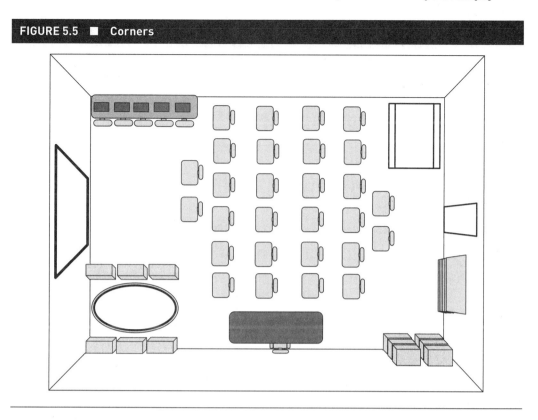

Remember, these designs serve only as a guide and a jumping-off point for you. Perhaps you'll try one of these ideas and find something even better that works for you! The students themselves may provide helpful feedback that will drive your decisions about classroom design and layout. As you become more comfortable as an MT teacher, you may find that your needs change and, in turn, so does the classroom setup. Again, embrace the trial and error and allow it to add to your level of expertise rather than discourage you from your mission for change!

## PLANNING AND PREPARATION

Now it's time to plan your space. Once you've selected a general classroom design, you need to consider a few things: Can you use what you already have in the classroom or do you need to acquire some new items? Perhaps you even need to scale down the amount of existing furniture you have or swap with a colleague for better choices. Will you be investing in kinesthetic furniture or flexible seating options? Is your technology portable or anchored? Making a wish list can spark your creativity, as can sketching out your layout ideas, scouring the Internet for inspiration, and visiting other classrooms to gain fresh ideas. If you need to gather items for centers or corners, now is the time to make that list as well. Take a good look around the classroom and make a plan for how you will use all the available space you have. Here are some key details to consider as you prepare your MT classroom:

- Location of interactive whiteboards, chalkboards, writing boards
- Location of outlets, fixed cords, charging carts
- Fluid walkways
- Open space for movement
- Unobstructed views for students
- Storage of materials

Every classroom is unique in its space and shape, and every educator will have his or her own unique challenges to contend with. With effective planning and a clear vision of what you want for your students, it will be more manageable to overcome these obstacles. Make your classroom arrangement consistent with your goals for balancing movement and technology. Depending on your grade level and subject, how do you see the children learning in a balanced MT classroom, and what role does the physical space play in this? Decide where you will deliver instruction, where students will engage with instruction, where movement will happen, and where technological devices will be located. A good setup for an MT classroom is essential for maximizing learning opportunities while minimizing transitional challenges. An effective MT classroom is a space that looks and feels comfortable for you and your students and doesn't get in the way of the teaching and learning experience. We encourage you to prepare a space that supports STRIDES (**s**tructuring and managing, **t**ransforming with A.A.A., **r**efining movement and technology, **i**nterconnecting communities, **d**efining the balance, **e**mploying SMART activities, **s**upporting a united approach) and your new way of thinking about the 21st-century classroom and removes any obstacles that may stand in your way. The classroom should support your new MT routines, allow for efficient transitions, and permit all students to move around safely.

## SAFETY AT THE FOREFRONT

Safety is the most important thing to consider in a balanced MT classroom. Students in an MT environment will understandably be eager to participate. The MT teaching methodology provides a school day filled with interesting and engaging activities that increase student motivation, so naturally, there will be feelings of excitement and anticipation. Safe practices will ensure the welfare of students and teachers and can help prevent damage to equipment. Making sure students can move around the room freely with a smooth flow is essential, which is why planning and preparation of the classroom environment is key. MT teachers may find that they need to redesign their rooms several times before finding the arrangement that is the best fit for safety. Routines and procedures in the MT classroom will need to be explicitly taught, retaught, and reinforced with the students, especially at the beginning of the school year and with new students. Safety procedures and regulations will need to be modeled and discussed, and a plan for students who do not follow those procedures will need to be put in place. Teachers and students alike need to work together to maintain a safe classroom environment. It's also important to keep in mind that just as in any other classroom, routines and procedures take time and practice in order to become second nature.

If you are starting your journey as an MTE, developing a management plan may be daunting, since you haven't gotten your feet wet and aren't exactly sure what your MT classroom will look like. When it comes to managing any classroom, experience is usually your greatest resource. As you embark on this exciting new movement in education, it may not be easy to predict the safety concerns that could arise. The following checklists were developed to give you a jumping-off point when thinking about safety for both movement and technology.

## Movement Safety Checklist ✔

Can students move around the room freely with a smooth flow?

Are key classroom objects (whiteboards, centers, etc.) easily accessible?

Are kinesthetic learning areas large enough to accommodate class size?

Can movement activities be done efficiently with minimal furniture movement required?

Is a plan in place for transitioning students smoothly from one area to another?

Can you ensure that students maintain safe speeds during movement?

Is the flooring in good condition (with no potential hazards)?

Are there any changes in floor level or the types of flooring that need to be addressed?

Is the furniture strategically placed to allow maximum movement and to eliminate tripping hazards?

Are movement rules and procedures posted in the room?

## Technology Safety Checklist ✔

Have materials and equipment been inspected for defects?

Are fixed devices (computer carts, desktop computers, etc.) located in areas that do not obstruct student view or movement?

Are mobile devices (laptops, tablets, etc.) stored safely out of the way when not in use?

Is a plan in place to move mobile devices safely around the classroom?

Are power cords, extension cords, and the like located out of walkways?

*(Continued)*

(Continued)

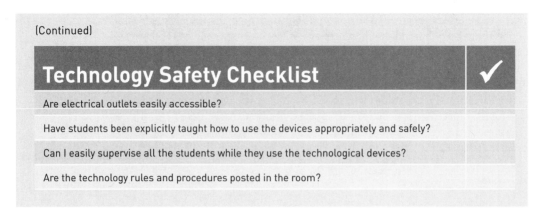

| Technology Safety Checklist | ✓ |
|---|---|
| Are electrical outlets easily accessible? | |
| Have students been explicitly taught how to use the devices appropriately and safely? | |
| Can I easily supervise all the students while they use the technological devices? | |
| Are the technology rules and procedures posted in the room? | |

Once you have determined your rules and procedures for safety, it will be important to introduce those routines with the students from the first day they enter the classroom. Establishing a safe environment and holding students to a high level of responsibility will be crucial to maintaining order in the MT classroom. This can be done in classrooms for all ages. Modeling and demonstrating safe behavior, positively reinforcing students who demonstrate safe choices, and quickly redirecting undesired behavior will allow you to set clear expectations that students understand and strive to meet.

# MANAGEMENT STRATEGIES

## Concerns and Expectations

Without a doubt, classrooms with clear rules and expectations foster student learning better than those without. The MT classroom is no exception to this. As educators, it is our responsibility to clearly define the boundaries for student behavior in order to meet the needs of all learners while keeping curriculum objectives at the forefront of the classroom. Teachers who embark on this new teaching and learning style may have many questions and concerns about effective management. Using both movement activities and technology in the classroom can certainly invoke a sense of worry that students will easily become distracted, overstimulated, silly, or unsafe. Teachers will need to establish order quickly and efficiently at the beginning of the school year and will need to revisit and reinforce the rules often to create a learning environment built on mutual respect between teacher and students.

One of the greatest misconceptions in education is that using teaching methodologies that students find engaging (such as kinesthetic learning activities or incorporating technology) will ultimately result in the teacher losing control of the classroom. This is not the case at all. As with any traditional lesson, students will be expected to maintain a level of respect and show appropriate behavior at all times in the MT classroom. Take a look at some common fears about movement and technology and simple solutions to overcome them:

| Movement Fears | Suggestions |
|---|---|
| Accidents | Remember: Safety at the forefront! Establish safety guidelines early. |
| Reluctance to participate | Model activities with the students—if they see you doing it, they will do it.<br><br>Hold students accountable for participation in all activities, movement or not. |
| Silliness/Giggling/Immature behavior | Encourage students to have fun while learning but be clear about your objectives and expectations. |
| Disorderly behavior | Movement activities are no different than any other lesson. Set clear consequences for disorderly behavior anywhere in your classroom and enforce them when needed. |
| Low student comfort levels | Be vulnerable: Show students when you step outside your own comfort zone and share your movement preferences. |
| Personal space | Have students reflect on their own spatial awareness and develop simple guidelines to identify personal space (arm's length, carpet squares, etc.). |
| Losing control | Practice simple methods for regaining the group's attention (claps, lights, sayings, etc.). |

| Technology Fears | Suggestions |
|---|---|
| Accidents/Damage to the equipment | Remember: Safety at the forefront! Establish clear expectations, thoroughly demonstrate safe usage, and reteach often! |
| Disorderly behavior | Set clear consequences for disorderly behavior anywhere in your classroom and enforce them when needed. |
| Using the technology inappropriately | Review your district's acceptable use policy (AUP) with students. If your district doesn't have an AUP, develop one together with your class at the beginning of the year. |
| Visiting social media or gaming | Look into your school's firewall system to see if these sites are blocked or can be blocked for students. |
| Cheating | Cheating while using technology is no different than any other form of cheating in the classroom. Define your rules and expectations for academic honesty and enforce them as needed. |
| Distracted students | Technology should always be used with purpose. Write the learning goal on the board and monitor students to be sure they are working toward it. |
| Overexcitement | Use technology consistently and often in the classroom, making it just another tool for learning. When the devices aren't novel, the overexcitement will wear off. |

Maintaining structure and organization in the classroom is essential to students' academic success. Effective management techniques increase time on-task and decrease time spent on redirection. Time is used more efficiently, students are respectful of both the teacher and one another, and there are fewer behavior problems. With increased curriculum rigor and teachers feeling the pressure of covering more in less time, sharpening those general classroom management skills is wise. Traditional classroom management strategies are very effective in the MT classroom. Here are some common strategies that you may want to consider as an MTE:

- **Allow students to help:** Making students an active part of your classroom management generates more buy-in and helps your class run more independently.

- **Make rules and expectations visual:** Students should be able to see and reference both expectations and consequences at all times.

- **Use positive reinforcement to encourage initiative:** Praising and rewarding students for making good choices will result in an increased likelihood of students repeating that behavior.

- **Use proximity wisely:** Certain students will do better in certain areas of the room. Organize seating charts and student placement wisely.

- **Be present:** Circulate the room. Be near the students. Make eye contact and let them know that you are an active part of the classroom alongside them.

- **Build excitement:** Let students know your goals and explain the reasoning behind them. Let them join in the passion you feel for making positive changes in their educational experience!

- **Offer choices:** Students like to feel empowered. Offer students some choice whenever possible. Decide ahead of time what is nonnegotiable and where you can allow the students to take the reins a bit.

- **Talk to your students:** Get to know them on a personal level. Understanding your students provides you with an advantage for preventing discipline or academic problems.

- **Partner with parents:** Reaching out to parents positively and early establishes a relationship that supports your classroom outside of the school day. Let parents know about your vision for the MT classroom and why it's important to you. Ask parents to reinforce your rules with their child at home.

- **Establish routines:** Routines provide comfort for children. Students are less likely to become disorderly when they can predict their day.

Students need boundaries to feel safe, and it's important that they understand what is expected of them. Often, the students themselves are encouraged when they are included as part of the rule-making process. You may want to consider developing your classroom expectations together with your students when the school year begins. Start with your vision for the MT classroom. Explain to the students that they will be using an abundance of both movement and technology and help them understand why each is important to their academic success. Then, make a list together of the concerns you may have and ask them to suggest solutions. From that list, you can develop a set of guidelines for the classroom. When students are involved in this process, they gain a sense of ownership over the classroom and are more likely to move about responsibly and independently and to care for materials and equipment. As the students become more enthusiastic and engaged, the teacher's confidence will grow and classroom management will fall routinely into place. Conversely, consequences will need to be set for when the rules are broken. Clearly explain these consequences to the students and be fair and consistent when using them. There should be no guesswork for students: They need to know exactly how they are expected to behave and what will happen when they choose to step outside the lines.

## Needs and Interests

Although easy to dismiss, getting to know the interests of your students is quite important and can have a positive impact on their classroom experience. Students have a wide variety of needs and interests; failing to understand them on this level does a great disservice to them and their potential academic success. It is important to prepare yourself for the fluctuating attitudes of students regarding both movement and technology in the classroom. You will surely encounter students who love one aspect or the other: Active and social learners may embrace the kinesthetic activities while tech-savvy kids and introverts may prefer the technology aspect. In a true MT classroom, though, students will be required to use both movement and technology in parallel and interconnected ways. What options will you offer to students who clearly have an interest in one over the other? Will you be reactive or proactive to students' needs? It's best to make a plan for this before you introduce your classroom on the first day. Perhaps you will offer multiple ways to complete tasks and allow for some element of student choice in completing assignments. Alternatively, you may decide that the movement and/or technology aspects of your lessons are nonnegotiable and require that students stretch their comfort levels and grow a little bit. Neither option is right or wrong; it's a personal preference.

Because students may not prefer some of the activities in the MT classroom, a valuable opportunity arises for life skills to be taught. In all parts of life, adults often encounter activities or circumstances that are not desirable. Being a responsible adult requires us to put our personal preferences aside, step out of our comfort zone, and put our best foot forward. Often, we find that although these activities might not be classified as our favorites, we are still able to take something away from them or learn something new. This is how we grow, by stepping into the unknown and going for it. Today's youth are often categorized as entitled and self-centered. The MT classroom is a gentle and encouraging place that can urge students to think about the needs and wants of others over themselves and can allow the students to try something new without fear. It is a place where MTEs can teach patience, perseverance, endurance, self-betterment, and courage. In an educational climate that promotes college and career readiness, wouldn't we want students who possess these admirable attributes?

## Rewards and Consequences

MTEs will find that both movement activities and technological devices are highly enjoyed by the students. The enthusiasm for this type of balanced classroom will be contagious, and the students (even if reluctant at first) will quickly embrace using both elements throughout the school day. Because of the student attraction to these items, there will inevitably be some temptation to use movement or technology as a reward or consequence for student behavior. But we must consider this: In the MT classroom, movement activities and technology devices are important *learning* tools that support the classroom objectives. Should academic tools be used to control behavior?

There are some possible positive outcomes of using movement and technology as a reward or consequence. Students who are motivated by either (or both) would likely be willing to work toward their incorporation. Students who enjoy engaging in either (or both) types of activities may also find that having them taken away is a miserable experience, thereby making it an effective consequence. However, it is advised that careful consideration be made about the purpose of your MT classroom. The decision to combine movement and technology through a balanced approach is based on research about what's best for the brain and body. Those who have committed to this methodology understand that MT improves attention and focus, increases academic success, decreases unwanted behavior, and increases student engagement. The elements of movement and technology in the classroom are tools for learning, and deciding to use them as a form of reward or punishment should not be considered lightly. MTEs must also establish consequences for times when the unwanted behavior is directly linked to either element (for example, a student visiting an inappropriate website or a student who continues to touch another student in the movement activity after being told not to). In your classroom, you will need to decide what your philosophy is on this and devise your plan for behavior management accordingly.

## Routines

Routines and classroom procedures improve structure, efficiency, and task management in the MT classroom. Establishing and practicing routines in the classroom eliminates the mental clutter students face regarding housekeeping and nonacademic tasks. Students are less likely to be distracted by tasks that waste time and interfere with the learning process. Guesswork is minimized, and the result of routines is more time on-task, fewer behavioral interruptions, and a fluid and organized classroom. These routines will improve good habits and time efficiency while supporting safety and learning goals. Students will come to depend on routines to stay focused and diligent. They will thrive from the repetition and reinforcement that solid routines provide.

The following list includes examples of movement routines to be taught in the MT classroom. This is not an all-inclusive list, but it is a starting point for developing a plan for your own classroom.

- Entering and exiting the kinesthetic area safely
- Traffic flow around the classroom
- Accessing kinesthetic corners or centers
- Maintaining adequate personal space
- Assessing spatial awareness and surroundings
- Variable voice levels and when to use them
- Variable safe speeds and when to use them

- Furniture movement, if needed

- Procedures for injuries

- Returning attention to the teacher/regaining group focus

Examples of technology routines to be taught in the MT classroom are included below. Again, this is not an all-inclusive list, but it is a starting point.

- Using each technological device appropriately

- Equal distribution of technology (how to share the technology if the ratio isn't 1:1)

- Guidelines for cooperative groups using single devices

- Handling devices with care

- Storage of devices when not in use

- Accessing technology corners or centers

- Procedures for personal cell phone use (or storage)

- Using power cords, extension cords, and outlets safely

- Procedure for turning in digital assignments

- Returning attention to the teacher/regaining group focus

It can be expected that these procedures will need to be taught at the beginning of the year, practiced and reinforced many times until students demonstrate understanding, and then retaught at any point during the school year when a refresher is needed. This attention to detail will establish an organized and fluid classroom that requires minimal teacher redirection and increases student responsibility.

## Transitioning

Transitioning may be the single most time-consuming task in the classroom. Teachers often complain that transitioning takes away precious instructional time, makes students hyperactive and difficult to settle, and is generally unpredictable. MT classrooms need smooth transitions in order to keep the focus on the learning goals and lesson objectives. Students need quick (one minute or less) and efficient transitions in order to prevent restlessness, distraction, and misbehavior. The importance of a smart classroom design cannot be denied here. The physical layout of the classroom will assist (or hinder) physical transitions among students. Again, it is highly advisable to spend some time thinking about the classroom design that works best for you and your teaching situation. In addition to the physical space, transitions must be taught, modeled, and practiced. There are three steps to a smooth and easy transition:

1. Gain the students' attention.

2. Give clear and concise directions.

3. Signal students to move.

If you consistently use these three steps and routinely use the same (or similar) wording for each step, the students will come to view transitioning as merely another routine that they are familiar with. MTEs will need to keep in mind that at times, students may be transitioning in or out of movement with or without technological devices. This means that in addition to transitions being efficient, they must be safe for both students and expensive devices. As students become more comfortable with your style of transitioning, you'll begin to see an increase in self-regulation as they move from one activity to another.

## WHAT DOES THIS MEAN TO ME?

### K–12 Teachers

1. Take a good look at your classroom shape and size. Identify ways to rearrange your furniture to create a safe and fluid space where MT activities can take place. Set a date to make these changes.

2. Work with your students to develop a list of rules and procedures for MT activities. Post your list in the classroom. Allow the students to be an active part of your classroom management.

### Administration

1. Ask your teachers what you can do to help them set up the best MT classroom possible. Listen to their suggestions and give them your full support.

2. Explore ways to purchase flexible and nontraditional seating options so that teachers can create fluid choices in smaller spaces.

### Educational Leaders/Affiliates

1. Develop and/or provide professional development workshops for schools on kinesthetic teaching and technology integration.

2. Highlight and recognize schools, classrooms, and/or teachers that are thinking outside the box when it comes to classroom design and routines.

## CHAPTER SUMMARY

- Balancing movement and technology in the classroom requires strategic thinking about the physical space and layout.

- The optimal setup of an MT classroom can vary widely from teacher to teacher and may take some trial and error to design.

- There are several options for a fluid MT space: perimeter, unified teams, centers, U-shaped, and corners.

- Planning and preparation are key when designing the MT classroom. MTEs will need to think about what technology and movement will look like in their classrooms.

- It's important to set goals for using movement and technology both independently and separately and to develop a plan for each.

- Safety is the number-one priority at all times in the MT classroom. Safety for both students and technology should be addressed, and rules and procedures to ensure classroom safety must be explicitly taught.

- Classroom management will play an important role in the MT classroom. MTEs will need to carefully consider the role that successful management plays when bridging the gap between movement and technology.

- Student interests and needs will vary with both movement and technology. Educators must prepare to address those needs and to be flexible.

- Routines and procedures must be developed and taught in order to establish a seamless and fluid flow between MT activities. Clear and concise expectations are essential to an effective learning environment.

# 6

# TRANSFORMING
# WITH A.A.A.

## MOVEMENT: IT'S ALL ABOUT YOU

When it comes to the role that movement and physical activity play in your life, it really is all about you and the value you place on your health and well-being. The battle of maintaining one's fitness level is a lifetime challenge for the majority of Americans. Some people are highly motivated to exercise and uphold their physical activity levels on a regular basis. Others have inconsistent behaviors: At times, their fitness is good; other times, it is minimal or nonexistent. The reality is that for a wide variety of reasons, a large percentage of people do not have a fitness regimen as part of their life nor do they place a priority on maintaining high levels of physical activity or daily movement. One of the most common reasons given for inactivity is not having the time to commit to a program or routine. Although demands can be overwhelming with careers, families, children, and other responsibilities, we should always make time to improve our health. Incorporating high levels of physical activity or leading active lifestyles is critical to our physical health and well-being.

Define your individual activity level and admit to the value you place on your health management. Are you currently making time to exercise regularly? Are you moving often enough throughout your day? Putting an emphasis on the amount of physical activity you do makes a statement about the value of movement in your life. Is it important to you? If your answer is *yes*, then it is essential that you make the time to add, increase, or continue with an exercise program or high levels of physical activity. If your response is *no*, then please reconsider your position. There are many benefits to leading an active lifestyle, such as improving your health and self-esteem, increasing energy, stabilizing sleeping patterns, reducing stress, and strengthening your body and brain. All of these are important to a high quality of life. Make movement matter in your own personal life, no matter how busy you are. This focus will yield incredible results, making you a better parent, teacher, spouse, friend, and sibling and helping you create an upgraded version of yourself. You deserve to feel this way! Movement's role in your life truly is all about you—a new and improved you.

# DIGITAL RESPONSIBILITY

When you think about the term *digital responsibility*, the first two things that might pop into your mind are how technology is being used and whether it is being used appropriately. Technology is used mainly for entertainment, information, and communication, and all of these uses can be beneficial as easily as they can be detrimental. Being accountable for your actions is important. Searching for inappropriate topics, sending insensitive information, or posting tactless pictures are a few examples of unacceptable digital usage. Digital communities are a current-day popular means for communication. Whether it is on social media or gaming sites, an important aspect of digital responsibility is being a conscious and considerate member of these groups. There are also several legal issues to be aware of when using technology, such as copyright infringement, plagiarism, illegal downloading, identity theft, sending spam, hacking, invasions of privacy, and cyberbullying. Unfortunately, in our society, digital functions are often misused and abused by all people with no exceptions to age, gender, ethnicity, and/or socioeconomic backgrounds. Failing to follow respectable technological guidelines and flaunting the ethical rules for digital use are prime demonstrations of irresponsible behavior.

When we think about digital responsibility, we also need to evaluate the timing of our usage. In other words, are we using our devices at proper moments throughout our day? Some examples of improper timing might be as follows:

- When engaging in face-to-face conversations
- While driving or walking
- When you should be sleeping
- At the dinner table or at a restaurant
- When you are spending time with family or friends
- When attending a professional event

Many of these instances are actually considered to be acceptable social behaviors in our current society. When was the last time you engaged in a full conversation with another person or group where no one glanced at their cell phone? Even at the movie theater, it is not uncommon to see a light coming from a phone throughout the movie. Consider all the automotive accidents that have happened over the years as a result of cell phone use. Just because these behaviors have become the norm, is there any part of you that can recognize that we may have taken a giant step backward in our ability to be mindful with our own time and with the time we spend with others? We are constantly multitasking (or feeding our distracted brain, as described in Chapter 3); this is a great skill to have in numerous circumstances. However, there need to be periods throughout our day where we focus on one thing, giving it our undivided attention. This inability to attend to something singularly is a weakening skill in our current culture. But should it be?

Another key component of digital responsibility that is often overlooked by our culture is the amount of time we devote to technology. Finding a balance between digital usage and other activities is important. This entire book is about defining this balance in educational settings. Digitally responsible people keep their technology time in check no matter where they are or what they are doing. One of the focuses of this chapter is to help you define how much technology is too much in your personal life and in your classroom. There is no exact science or specific time frame to place on this concept, but we must still try to identify this notion so that we can make applicable modifications if need be. Is it feasible that some days we have more opportunity for screen time or surfing the Internet than others? Of course. The concern comes from overuse, which is when technology plays such a large part of our life that it consumes our time, energy, and thoughts. This is the case for many of us; we have become dependent upon the idea of being well-informed instantaneously and constantly. We are losing the concepts of wait time, patience, and delayed communication. Digital advantages are amazing in times of urgency and during emergencies. But we are starting to live as though everything is a crisis or traumatic. Technology dependencies are the polar opposite of digital responsibilities. We need to take immediate measures to ensure that this does not become or continue to be our norm.

# DEFINING A.A.A.

## Self-Awareness

### Movement

To be *self-aware* is to be conscious of your feelings, sensations, motivations, behaviors, thoughts, and actions. For example, to be self-aware might mean admitting that the real reason you aren't exercising isn't that you don't have the time but that you aren't motivated. Being aware of the value of physical activity in your life is significant in helping you keep up or expand your activity levels. Also, if you have been leading a sedentary lifestyle, being self-aware to the true causes behind this can help you change it. We must learn to be cognizant of our feelings and thoughts about physical activity so that we can attend to our desired growth. We also need to recognize the advantages we gain when we are being more active and committed to increased levels of exercise or movement.

Upholding consistent, high-level physical activity goals is crucial to our overall health and well-being. Therefore, we must strive to build awareness of our behaviors and ways of thinking so that we can embrace this goal. We all have the ability to lead active lives and make movement a significant part of our existence. Understanding our physical, emotional, and cognitive awareness is the first step in tackling this endeavor. This allows us to know ourselves as we modify our negative thoughts and reframe them to a new order of thinking. As we develop our conscious mind, we will uncover an internal strength that will support an increase in our activity and movement levels while boosting our physical health.

## Digital

Digital self-awareness is being conscious of the role technology is playing in one's life. One example is having the ability to identify a practical reason for checking your cell phone. In many cases, people glance at their phone habitually for no reason other than they have developed a compulsion to do so. Building an awareness of how and why we use technology will help us define whether we are maintaining a sense of balance in our usage. Some of our reasons for digital practices are appropriate and practical. Here are a few examples:

- Watching television to relax or unwind (this would not include binge watching)
- Calling a loved one or chatting on a social media site during windows of opportunity
- Searching the Internet to research an item prior to a purchase or when needing to gain knowledge about a topic
- Sending or replying to a text when trying to catch up with someone or arrange a get-together
- Searching for a friend or match on a safe and trusted site

The truth is, there are countless times when technology is exactly what we need. However, if we look at the harmless examples above, every one of them can become destructive or dangerous if overused. Imagine the damage that can be caused by watching television constantly or searching the Internet incessantly with minimal breaks for rest, hobbies, or other interests. This is where healthy usage ends and addiction begins. Trying to find the line between toxicity and nontoxic behaviors is the key to defining balance. Building an awareness of how we are spending our time and the length of this time is our starting point to define whether we are happy with the decisions we are making and the behaviors we are choosing. Chances are, you may have at least one area of technology that you are overusing. It may be watching too much television, checking your cell phone too frequently, or even reading for extensive hours on your iPad (which can be harmful to your eyes and the rest of your body). As we strengthen our awareness and pay attention to our feelings, thoughts, and sensations, we can begin to see areas for concern and potential dangers to our well-being.

## Attention

*Attention* is the action of dealing with or taking special care of something or someone. When we develop our self-awareness regarding the part that movement and technology plays in our lives, we can attend to the alarming areas. Sedentary lifestyles, digital dependencies, and/or addictions are detrimental to our existence. We must make these worries into priorities so we can find and maintain balance. One of the best ways to bring attention to apprehensive areas is to set goals that help us improve our weaknesses.

### Movement

- Walk around the house during commercials.

- Add exercises to house chores or join a gym.

- Choose parking spots farther away from store entrances.

### Technology

- Silence your device or completely detach from it—for example, go for a walk and leave your device at home or read a book in one room of your home and keep your devices in a different room.

- Close your screens or turn your phone face down. This sends a message to your brain that you are detaching or disconnecting.

- Designate moments in your day where you do not multitask or use any technology. This will remind you how important it is to give things your full attention.

There are numerous ways to set goals that help you focus on or give attention to the areas you wish to strengthen. You may be focused solely on increasing movement or technology time in your routine or decreasing one or both of them. Even excessive exercising can be harmful to the body, as the body requires time to rest and repair. The concept of being attentive to this balancing act in your own life choices and actions is meaningful to your outlook on what it means to be a movement and technology educator (MTE).

## Action

Awareness and attention are major components of transforming with A.A.A. However, they must be followed by action. Words and intentions are the starting point, but the follow-through of making changes in unwarranted behaviors and thoughts is what really strengthens our balancing act. For example, if you say you are going to increase your physical activity and you fail to do so, have you succeeded in your mission? Your plan was set in good faith, but the execution crumbled. Or if you commit to limiting your time on social media sites to an hour a day but you are on them for two or three hours, have you made a difference in your behavior?

Taking action is often the most difficult step in this process, especially if you are dealing with addictive behaviors or dependencies. Discovering intrinsic motivations is also very problematic but necessary in order for actions to be long lasting. If we are truly going to transform our own lives or our classroom tactics, we must be self-aware, focus our attention, and respond with consistent actions. Once these skills are matured, we will find the balance between movement and technology in our own lives and in our classrooms. Transforming with A.A.A. is a significant component of STRIDES (**s**tructuring and managing, **t**ransforming with A.A.A., **r**efining movement and technology, **i**nterconnecting communities, **d**efining the balance, **e**mploying SMART activities, **s**upporting a united approach) and becoming an MTE. If we are unable to recognize areas that need change or if we can identify them but are unable to take action, preserving a lasting balance will be strenuous. As we concentrate on these skills, they will improve and we will learn ways to progress and stabilize our values and our actions. This personal and professional renovation is the essence of A.A.A.

## A PERSONAL OUTLOOK

Even though the goal of this book is to focus on education, you will be asked to consider your beliefs about movement and technology in your own life. If you are not a physically active person, you can still incorporate daily movement into your classroom setting; if your personal technology usage is minimal, you may use it regularly in your teaching. How you live personally can be completely different from how you function in the classroom and what you value professionally. However, it is beneficial to find the balance between movement and technology in your personal life and professional life; that is why we will take time to evaluate both. It is easier to support the importance of increased physical activities in your classroom when you make this a priority in your personal life. Also, it might be more difficult to educate students about the serious concerns of overusing technology if you suffer from digital dependencies and addiction. It makes sense to try and align our private and professional opinions about movement and technology; this will also make it easier for you to make these connections with your students.

Everyone has the ability to be physically active at a level that fits each individual. Everyone also has the ability to gain digital literacy. Effort, work, interest, attention, and action are required. People of all ages might find this difficult to do. Perhaps if we change our frame of mind and the way we view these concepts, they will be less intimidating. This will not change the labor involved in reaching your highest potential, but it may heighten your self-motivation when you believe and have faith that you have the capability to accomplish these tasks or goals. This requires a new perspective related to the necessity of balancing movement and technology. Physical fitness and activity are not for the elite. These concepts should have nothing to do with talent and/or skill. Instead, your activity levels are about *you* and becoming a stronger version of yourself. Similar to movement, technology is also for everyone, not only the youthful. Having responsible digital behaviors is a goal for all members of our society.

## Movement

Answer the questions below to uncover your personal outlook on movement. These questions will strengthen your awareness of and attention to your values for movement while asking you to write objectives for taking action.

- Do you believe it's important to lead a physically active lifestyle? Why or why not?
- Are you currently incorporating a lot of movement activities in your life right now? Why or why not?
- List some examples of things you do to strengthen your physical health.
- What are your weaknesses in this area and what keeps you from increasing your movement levels or moving regularly?
- What changes can you make in your life so that you can increase your physical activity levels?
- Please write two or three objectives or goals to help you increase your movement levels.

## Technology

Answer the questions below to uncover your personal outlook on technology. These questions will strengthen your awareness of and attention to your values for technology while asking you to write objectives for taking action.

- Do you use technology regularly and do you uphold digital responsibility standards? Please list your uses.
- Are you overusing technology in your life (for example, binge watching television or gaming excessively)? Please explain.
- Do you avoid technology? List some examples of things you can do to improve your knowledge and comfort with technology.
- What are your digital strengths and weaknesses?
- What changes can you make in your life so that you can balance your technology usage?
- What are two or three objectives or goals that can help you increase or decrease your digital usage?

# A PROFESSIONAL AGENDA: FINDING YOUR BALANCE

Once you have outlined your goals for personal balance between movement and technology, it will be easier to define your professional needs. This is the main intention of this publication, and we must take these considerations seriously. In order to discover our balancing act, we must become aware of our shortcomings, place attention on our areas of change, and take action to make these changes happen. These are critical to becoming an MTE. In Chapter 4, you were given the opportunity to rate your comfort level and usage of both movement and technology in your current teachings. These questions provided the first step in making you aware of your present standings. We will now direct our focus to the areas we will attend to, the pace in which we will move at, and what we will accomplish to become an MTE. You can't say, "Oh, yeah, I need to use more movement in my class" or "I am utilizing technology too frequently." Those generic statements are not enough to cause direct, consistent change in your methodologies and practices. You will need to set specific goals and visions on how to achieve them in order to optimize your growth and success.

In Chapter 4, we also identified the significance of setting goals and mentioned that having support from administrators is vital to this process. The magnitude of these two notions cannot be stressed enough. Too often, as human beings, we make blanket statements about our intentions to make changes in our lives without creating a detailed plan of how to accomplish our wishes. As a result, we have already set ourselves up for failure. Teaching and learning about proper goal-setting is an important step in the process of becoming an MTE. To modify our standard routines, practices, and deliveries, we must design a solid, realistic approach. Goal setting and steps for follow-through are two areas that can't be glazed over. They are the pillars to making change possible.

A common mistake when setting goals is creating goals that are not practical. This, too, becomes a balancing act. It is important to push yourself, but not too much or failure will be inevitable. You must think big, but not too big or you can be turned off to what will soon seem impossible. Here are some components of goal setting that should always be considered:

- **Describe the objective in detail:** Consider what exactly you want to achieve, where, how, with whom, when, under what conditions, with what limitations, for what reasons, and so on. A clear description is essential to writing and achieving goals.

- **Make your objectives measurable:** Identify what you will see, hear, and feel when you reach your goal. Break your goal down into measurable elements with concrete assessments. How will you determine when you have found your balance? Defining this physical manifestation will make your vision clearer.

- **Make your objectives and goals reachable:** You have to be honest with yourself as you consider whether the goal is really acceptable for you.

Teachers already have such high demands and heavy workloads; goals for changing methodologies must be realistic. If you don't have the time, knowledge, or skills to make specific changes, keep this in mind and don't be hard on yourself. We all have limitations. Sure, we can grow, stretch, and build our skills, but our goals must be reachable and realistic.

- **Be sure your goals are practical and relevant:** There's no question that balancing movement and technology in schools is practical and relevant. But the pace and weight of your goals needs to be sensible and pertinent to your conditions. You may need to attend trainings or take graduate courses to prepare for your challenges. This takes time, and you will need to demonstrate patience and understanding.

- **Identify your timing and pacing:** Your personality will factor into this component of goal setting. By nature, some of you will want to move quickly because you are convinced of this need and you want to make it happen as fast as you can. Others may want to test the waters and see how effectively these methodologies coexist with one another. Some of you may feel immediately convinced of this blended philosophy but will need to move slowly for a variety of reasons. All approaches are valid, as long as you are willing to move forward to find your balance.

Now that you have been introduced to or reminded of the key components of goal setting, let's move forward and get you started on this process. View the sample for goal setting below.

## Goal-Setting Sample

### Goal #1

- I will use one movement activity every 30 minutes in my learning environment every day, beginning with brain breaks.

- I will write the specific activity in my lesson plan and only keep track if or when I fail to meet this objective. I will also explain my reason for not implementing the activity to see if I can identify a pattern.

- I need to make a list of a variety of brain breaks, and I will give myself one month to accomplish this task. For now, I will start with using GoNoodle (or a similar computer site that provides brain breaks with movement) every day so I can reach my goal.

- My short-term goal is to incorporate different types of brain breaks, even though I am starting off with computer games and activities in isolation. My long-term goal is to use fewer brain breaks over time as I learn to unite my academic standards with movement. I will try to do this once a month for now and increase my frequency as I increase my knowledge and comfort.

# Movement

Write two or three goals to reveal your professional agenda for balancing movement in your classroom.

### Goal #1

1. List one detailed, reachable, practical goal.

2. What will you use to measure the level of success?

3. What will you need to do or get to accomplish this goal?

4. Is it a short- or long-term goal and when will you reach it?

### Goal #2

1. List one detailed, reachable, practical goal.

2. What will you use to measure the level of success?

3. What will you need to do or get to accomplish this goal?

4. Is it a short- or long-term goal and when will you reach it?

### Goal #3

1. List one detailed, reachable, practical goal.

2. What will you use to measure the level of success?

3. What will you need to do or get to accomplish this goal?

4. Is it a short- or long-term goal and when will you reach it?

# Technology

Write two or three goals to reveal your professional agenda for balancing technology in your classroom.

### Goal #1

1. List one detailed, reachable, practical goal.

2. What will you use to measure the level of success?

3. What will you need to do or get to accomplish this goal?

4. Is it a short- or long-term goal and when will you reach it?

### Goal #2

1. List one detailed, reachable, practical goal.

2. What will you use to measure the level of success?

3. What will you need to do or get to accomplish this goal?

4. Is it a short- or long-term goal and when will you reach it?

**Goal #3**

1. List one detailed, reachable, practical goal.

2. What will you use to measure the level of success?

3. What will you need to do or get to accomplish this goal?

4. Is it a short- or long-term goal and when will you reach it?

## A Constant Repeat

There are two essential ideas to keep in mind when it comes to transforming with A.A.A. The first is that you will have to revisit this chapter and your goals upon the completion of this book. You will not be aware of all the applicable ideas that can affect your objectives until you finish each chapter. There is a plethora of activities and means for finding your balance as we progress through each step of STRIDES. The second point, which is also critical and never-ending, is realizing that you must constantly revisit your goals to evaluate your accomplishments as an MTE. You will need to continually write new goals as your knowledge, comfort, and experiences increase. This is inevitable. As you work through STRIDES and master your practices, you will be motivated to continue your efforts and develop your expertise. This is when you will mature your balancing act and become a leader in this groundbreaking educational philosophy. Remember to always push yourself along your journey while maintaining a sense of patience and understanding of the potential challenges in this evolution. Be sure to surround yourself with like-minded colleagues and friends who will support your struggles, determination, and victories.

# AN EDUCATIONAL MISSION

Up to this point in transforming with A.A.A., we have focused on your personal and professional beliefs and endeavors. As an MTE, it is equally important to discover ways to help our students find this balance in their personal lives and in their learning. The educator is urged to play a fundamental role in this process. Students look to teachers to learn behaviors, values, and beliefs. Some children and adolescents undoubtedly have respectable parental/family guidance to channel these opinions and principles aside from the school environment. Even in these instances, educators can still be a part of developing students' thinking and viewpoints. Consider the countless students who come from unstable homes where life choices are questionable and, at times, illegal. This is a dark reality for many of the children's lives we touch year after year, decade after decade.

Educators and schools will need to take ownership about what we teach our students regarding the movement and technology (MT) balance. Some of these perspectives will be demonstrated naturally as educators physically provide this balance in their daily lessons. Students will be **m**oving **o**ften while receiving a **s**teady flow of **t**echnology (MOST) as teachers make the most of their time and content deliveries. Do you think that having educators lead by example will be enough to reverse the current trends of declining movement and accelerated digital use? It is more likely that educators will need to teach this balancing act and what it means to transform with A.A.A. in order to make a notable difference. Many students will need guidance to increase their movement levels or decrease their technology use. Who can our society count on to provide this assistance to all students across the board? Schools and teachers.

Educators are a constant in students' lives and can build awareness, give attention, and support action. Below is a five-step approach for schools and MTEs to consider when promoting this balancing act.

1. Provide a visual approach by demonstrating balance in your classroom.

2. Create an internal buzz by talking frequently and passionately about the importance of maintaining the MT balance.

3. Share facts and data about both movement and technology so students understand the significance of sustaining a balance.

4. Make the challenges of upholding the balancing act relatable and understandable.

5. Provide educational opportunities for students to set goals and work on their balancing act.

Teachers are encouraged to take our youngsters through the same process you previously went through when you evaluated your own personal outlooks and professional agendas to find your balance. You can create awareness by talking with students about how we have gone from a society of movers to a society that is sedentary and inactive. Sharing information with students about the benefits of movement and the pros and cons about technology (presented in Chapter 2) is another avenue to promote awareness. Once your students are made mindful of these alarming facts, you can start to direct their attention to how often they move or use technology. You can ask them to identify areas of concern in their personal or home lives. This stage alone will get them to start thinking about the concept of a balancing act and why and how it is important to their overall health and well-being.

Provide educational opportunities that encourage students to find their own sense of balance between movement and technology. Share your own personal or professional experiences or goals, if you feel comfortable doing so. Assure them that this is a process we all need to go through to get the most from our learning, health, and overall happiness. Offer an opportunity for them to write goals in your class when an appropriate time arises. Talk with them about the fears or doubts surrounding addictions and digital dependencies. Many of your students may already be on this path. Leading by example will have its benefits, but teachers are urged to go one step further and educate students about the MT balancing act. This is essential in order to redirect and transform our current societal directions.

# PREVENTION AND URGENCY

*To prevent* means to stop something bad from happening. Unfortunately, something damaging to our future has already occurred: We have become a sedentary society who overuses technology to the point that our health has been compromised. Some might say we have passed the point of being preventative when it comes to technology use and movement levels in our society. This statement contains some truth, but it is not completely accurate. There is still time to reverse our thinking. This redirection may not occur if we don't immediately start making changes to the way we educate our children and adolescents. If teachers change their content delivery and teaching methodologies, this will provide a clear demonstration of the importance of maintaining the balance between movement and technology. As educators teach students how to transform their thinking and behaviors with A.A.A., the younger generation can reevaluate their use of their time, interests, hobbies, and learning practices.

Schools and educators cannot delay this evolutionary makeover any longer. The urgency for this transformation and becoming an MTE is evident in the research and the lifestyles of our children and adolescents. Teachers are recommended to lead the way to this societal renovation without haste so that we can regain our health at a steady, deliberate pace. Technological advancements will still benefit our daily activities, but they will no longer consume us. Educational leaders who act with urgency will be the frontrunners in defining the standards for this comprehensive philosophy. This new design should become a mandatory overhaul, as students' future physical, social, mental/emotional, and cognitive well-being depends on it.

## WHAT DOES THIS MEAN TO ME?

### K–12 Teachers

1. After answering the questions regarding your own outlook on movement and technology, focus on one personal and one professional goal for each (two total). Take an active step toward reaching each goal.

2. Lead your students through an activity to help them recognize the role that movement and technology play in their lives. Encourage them to find a sense of balance between the two while helping them write two realistic goals (one movement, one technology) and the immediate steps they can take to achieve these goals.

### Administration

1. Complete an analysis of your school's philosophy regarding the value of movement and technology in day-to-day routines and activities. Be sure to include your faculty's perspective.

2. Lead your team by setting small, realistic goals for movement and technology as separate but equal concepts.

*(Continued)*

(Continued)

**Educational Leaders/Affiliates**

1. Support increases in physical education programs and budgets for technology equipment, devices, and programs for Grades K–12.

2. Develop guidelines that require schools to place equal value on movement and technology in all school settings.

# CHAPTER SUMMARY

- Although the demands can be overwhelming, we should always make time to improve our health by incorporating higher levels of physical activity.

- Movement's role in your life truly is all about you: a new and improved you.

- Whether it is on social media or gaming sites, an important aspect of digital responsibility is being a conscious and considerate member of these groups. Finding a balance between digital usage and other activities is important.

- Digital advantages are amazing in times of urgency and during emergencies, but technology dependencies are the polar opposite of digital responsibilities.

- As we strengthen our awareness of how we use movement and technology, we can begin to see areas for concern and potential dangers to our well-being.

- Awareness and attention are major components of transforming with A.A.A., but they must be followed by action.

- Transforming with A.A.A. is a significant component of STRIDES. If we are unable to recognize areas that need change, preserving a lasting MT balance will be difficult.

- In order to discover our balancing act, we must become aware of our goals, place attention on areas of change, and take action to make those changes happen. Our goals should be detailed, measurable, reachable, practical, and timely.

- When transforming with A.A.A., educators must constantly revisit their goals.

- The urgency for this transformation is evident in the research and the lifestyles of our children and adolescents.

# 7

# REFINING MOVEMENT AND TECHNOLOGY

## THE INEVITABLE CLIMB

The modern-day student requires active engagement, novelty, and content deliveries that are fun and exciting. Educators are always looking for ways to inspire the learner in order to motivate them and hold their attention to the designated content. As a result, both movement and technology (MT) usage have increased in K–12 classrooms over recent years. There has been notable growth in research conducted on the relationship between movement and academic achievement. These studies suggest that using movement in the classroom yields positive academic results and students who enjoy being physically engaged in the learning process. Technology always brings its A game when it comes to delivering exactly what the brain wants and desires. It is fast, provides instant feedback, and is bright and shiny—almost like a new toy. Technological uses seem to hold the focus of its audience without fail, despite the deterioration of the current-day attention span. It's no wonder why schools have jumped on the "digital bandwagon" almost the second it began to build steam in our culture.

The benefits of both movement and technology are ample. Utilizing combined strategies and techniques are worth the educator's energy to absorb, apply, and eventually master.

These emerging trends are only expected to continue and intensify their inevitable climb as more educators become aware of the benefits and ease of implementation when combining these powerhouse teaching tools. Here are the top ten benefits for including daily movement and technology in academic environments:

1. The health and well-being of students is plummeting, and creating an MT balance can help

2. The brain and body are always connected and affect one another

3. Increased academic performance and achievement

4. Enhanced brain function and memory

5. The body and brain are fueled with chemicals and novelty for optimal learning

6. Improved concentration refocuses and stimulates the brain

7. Increased motivation while differentiating

8. Increased attendance while decreasing behavioral challenges

9. Engaged senses and increased student involvement

10. Improvement for the learner as a whole

## THE SIGNIFICANCE OF ALL

*ALL* stands for *academic achievement*, *learner attention and focus*, and the *learner as a whole*. When you form a balance between movement and technology in classroom settings, you are creating an environment for increasing academic achievement, which is the essence of being a movement and technology educator (MTE). Based on research and common sense, physical activity releases chemicals in the students' brains that are ideal for optimal learning. This learning state will aid in cognitive functioning while improving academic achievement. These chemicals will also help to refocus and reenergize the brain so students can attend to the content for longer periods of time without distractions. Attention spans are shrinking, leaving teachers in need of strategies to redirect and hold their students' concentration and focus. Technology naturally provides brain excitement through quick-changing screens and visuals that entice the learner while holding their attention. Another profound benefit of incorporating daily movement and technology into all classrooms is that these activities will educate the learner as a whole. Balancing movement and technology will provide opportunities to produce well-rounded physical, social, mental/emotional, and cognitive growth. This is significant to educating every aspect of students' lives while enriching their entire existence.

## Academic Achievement

Even though educators are always searching for the newest cutting-edge strategies to improve student learning and success, they are often apprehensive about change. These combined, innovative teaching methods will help to improve cognition and recall through easy activities that have great value. Movement and technology can operate in harmony and become imperative for enhancing learning, memory, and retention in today's classroom. The practicalities behind the activities presented herein are impressive and will be welcomed by students and teachers alike. This chapter will detail a variety of options while sharing applicable ideas for uniting movement, technology, and academic content.

Let's face it—the primary goal of most educational environments is to improve academic achievement and test scores. Balancing movement and technology attends to the child's requirements for optimal brain functioning. The reality is that most school settings direct their time and energy to cognitive programs that are geared toward making improvements on academic standards alone by increasing workload. Some school districts have strengthened their physical education programs, but many have actually reduced physical education's time, value, and importance while minimizing students' physical activity levels in the process. This makes daily movement in the classroom an irrefutable priority. Many schools have also reduced their tech time by eliminating computer classes and teachers while expecting students to grasp the skills on their own or from their primary classroom teacher. Cognitive performance dominates schools and demands that teachers produce data-driven improvements that reach and exceed the district's expectations. This growth should definitely be a primary goal in schools, and balancing movement and technology can play a significant role in helping students make the grade, along with providing supplementary benefits.

## Learner Attention and Focus

You will need to estimate your students' attention spans when combining movement and technology with STRIDES (**s**tructuring and managing, **t**ransforming with A.A.A., **r**efining movement and technology, **i**nterconnecting communities, **d**efining the balance, **e**mploying SMART activities, **s**upporting a united approach). Even though student focus can change from day to day, it is still important to decide on a class average. Statistics suggest that attention spans have shrunk as much as 50% over the past decade (Gaille, 2017). Whether you teach elementary or secondary students, their ability to maintain focus is decreasing at discouraging rates. Some findings show that attention spans fell from twelve minutes to eight minutes in the year 2000, while some claim that average attentions spans are as low as five seconds with an increase in children diagnosed with attention deficit hyperactivity disorder (ADHD) to 9.5% in the past decade (Gaille, 2017). When providing daily movement activities and interactive digital programs, there is a direct emphasis on refocusing and reenergizing the brain to heighten academic performance and improve students' ability to attend to learning objectives.

How can attention spans be diminishing when students can sit for hours while focusing intensely on a computer game or social media? This example supports the idea that students' ability to concentrate is increasing. Social media, games, and other technological offerings attract the brain. They are engaging, stimulating, bright, colorful, quick changing, and exciting, all of which seduce the brain. Making the classroom environment just as appealing to the learner must be an educational priority. We must give the brain what it craves. Movement works perfectly with technology to stimulate and appeal to the brain and body of learners; these are natural benefits. We need to tap into this resource to increase attention spans for cognitive performance. Balancing movement and technology in the classrooms on a regular basis allows for continual student engagement.

## Learner as a Whole

What does it mean to educate students as a whole? It refers to caring about the mental/emotional, social, physical, and cognitive growth of each child. Many educational environments devalue this notion. Although academic achievement is consistently the focal point of school settings, isn't it important for education to play an equal role in trying to help children become happy, healthy, caring, productive adults? This would mean that standards and goals would equally attend to all areas of growth for each student, cognition only being one quarter of the consideration. Utilizing movement and technology equally helps to develop each aspect of the child. This is a reputable strength of this balanced teaching philosophy.

- **Mental/Emotional:** Physical activity and movement have a direct, physiological effect on mood. It is stimulating and calming at the same time, which can benefit all learners. Technology can help students feel more confident and build self-esteem as they progress at an individual pace while receiving constant feedback and support.

- **Social:** Chapter 4 is devoted to community connectors for both movement and technology. These will foster respectful learners and help to improve social skills.

- **Physical:** Active learning increases physical activity and improves the overall health and well-being of students. When technology is coupled with movement, the rewards double.

- **Cognitive:** The previous section of this chapter, along with Chapter 2 and Chapter 3, outlined extensive research that shows a positive connection between movement, technology, and academic achievement.

## THE ABCs OF MOVEMENT FOR ALL

The ABCs of movement for ALL (academic achievement, learner attention and focus, and the learner as a whole) are categorized into three specific groups: *academic activities*, *brain boosters*, and *community connectors*. Each category has specific goals, but they all can be used to increase student achievement and learner attention while educating the child as a whole. As we move through the rest of this chapter, each section will be explained and activities will be suggested. This chapter is intended to be a starting point in your thinking. There are multiple books that serve as comprehensive resources. Active learning is an exciting teaching philosophy that is memorable and motivating for learners. Two suggested books to consider when you are ready to add to your list of strategies and activities are *Ready, Set, Go: The Kinesthetic Classroom 2.0* and *The Kinesthetic Classroom: Teaching and Learning Through Movement*.

These two books provide extensive examples on how to incorporate movement into learning environments. In Chapter 4, an *active educator* was defined as a teacher who uses movement daily to reach academic standards. You must develop these teaching tactics, as well as the skills of a tech teacher, in order to become an MTE and excel at STRIDES. Incorporating movement into the classroom is very intimidating to newcomers. Therefore, it is recommended that you *start small, think big*. This means that you implement activities that you are most comfortable with first. This may be body blasts or body breaks. Physical activities, such as exercise or brain breaks, are often the most popular forms of movement utilized in the modern-day classroom. These activities are wonderful, effective, and an important component of the ABCs movement for ALL.

As each section is detailed in the pages that follow, envision the role it will play in your classroom. All three components are appropriate for every educational environment, and no grade level is excluded from the vast benefits that each one provides. If you look at Figure 7.1, academic activities bridge movement and content through three active means. Brain boosters also involve three types of body movements that reenergize and refocus the brain. Community connectors concentrate on building a cohesive classroom environment that fosters kindness and respectful learning.

**FIGURE 7.1 ■ The ABCs of Movement for ALL**

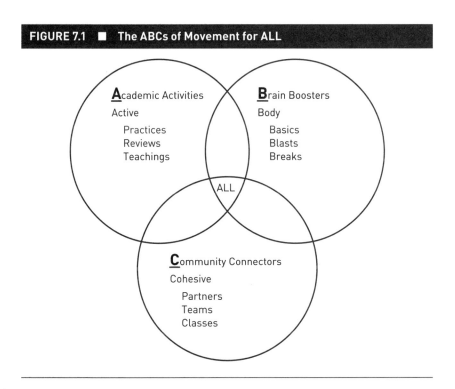

## Academic Activities

Academic activities are perhaps the most important of the ABCs of movement for ALL because they unite movement and academic content into one. This is an attractive quality for teachers who constantly feel pressed for time. Some educators reject physical activities, such as body boosters or community connectors, because they are disconnected from the subject matter in certain instances. Some teachers feel there is not enough time in their schedule to include non–content-based movements. This way of thinking is not supported by the research; however, educational demands are particularly high, and it can be easy to adopt this perspective as a reactionary thought. Academic activities bring the content to life and fall into three categories: active practices, active reviews, and active teachings. They are lively, stimulating, and energetic as they engage students in the learning process. They are also ideal for memory and recall because they strengthen episodic memory. During test taking, students will be able to recall the physical movements and experiences that helped them to understand and connect with the content.

This book, along with other well-designed sources on active learning, will encourage you to go deeper into your philosophy by directly linking movement and academics to meet content standards on a regular basis. This skill takes time for educators to master because it requires out-of-the-box thinking while breaking away from traditional teaching methods. It also demands a creative mind in order to teach higher-level standards through kinesthetic means. However, once these lessons are developed and fine-tuned, they are priceless due to their massive effects on memory, recall, depth of understanding, and achievement. An additional advantage is that they often naturally help to build peer relationships. This is represented by the overlapping circle between academic activities and community connecters in Figure 7.1. Many of these activities require students to work with partners, teams, or an entire class to accomplish the task or learn the subject matter. As a result, emotions are raised that aid in the learning process and the recall of the content at a later time. Movement and physical activity are always emotional at some level. This means the brain is alert, attentive, and ready to absorb experiences. Educators can take advantage of these benefits to improve students' accomplishments in all areas of education. Each category will be defined and followed by classroom applications.

### Active Practices

*Active practices* are academic performances that utilize movement to study or repeat content or skills in order to improve or maintain one's proficiency. The following list describes five examples.

1. **Seat shuffles:** This is a great way to incorporate movement into traditional worksheets. Place a worksheet on every desk or workstation. Play music and allow students to walk around the classroom. Students can also skip, slide, gallop, or perform any other movement you would like. When this music goes off, students sit at the closest desk and complete the first question on the worksheet. When the music comes back on, they begin to move again. The next time they sit down, ask them to check or grade Question 1 before they complete Question 2 on the worksheet. Continue for your allotted time.

2. **Paper passes:** In this activity, ask students to mill around the classroom with a worksheet in their hand. Every time they pass a peer, they will politely say "Hello" or share a nice comment as they exchange sheets with one another. Upon your direction, they will go back to their seat and complete Question 1. When they are finished, they get up and begin to move again, using positive comments and words of kindness. The next time they sit down, ask them to check or grade Question 1 before they complete Question 2 on the worksheet. Continue for the allotted time.

3. **Academic exercises:** Use exercises from the body blast examples listed starting on page 107 to practice academic content; for example, have students practice their spelling words while performing a jumping jack for each letter of the word. This works well for material that needs constant repetition.

4. **Paired solutions:** While utilizing movement, have students work with a partner to solve a problem or complete a worksheet. For example, have partners pass a ball back and forth while practicing how to count by twos or discussing character details from a recent class reading.

5. **Team activated:** These activities have the same concept as paired solutions, but you use movement activities with small teams to practice content. An example would be asking a team of five students to stand in a circle and pass a ball around. The person who has the ball shares a noun (or any part of speech they are currently working on) with the team. With each pass of the ball, a different noun is shared.

## Active Reviews

*Active reviews* are academic performances that utilize movement to restudy or reexamine content or skills in order to improve or maintain one's proficiency. The following list describes five examples.

1. **Team relays:** Separate your class into small teams of four or five. Review content while incorporating relay races into the process. An example of this would be asking team members to race from the back of the classroom to the front and write an answer to a review question on the board; multistep math problems work very well in this example. Keep in mind, *race* doesn't mean run. Choose movements that are appropriate for your space and circumstances.

2. **Stomp:** Place your class into equal teams of 8–10 and ask them to split in half and face one another. For example, you may have five students in a line facing the other five while each team is standing approximately 5–10 feet away. Place *stomp* cards in the middle of the line. These cards should have answers on them (A, B, C, D; noun, verb, adjective; scalene, acute, obtuse; etc.). Number the students on each side of the line 1–5. Read or display a question and call a number. The student whose number is called races into the center and stomps on the answer. Whichever side of the line stomps the correct answer first wins the round.

3. **Fast hands:** This game is the same concept as stomp, but students will use their hands to tap or grasp the correct answer. Fast hands works better in small groups of two or three. For example, have students sit and face one

another with a *true* and a *false* answer card in front of them. The teacher reads or displays a true/false question while the students race to tap the correct response with their hand.

4. **Popcorn:** Have students get into small teams of 3–5 and "pop" (throw and catch) a ball around their circle. When the teacher makes a sound or says "stop," the student with the ball has to answer the review question for their team. They can refer to their peer to the right or left of them as their "lifeline" if they need help with the answer. If no one knows the answer, this lets the teacher know she or he needs to revisit the content.

5. **Speed racers:** Have students mill around the classroom with a small whiteboard. When the teacher says "match," students will pair up with the person closest to them and face them. The teacher reads or displays a question and the students race against their peer to write the correct answer. After they correct each other's work, they begin to mill around the room again. They should face a new partner each round. Points can be given for correct answers and speed of completion.

## Active Teachings

*Active teachings* provide instruction or knowledge through movement for students. The following list gives eight examples taken from the two books listed earlier.

### Language Arts

- **Editing on the move (punctuation and mechanics):** Allow students to work alone or with a partner. Give students a list of sentences. Have them walk while editing one sentence at a time. Students will raise their two arms to demonstrate a capital letter, pause for commas while bending their knees, and add one of the following end marks: squat into the tuck position for a period, jump up and down for an exclamation point, or make a hooklike motion with their arm while lifting their leg for a question mark.

- **Colon/Semicolon fist bump (conventions of standard English):** Have students stand face-to-face with a partner. Read a sentence that contains a colon or semicolon. Partners will use a double-knuckle fist bump (two fists in front of the body, one above the other) if they believe a colon should be used in the sentence or a double-knuckle fist bump with a bottom fist swoop (two fists in front of the body, the bottom fist makes a swooping action, swaying back and forth) for a colon. Use a variety of sentences at different levels and allow students to discuss their choices.

### Math

- **Integer lineup (adding integers: positive and negative):** Give half your students positive signs and the other half negative signs. Have students mill around the classroom and then ask them to show you zero (a positive sign must link with a negative sign or two positives with two negatives, etc.). Once the idea is solidified, have the positives on one side of the room and the negatives on the other. Display the problem $5 + (-2) =$ and designate a meet-up line in the center of the room. Five positives come to the line and so do two negatives. They stand across from one another making 2 zero pairs with 3 positives left over. Therefore, the answer is 3. Have students return to their groups and continue with multiple problems.

- **Solving an equation (any multistep math problem):** Put students into teams of six or seven. Make a set of laminated cards 0–9, an $x$ for the variable, and a set of $+$, $-$, $=$, and $/$ signs for each group. Have a group demonstrate (in front of the classroom) how to physically solve an equation while using the signs, movement, and their bodies. Students should be able to see each step of the process as it physically happens. After the demonstration, have each group try to solve a few problems with their team.

### Science

- **Magnet tag (experience magnetic force):** Discuss polarity; repel and unite while making the human body a magnet (the front is the north pole and the back is the south pole). Choose someone to be "It." When players come face to face, they say "repel." When students come at each other from north and south poles, they can link up (the person in the back puts their hands on the front person's shoulders). They can stay linked for five seconds, then they must disconnect. The player or players who are "It" can only tag single magnets. Linked magnets cannot be tagged until they disconnect. If a student is tagged by someone who is "It," they switch roles.

- **Neural network relay race (neurons and order of events):** Divide your class in half so they can become two separate neurons or neural networks (depending on class size and the teacher's goal). Make notecards to explain the job of each person (part of the neural network). The first dendrites (1–3 people) spread their arms like tree branches; their job is to observe. Dendrites in the second neuron catch the information. Nucleuses (1–3 people) store the information (a ball) and say "buzz" to show excitement. They pass the ball to the axons (as many people as needed), who will stand in a straight line and say "Pass the information" as they pass the information (ball) down the axon. The axons give the ball to the synaptic gaps (1–2 people) who say "From one neuron to the next" as they pass the information to the dendrite of the second neuron. The process continues as the information is passed through the second neuron, creating a neural network. Teachers may want to have multiple neural networks racing against each other to increase motivation once the parts are learned.

### Social Studies

- **Link up America (maps and organizing information in a spatial context):** Allow students to use a map of the United States. Turn your classroom into the United States and point out Washington, Maine, Florida, and California. Ask your first student to become a state (they can pick anyone they want). After they stand in the appropriate place in the room, ask another student to link up. They can become any state that borders the first state that was chosen. Continue by asking students to link up one at a time. Also, you can ask students to relink at any given time to make sure everyone is paying attention, as they never know when they will be called. Eventually, you can ask students to put their maps away and perform the activity without it.

- **Conquering of the Aztecs (war):** Split the class into two teams (Aztecs will be two thirds of the class and the other third will be Spanish conquistadors). Choose two students; one will be Montezuma and the other Cortez. The war is a tag game based on the following rules:

  a. Aztecs walk while conquistadors gallop (since the Spaniards had horses).

  b. Conquistadors can use some type of shield to block tags made by the Aztecs (for example, a book).

  c. Aztecs tag with their hands to represent spears, while conquistadors use balls to tag (this represents bullets and smallpox; both of which are more deadly than spears).

  Students move around the space trying to tag each other.

  a. One tag with a ball kills the Aztecs, but Aztecs must tag a conquistador twice to kill them; in the first tag, students lose the use of that body part.

  b. As an extra part of the game, the teacher can assign a student to play Dona Marina, an Aztec woman who many believed persuaded her own men to switch sides and fight for the conquistadors. This player can give a ball to any Aztec player at any time, automatically putting them on the conquistador's team (this guarantees that the conquistadors win).

Play multiple games if time allows, allowing students to have different parts.

## Brain Boosters

What's good for the body is good for the brain! There are three examples of brain boosters: body basics, body blasts, and body breaks. Each category will be defined and followed by classroom applications.

### Body Basics

*Body basics* are physical activities that prime the brain for enhanced learning. They are developmentally appropriate movements that stimulate and ready the brain to absorb academic content and meet challenges. Using body basics to improve and fill developmental gaps is important for increasing academic achievement. Implementing these brain-compatible activities improves neural connections and heightens cognitive functioning and abilities. Many theorists believe this developmental research is still young and inconclusive. Other experts in the field confirm that specific, directed physical movements prepare the brain for heightened cognitive performance and should be utilized on a regular basis in all classrooms and/or physical education programs. The intention of these coordinated motor movements is to open up channels of communication between different regions of the brain for complex cognitive function and processing. Incorporating these movements to improve the functioning of systems will develop both the brain and body to boost student learning (Moize & Hess, 2017).

Body basics can be used at any time during the lesson, but they are most effective prior to learning or during transitioning from one topic to another. These activities have three objectives: (1) to fill developmental gaps in the brain and body, (2) to stimulate the brain to open up channels of communication between brain regions, and (3) to prepare the brain and body for peak performance as an interconnected unit (Moize & Hess, 2017). Students can improve an array of both physical and academic skills when these activities are incorporated into academic lessons. The physical–cognitive connection plays a significant role in learning; therefore, it stands to reason why such specified physical movements belong in an academic setting and should be practiced consistently. If the mind and body function in unison, they must be strengthened equally for optimal learning and performance. Body basics can increase cognitive functioning while improving memory retention and retrieval. Body basics include the following skills:

- **Vestibular development:** The vestibular system is located in the inner ear and is involved in stability and spatial orientation. This system is often referred to as the *human balance system*. The vestibular system is the first sensory system to develop and will affect the auditory, visual, and kinesthetic senses, which play a direct role in learning.

- **Cross lateralization:** *Lateralization* is the tendency for some neural functions in the brain or cognitive processes to be more dominant in one hemisphere than the other. Physical movements that allow students to cross the midline of the body (moving the arms and/or legs across the body's center) recruit more parts of the brain for well-developed attention systems (Moize & Hess, 2017).

- **Balancing:** Having learners practice and improve their ability to maintain balance is crucial to the learning process and student success because they receive information about where they are in space through motion and active engagement.

- **Visual tracking:** *Visual tracking* is a term that is universally recognized by classroom teachers and refers to the ability of the eye muscles to focus near and far, left and right, and up and down. The eyes move in similar pathways to the limbs, and strengthening these muscles through appropriate exercises helps to increase the length of time the eyes can focus on reading and math computations.

- **Gross and fine motor movements:** The brain uses gross and fine motor skills to lay the foundation for learning. Agility, coordination, and motor skills are controlled by the cerebellum. Cognitive functioning and processing in the brain increase when the cerebellum is operating efficiently.

- **Muscular strength:** The muscular system is responsible for the movement of the human body. Developing core strength in the back and abdominal area supports the spine and improves posture, which is beneficial in learning and everyday life. As a result, oxygen and blood can flow freely, supplying fuel to the brain to help achieve peak performance.

- **Cardiorespiratory endurance:** Cardiorespiratory endurance measures how well the heart, lungs, and muscles work together to keep the body active and physically engaged. Research reports that physically fit students perform better academically while balancing the hormones, brain chemicals, and body system, allowing the brain and body to go into a homeostatic state that is beneficial to the learning process.

The following lists describe body basic moves that work well in classroom environments.

### Spinning and Visual Tracking

- **Traditional spins:** Students spin in a specified boundary and at a teacher-directed speed. (Students should freeze if they get dizzy and should not fall.)

- **180–360 spins:** Students jump (or keep one foot planted) and do a 180 or 360 spin clockwise or counterclockwise for a specified number of turns.

- **Fitness spins:** Students spin while performing an exercise at the same time (teacher directed or student chosen). Some examples include jumping jacks, heel tapping (left then right), air climbing (pretending to climb a mountain), hopping on one leg.

- **Creative spins:** Any activity that students can do while spinning at the same time (one example is animal imitations).

- **Visual tracking exercises:** Visual tracking exercises include shape tracers (trace shapes while having the eyes follow), air trackers (follow an object or hand/finger through the air; a figure-eight pattern works well), written trackers (trace a picture or draw a figure-eight pattern with a writing utensil while the eyes follow), and object trackers (games or activities that have the eyes follow in a variety of directions).

### Balancing

- **Single-person or partner yoga balances:** Students, partners, or small groups will perform any yoga balancing postures per the teacher's discretion. Poses should be held for a specified time. Hold poses on the right and left sides of the body when appropriate. Single person poses might include tree, warrior, triangle, and standing forward bend. Partner poses might include V pose, Y pose, supported warrior, and twin trees. (Posture descriptions and pictures are easily accessible on the Internet.)

- **Fitness balances:** Students will perform fitness challenges that include balancing. Some examples include chair balance with leg lift, wall push-up with leg lift, lunges, wall-sit with leg lift, and so on. (Activity descriptions and pictures are easily accessible on the Internet.)

### Cross Lateralization

- **Body cross taps:** Students connect or tap any body part on the left side of the body to a body part on the right side (and vice versa) for a specific time or number of repetitions. Some examples include left elbow to right knee, left fingers to right toes, left fingers to right ear, left hand to right shoulder, left elbow to right hip. Always have students reverse sides.

- **Dances with body crosses:** Students perform any dances that cross the midline of the body (the Macarena, for example).

- **Moves with crosses (move from one place to another):** Students perform any movements where they move about the room while crossing the midline of their body (skipping while touching the left elbow to the right knee and vice versa, for example).

- **Fitness exercises with body crosses:** Students perform fitness exercises that cross the midline of the body.

### Fine Motor, Gross Motor, and Coordination Activities

- **Gross motor movements:** Students perform any gross motor movement (see body blasts for ideas). Use a combination of activities for both muscular and cardiorespiratory improvements.

- **Locomotor and non-locomotor movements:** Students will perform a variety of locomotor movements (moving from one place to another) around their classroom, such as walking, hopping, galloping, jumping, skipping, sliding, and leaping. Students will perform a mixture of non-locomotor (stationary) movements as well; some examples include bending, twisting, turning, lifting, stretching, and extending.

- **Hand–Eye coordination activities:** Some examples of hand–eye coordination activities include toss and catch (throw an object slightly into the air and catch it), side-to-side toss and catch (throw an object side-to-side between the hands), and around-the-body passes (pass an object around the body clockwise and counterclockwise). Objects can be balls, beanbags, juggling scarves, and so on.

- **Fine motor movements:** Fine motor activity examples include cup stacking, manipulating objects, and scissors usage.

- **Foot–Eye coordination activities:** Students perform foot–eye coordination activities. Some examples include foot taps (tap the right foot on an object, then the left foot; repeat at directed speed), side-to-side foot passes (pass a ball or an object between the feet), object balances (balance an object on the foot), and object passes (pass an object from one foot to another person's foot).

- **Rhythm and beat challenges:** Students perform rhythm and beat movements. Some examples include scarf juggling, hand clapping rhythms, body percussion rhythms, manipulative and rhythms.

## Body Blasts

In most cases, adding fitness activities (also referred to as *fitness blasts*) to a classroom setting requires minimal knowledge. Obtaining some background information can be useful to teachers so they feel confident in including these simple activities effortlessly in to their daily lessons. Fitness is generally broken into two categories: health and skill. Health-related components of fitness are often seen as more important because they are directly related to improving students' physical well-being. Below are five health-related components of fitness:

1. **Muscular strength:** The extent to which muscles can exert force

2. **Muscular endurance:** The ability of the muscles to perform continuously without fatiguing

3. **Cardiovascular/Respiratory endurance:** The ability of the heart and lungs to work together to provide oxygen and fuel to the body during sustained movements

4. **Flexibility:** The ability of the joints to move through a range of motion

5. **Body composition:** The amount of fat mass compared to lean muscle mass, bone, and organs

Additionally, there are five skill-related components of fitness. These components enhance performance in motor skills and sports. They are as follows:

1. **Power:** To exert maximum force in minimal time (includes strength and speed)

2. **Agility:** The ability to minimize transition time from one movement pattern to another

3. **Balance:** To control the body's position (stationary or moving)

4. **Coordination:** The ability to combine several distinct movement patterns into a singular movement

5. **Speed and reaction time:** The ability to minimize the time cycle of a movement; reaction time is a subcomponent and refers to the time it takes for the neuromuscular system to produce movement from stimulus to reaction

This may seem like a lot of information to an educator who has minimal or no experience with any type of fitness training. However, increasing fitness levels simply means educators will move students in as many different ways as possible, with a variety of time frames and intensity levels. Incorporating body blasts in a classroom environment is not meant to be time consuming or to become a distraction from the content. Typically, teachers can include these activities in the 2–3 minutes prior to learning or transitioning. Upon completion of the physical movements, students will feel energized, alert, and ready to proceed to academic challenges. These exercises can be used efficiently by educators for the purpose of increasing cognitive output.

Making fitness attainable for everyone is important; therefore, suggest and explain modifications when defining the physical challenges you offer to your students. Students, and really anyone for that matter, should never feel bad about making adaptations to their exercises. The key is to move your body in a variety of ways and to participate at your best level. Jumping is a good example of a popular movement that can easily be modified. Even though it is used in many of the cardio exercises, every movement can be adjusted so that jumping is completely eliminated. In most cases, the student can step with their feet, slow down the exercise, or work one side of the body at a time to reduce the high-impact movement to a low-impact activity. Students can also decrease their range of motion in exercises, slow their speed when necessary, or modify the movement completely.

The main goals of the suggestions listed in this section are to provide students with opportunities to move while increasing heart rate, contracting muscles, improving balance, and strengthening the core. Students of all abilities can participate in exercises that enhance fitness levels while improving academic achievement. Utilizing modifications and encouraging students to participate at a level where they safely push themselves and give their best effort is ideal for brain–body health.

Body blasts/fitness blasts can be performed two different ways: for a specified time or number of repetitions. They are also presented with three distinct efforts, as described below:

1. **Body blasts:** Students participate at an increased speed for 90 seconds or 90 repetitions. Pacing is consistent and steady.

2. **Fast body blasts:** Students participate at a speed that is faster than body blasts and last for 60 seconds or 60 repetitions. Pacing is noticeably faster.

3. **Super-Fast body blasts:** Students participate at their all-out fastest speed (while maintaining safety) for 30 seconds or 30 repetitions.

What follows is a list of cardio blasts, muscular blasts, and balance/core blasts that can be used in your classroom. Many of these movements are common terms that can be searched for on the Internet for a visual demonstration.

### Cardio Blasts

- **Jumping jacks:** Stand with your feet together and arms at the side of your body. Jump while moving your feet apart and swinging your arms above your head until your fingers touch, then jump and come back to the starting position. Repeat as many times as you'd like.

- **Jump twists:** Stand with your feet together. Jump and twist to the right, jump back to the center, jump and twist to the left, jump back to the center, and repeat.

- **Heel taps:** Stand and touch your right hand to your right heel behind your body. Repeat with your left hand to your left heel.

- **Instep taps:** Stand and touch your right hand to your left instep in front of your body, then repeat with your left hand to your right instep.

- **Line jumps:** Jump side to side or front to back over an imaginary line.

- **Squat jumps:** Squat down and touch the floor (or get as close to it as you can) while keeping your back as straight as possible. Jump up into the air, then repeat.

- **Switch jumps:** Stand with your right foot in front of your body and your left foot behind your body; jump and switch feet.

- **Crisscrosses:** Stand with your feet slightly more than shoulder width apart. Jump and crisscross your feet so that one is in front of the other, then jump back to the beginning. Repeat with the other foot in front.

- **Air climbers:** Stand and lift your right knee into the air while reaching your left arm above your head. Switch and lift your left knee and your right arm.

- **Squat punches:** Stand with your feet apart. Squat and punch your right fist out in front of you, then bring it back to the center of the body. Repeat with your left fist, and bring it back to the center, all while maintaining the squat.

### Muscular Blasts

- **Squats:** Stand with your feet slightly more than shoulder width apart (toes slightly outward) and put your arms out in front of your body (parallel to the ground). Looking straight ahead, tip your hips backward and bend your knees (no lower than parallel to the floor). Keep your back straight and shoulders and chest up, then rise up to return to the starting position.

- **Lunges:** Stand with your feet in a wide-stride stance (one foot in front of the body, one behind). Keeping the body and back straight, the shoulders back, and the chin up, look ahead and lower your hips until both knees are bent (about 90 degrees, making sure the front knee is directly above the ankle), keeping your weight in your heels. Push back up to return to the beginning position. Do the same for both sides.

- **Wall-Sit:** Stand with your back against the wall, place your feet out away from the wall, and squat down until your legs are parallel to the floor (or less). Hold this position for a specific amount of time.

- **Wall-Sit with leg lifts:** Do the same as the wall-sit listed above but extend one leg out in front of your body and hold for a designated time, then switch legs.

- **Side leg lifts:** Stand with your hands on your hips and lift your right leg out to the side of your body as high as you can. Bring your leg back down and switch to the other side.

- **Floor/Wall push-ups:** Perform traditional or modified push-ups on the floor or wall; be sure to keep the body straight and in line with the spine.

- **Floor/Wall shoulder taps:** Get in the push-up position on the floor or against a wall and tap your left hand to your right shoulder, then your right hand to your left shoulder. Be sure to keep your body straight.

- **Chair/Floor tricep dips:** Sit at the edge of a chair, place your hands behind your hips, lift your bottom off the seat, and walk your feet forward (the farther away from the chair, the harder the exercise). Lower your body downward, then lift your body back up with your arms.

- **Weightless chest flies:** Stand with your arms spread out wide to the side of your body. Bring them in front of your body, crisscrossing one over the top of the other. Next, move your arms back to the side of the body, and then bring them forward with the other arm crisscrossing over the top.

- **Arm circles:** Stand with your arms out to your side and make small or large arm circles, forward and backward. Keep the speed safe for joints and muscles.

### Balance/Core Blasts

- **Tree pose:** Stand with your arms at your side. Shift your weight to your left foot and place your hands on your hips. While looking straight ahead, lift your right leg and place it on your inner thigh (or as high as it can go) while lifting your arms above your head. Hold and repeat on the other side.

- **Triangle pose:** Stand with your feet wide apart and your right foot forward. Align your heels and turn your right foot out 90 degrees. Pivot your left foot inward 45 degrees and raise your arms until they are parallel with the floor. Extend your torso over your right leg and bend at the hip. Rest your right hand on your shin, ankle, or the floor outside your right foot. Stretch your left arm toward the ceiling, keeping your head neutral. Hold and repeat on the other side.

- **Warrior 1 pose:** Bend your right knee directly above your foot and place your hands on your hips. Square the hips and shoulder to the front wall and open your chest. Lifting your arms straight above your head, arch your back and look to the ceiling. Hold and repeat on the other side.

- **Chair pose:** Stand with your feet together. Place your hands on your hips, bend your knees, and push your bottom out behind you (as if you were sitting in an imaginary chair) with a straight back. Tighten your body and raise your hands overhead with your palms facing one another. Hold this position.

- **Eagle pose:** Stand with your arms and legs by your side. Balance on your right foot while bending slightly. Cross your left thigh over your right (hook your toes on your calf if possible), fix your gaze, extend your arms, and drop your left arm over the right. Bend your elbow and wrap your arms to try and press your palms together (or as close as you can). Square your body and hold this position. Repeat for the other side.

- **Standing cross crunch:** Stand with your arms at your side and your feet spread comfortably apart. Take your right elbow across your body and touch it to your left knee as you lift your knee (or as close as you can get to it) and tighten your core. Go back to the beginning to repeat for the other side.

- **Standing side crunch:** Stand with your arms at your side and your feet spread comfortably apart. Lift your right knee and connect it to your right elbow while tightening the core. Go back to the beginning to repeat for the other side.

- **Standing twist:** Stand with your elbows bent and fingers interlocked at the center of your chest. Spread your feet apart, slightly bend your knees, and twist right to left while tightening your core. Continue to go side to side.

- **Wall swimmers:** Stand with your entire body facing the wall with your hands straight above your head. Lift your right arm and left leg away from the wall at the same time while crunching your back muscles and tightening your core. Repeat with the other side.

- **Hip hinge:** Stand with your hands on your hips and your feet slightly farther apart than your hips. Bend forward at your waist while keeping your body tight until you are parallel to the floor (or slightly above). Keep your back straight and your neck and shoulders in line with the body. Stand up, then repeat as many times as you'd like.

## Body Breaks

When we take time away from sitting to incorporate movement, we are engaging in a body break, which in turn gives the brain some recovery time. As a learner, we can only retain so much information before the brain feels like it's on academic overload. This is true for students of all ages. When it comes to learning and brain functioning, sometimes less is more. In other words, educators should give short bursts of new content and then allow for processing and practice time for increased student learning. Content chunking is an effective strategy in which academic information is broken into shorter pieces so it is easier to manage and remember. Working memory and the hippocampus (which converts working memory to long-term memory) have capacity limits, especially when dealing with new information that may not be a priority to the learner. Prime time teaching moments typically occur at the beginning of class, when the brain is fresh and energized. Additional peak teaching moments occur during the last few minutes of class, after transitioning from one subject to another, or following a physical activity, movement, or body break. Even when academic content is presented in smaller amounts or creative teaching techniques are used for delivery, students still require a brain break for heightened cognitive functioning.

Body breaks give the brain time to rest or disconnect from the academic content. They are short and should last only a few minutes. Some educators cringe at the suggestion of giving students a break from content because they feel the curriculum doesn't allow for this. This fear is understandable but does not align with what the brain can handle when it comes to learning. Body breaks do take a small amount of time away from the subject matter; however, they also give the brain what it needs and requires. Therefore, it can function more efficiently. Body breaks boost the brain while refocusing and reenergizing it for another round of academic tasks. This boost is what makes up for the 2–3 minutes that were allotted for the break in the first place. Now the brain is recharged, allowing it to quickly catch up. Students need both the break and the boost during lengthy academic lessons so that information can be processed, stored, and retrieved. As you teach your content through active means and incorporate STRIDES regularly, you will not need body breaks as often. The break and boost are natural advantages of active learning and blended teaching.

Below are five examples of body breaks that work well in classroom environments.

1. **Computer games:** Use computer games that incorporate movement, such as GoNoodle or similar sites, to give quick 2- to 3-minute brain breaks. One consideration with many of these activities is they often use creative movements that can be intimidating for some students. When implementing physical activity, whenever possible, use concrete movements (such as basic exercises) until you establish comfort with physical activity in your classroom.

2. **Partner challenges:** Take a few minutes to have students complete a challenge that involves movement with a partner. Some examples include how many beanbag (or any object) tosses and catches partners can perform in one minute, how high they can build a LEGO tower in one minute, how many foot taps (one partner's right foot taps the other's right foot in the air, then left to left and alternate taps at a steady speed) they can get in 30 seconds, or if they can complete a challenge walk (pinching a ball between each other's elbows) around the classroom without dropping the ball.

3. **Body blasts:** Any of the body blasts previously listed serve as ideal brain breaks.

4. **Nature/Mindful walks:** When appropriate, allow students to take a 3- to 5-minute nature/mindful walk (preferably outside) to clear and relax their minds. Encourage them to focus on something positive while disconnecting from the academic content.

5. **Creative moves:** Give students 2–3 minutes to dance or move their bodies creatively. For example, you may ask them to pretend they are an animal, a tree, or an object. Again, this type of movement can be intimidating for some students. Concrete movements are preferred until you establish comfort with physical activity in your classroom. There are many students who will love being creative with their movements; therefore, these brain breaks can be fun and well-received by students.

## Community Connectors

Movement community connectors promote cohesion in three areas: partners, teams, and classes. There is no questioning the importance of communal relationships in life, in schools, or in becoming an MTE. The following chapter details this significance and provides activities for fostering connections in your classrooms. Similar to brain boosters, it can be uncomfortable for teachers to dedicate time to a need other than academic standards. Sometimes community connecters are linked to the content, but sometimes the sole intention is to attend to the relationships between students. These particular activities are interrelated with brain boosters and are represented in the overlapping area between the two in Figure 7.1. Cohesion interactions that do not include content serve as great body breaks. Remember, sometimes the brain needs a few minutes away from the subject matter to operate more efficiently and productively.

Movement community connectors and tech community connectors should be incorporated into all classrooms. At times, educators view these activities as more appropriate for elementary students. However, countless schools exist where students do not even know their peers' names. This is a misfortune and makes a statement about our priorities in education—unfortunately, it is not a positive one. How we treat one another as human beings is one of the most important aspects of our society. How can we not give it the same value in our schools? As you implement community-building activities, you will see a welcomed change in the way students treat each other. Kindness and respect will become apparent and communication skills will strengthen. As a result, it only makes sense that grades will improve, happiness will increase, and students will feel accepted and united. Community connecters are an instrumental component of the ABCs of movement for ALL as well as STRIDES.

## THE ABCDs OF TECHNOLOGY FOR ALL

The ABCDs of technology for ALL are categorized into four specific groups: *academic applications, boosting benefits (for ALL), content consumptions,* and *differentiated deliveries.* Each category has specific goals, but they can all be used to increase student achievement, learner attention and focus, and to educate the child as a whole. As we move through the ABCDs of technology for ALL, each section will be explained, and suggestions will be shared. These ideas are intended to be starting points in your thinking. Technology is advancing so quickly that you will always need to rethink and revisit the ways in which you will use it effectively in your classroom. The suggestions made in the text that follows may be outdated in no time and replaced with more advanced programs and devices to take the place of what's relevant today. Many of the basic concepts will be transferable to new designs and products, but you may need to expand your own thinking to make these connections.

All educators must develop both skills and knowledge to become successful tech teachers. These are essential components in order to grow as an MTE and excel at STRIDES. Incorporating technology into your classroom can be very intimidating to newcomers or teachers who prefer to use "old school" methods. Similar to becoming an MTE, it is recommended that you *start small, think big.* Implement activities and use technologies that you are most comfortable with first. This may be as simple as having students Google content on the Internet or write a paper with a computer. Teachers who are overwhelmed by the fast-paced world of technology need to start somewhere. Just as some teachers fear movement in the classroom, others are equally frightened by new technologies that are ever changing, especially in situations where proper training is not provided. Too often, demands are made for educators to implement technology, but educators receive minimal training on the objectives, implementation, and execution for this technology. This can result in fear and paralysis. It is hard to grow and move forward when self-confidence is nonexistent. Educational leaders must take appropriate measures to keep this from happening.

As each section in the subsequent text shows, you must envision the role that technology will play or currently plays in your classroom. All four components are appropriate for every educational environment, and no grade level is excluded

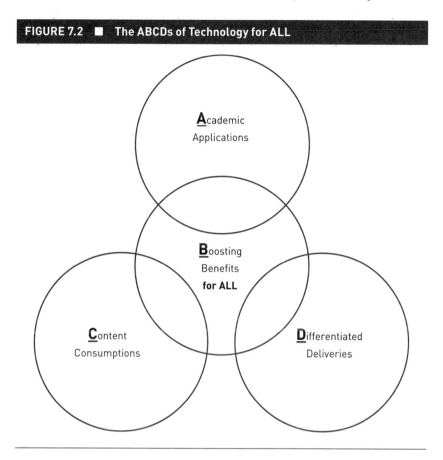

**FIGURE 7.2  ■  The ABCDs of Technology for ALL**

from the vast benefits that each one provides. If you look at Figure 7.2, academic applications, content consumptions, and differentiated deliveries are all used to boost benefits for ALL. Some of the suggestions that follow are geared toward the novice tech teacher, while others require more advanced knowledge and experience. Decide what works for you now and what might work better down the road as you grow. Veteran tech teachers will be able to implement ideas beyond the lists provided. This is a positive and allows them the opportunity to add to their knowledge and skill base as they grow as an MTE. Whether you are just getting your feet wet with technology usage or you are a master of the digital world, analyze the four categories and identify your strengths and weaknesses as you look ahead to improve your goals and direction.

## Academic Applications

Achievement and academic success have newly defined expectations in the 21st-century classroom. Learning individual skills or pieces of knowledge are simply not enough when it comes to the cognitive depth that students are now required to demonstrate. Focusing on underlying concepts, principles, or theories allows students to master the content and apply it. Practicing skills such as integration and synthesis are critical for higher-level learning and transferring information from one context to another. Utilizing technology in the classroom assists students in gathering information for deeper understanding while providing avenues for them to apply their learning. Here are some examples:

- **Collaborative assignments and makerspaces:** Interactive experiences and assignments are not only desired by the student, but they are also an excellent way for teachers to evaluate student engagement and understanding. There are many online platforms for students to work together on assignments (Google classroom and Twiddla are two examples), allowing them to participate in blended and varied groups and easing the accessibility to the group for students.

- **Modeling and drawing software:** There are a variety of programs that students can use to demonstrate their understanding of actual concepts through the element of design. From modeling software such as CAD to editing programs such as Photoshop, students interact in a productive learning environment and provide teachers with a big-picture view of their understanding.

- **Open-ended projects:** Creating open-ended projects, in which students explore their own ideas and draw from their personal experiences to meet an objective, has limitless options when technology is included. Technology can play an integral part in all aspects of the project, from gathering information and resources to creating a final product. Technology allows open-ended projects to truly take on a life of their own.

- **Discussion forums:** Social media sites and blogs have paved the way for more collaborative and engaging discussion forums in which students can apply their learning. Students can participate in thoughtful, detailed dialogue in a community environment. Responding to peers' perspectives, validating others' ideas, creating their own arguments, and providing support for their ideas builds important social and communication skills in a comfortable environment for the students.

- **Student-created wikis and web pages:** Creating wikis and web pages not only enables students to be producers of their own learning, it creates a unique opportunity for students to edit, teach, and guide each other. Students can create resources to be shared with their peers both in and out of the classroom. Teachers can observe as students work together to solve a problem and engage with each other in real-world ways.

- **Multimedia projects:** Creating spreadsheets, presentations, documents, video clips, movies, and music cannot be underrated for student content products. Multimedia projects are visually stimulating, maintain student interest, and present clear representations of student learning.

## Boosting Benefits for ALL

Academic applications, content consumptions, and differentiated deliveries can all be used to boost benefits for ALL. The reality is that technology is a part of everything we do in the classroom, as well as outside of it; it only makes sense that we utilize these advancements to deliver, consume, and apply academic content.

These strategies can improve student connections, understanding, interest, and productivity. Some benefits from utilizing technology in the classroom with content include the following:

- Strengthening community connections

- Increased academic achievement

- Improved relationship skills

- Increased attention and focus

- Improved self-esteem and self-concept

- Increased student engagement

- Energizing and exciting the brain

- Increased learning motivation

- Increased attendance

- Improved student feedback and support

- Reaching individual's needs, abilities, and interests

- Increased higher-level thinking

There are a multitude of learner benefits that are directly linked to frequent technology use or 1:1 computing. Examine the list below to see if or how you use technology in your classroom to reap these rewards:

- Use tablets, laptops, interactive whiteboards, and other devices to personalize the learner's experience.

- Create technology-based, student-centered lessons.

- Design technology-influenced lessons/activities that cater to students' abilities, interests, personalities, cultural differences, and so on.

- Use technology to allow students a sense of choice over their learning.

- Incorporate technology-based flexible pacing opportunities through websites or software platforms so students can move at their own pace.

- Utilize digital software programs to develop instruction to remediate struggling students.

- Include online programs that provide formative assessments to measure and track student performance and differentiate instruction.

- Use social media platforms, apps, and websites to allow students to collaborate and take their learning beyond standard classroom instruction.

- Encourage students to take charge of their own learning through WebQuests or independent investigations.

- Build personal, individual comfort with students by using technologies that connect to their digital identities.

## Content Consumptions

Content consumption typically requires interest and motivation. Today's digital learners demand a multifaceted approach to reach their full potential and hold their attention. Students crave a variety of ways to get information, and traditional textbooks and workbook pages are considered old-fashioned resources. With overloaded curriculums, there are more objectives to meet and not enough time to meet them. Students have to consume some of their instruction independently, and technology is a highly desired option for gaining this knowledge. Technology provides a variety of ways for students to get the information they need outside of explicit teacher instruction; some suggestions for technology use are listed below.

- **Teacher-created wikis and web pages:** Wikis and web pages are a great place for teachers to provide content that students can use for both exploration and review. Wikis allow for a collaborative learning environment and foster a social approach to learning. Students are able to access this online information both in and out of school, making the content more accessible.

- **Simulations:** Using technology enhances the experience of simulations in the classroom, where students participate in experiential learning designed by the teacher. In other words, it's using a real-life situation to teach a lesson. There are a variety of simulation sites available for students to engage with. Students can learn what it's like to live as a wolf at http://wolfquest.org, play the stock market at http://nationalsms.com, or sharpen their business management skills at http://www.informatist.net

- **Online/digital textbooks:** With more and more schools facing budget constraints, digital textbooks are one way for every student to have access to content at a fraction of the cost of traditional books. Digital textbooks are accessible and portable, and many students actually prefer them.

- **Podcasts:** Podcasts are a unique way for students to engage in instruction not only from their own teacher but from guest lecturers, experts, and interviews as well. Podcasts are portable, are easily accessible, and increase the listening comprehension skills of the student. Teachers can create or share content on an endless variety of subjects geared toward specific student goals.

- **Videos:** Studies have shown that video can be a highly effective educational tool (Hsin & Cigas, 2013). Using video increases student motivation, student engagement, and information recall.

- **Games:** Games can be a powerful instructional tool. Games are an opportunity for students to interact with content that satisfies the brain's desire for entertainment and novelty. Students are attracted to the freedom and choice that learning games provide while they develop crucial problem-solving and critical thinking skills.

## Differentiated Deliveries

All students have strengths or preferred ways of learning as well as weaknesses that can force them to stretch outside their comfort zone. Differentiating content delivery is essential and expected in today's classroom to meet learners' needs. Best practice in instructional delivery is always being examined and determined, from lectures to more modern small-group instruction to the MT classroom. By differentiating instructional methods, teachers can provide a variety of ways to get information and content to their students while adding excitement and creativity. Technology has created new means for content delivery: It has broadened our global reach for teachers and students alike. Technology has made the *impossible* into the *very possible*. You can find some different examples of content delivery in the following list:

- **Virtual field trips:** Teachers can deliver immersive learning experiences for their students through virtual field trips. Bringing the outside world into the classroom provides opportunities for teachers to guide their students into new discoveries about the world around them. Many companies such as Discovery Education, the Smithsonian, and Google Earth offer ways for teachers to easily explore the world with their students.

- **Mini lessons:** Using small, skill-specific lessons with students is a great way to ensure that every student has access to the content they need. Technology makes it easy for teachers to create these mini lessons through means as simple as PowerPoint presentations, YouTube tutorials, or recorded lectures.

- **Live video conferencing:** Whether it's collaborating with another school across the country or engaging in collegiate group discussions, platforms such as Skype and Google Hangouts allow teachers and students to connect with others near or far at any time. Allowing students to engage with others through video conferencing exposes students to more than one educator's ideas and experiences.

- **Virtual manipulatives:** Providing instructional materials these days is tough, especially as the trend of slashing educational funding continues. Hands-on materials that support instruction can be hard to come by as class sizes are rising and budgets are shrinking. But virtual manipulatives provide teachers with a way to make sure that their students can explore concepts in concrete ways. From virtual geoboards to pattern blocks to base 10 blocks, students can visually understand the concepts that are being delivered.

- **Multimedia elements:** Inserting multimedia elements into instruction is an easy way for educators to make sure their instruction is engaging and appealing to a variety of learning styles. From adding movement or videos to the lecture, creating PowerPoint presentations, inserting graphs and charts, or adding music, technology has opened up the door for more interesting and stimulating content delivery.

- **Whiteboards:** Long gone are the days of chalkboards and dry erase markers: Today's whiteboards are interactive. Both teacher and student can manipulate what is being projected; online links, videos, and images that can be explored throughout instruction are encouraged.

- **Hybrid courses and distance education:** There is a lot of focus on providing education to students who are not physically present. From collegiate courses to elementary school snow days, educational institutions are creating ways to deliver content to anyone from anywhere. In addition, distance education is being used for teachers in professional development and higher education.

- **Class communication:** Keeping students and parents informed is easier than ever with technology. Teachers are using e-mail lists, Facebook group pages, and apps such as Remind and ClassDojo to communicate assignments, report behavior, send reminders about upcoming activities, and upload pictures and video.

## EDUCATION'S ASCENDING CHAMPIONS

When you get right down to it, traditional teaching methodologies are still at the forefront of most or many educational settings. However, this is a temporary situation because education's top two ascending champions for best-practice tactics are movement and technology. Increasing, combining, and balancing movement and technology in the 21st-century classroom is simply inevitable. These educational elements are aggressively expanding and are commonly considered model methods for improving learning potential while preparing students for future challenges. Classroom environments are often quiet, while laughter and fun are not considered productive. Standardized test scores are the center of attention and rule most decisions and programs. The time to redefine education is long overdue, and refining movement and technology is a credible solution that should be implemented and fostered instantaneously. Movement combined with technological advancements provides the educational edge we have been longing for. This generation of students needs more motivation for learning than their predecessors. They want more laughter, opportunities to move often, advanced digital usage, opportunities to connect with their peers, and choices regarding the assessment of their own needs. Incorporating the ABCDs of movement and technology for ALL, along with STRIDES, makes a significant statement that defines a new era of learning. This innovative environment will outline a novel approach to learning that creates a fresh start and escalates its rise.

## WHAT DOES THIS MEAN TO ME?

### K–12 Teachers

1. Incorporate a wide variety of movements in your classroom to serve different purposes.
2. Use different forms of technology regarding the delivery, consumption, and application of your content.

### Administration

1. Encourage your faculty to include movement in their lessons (even if it's only a one-minute body break/brain boost) a minimum of 2–3 times a week with the goal of building on this request.

2. Encourage your faculty to include technology in their lessons a minimum of 2–3 times a week with the goal of building on this request.

### Educational Leaders/Affiliates

1. Establish and support agendas, curriculums, and schools that increase movement in their facilities in conjunction with physical education programs.

2. Place an emphasis on all schools to provide a balanced teaching approach that reaches the needs of ALL learners.

## CHAPTER SUMMARY

- Movement is growing in leaps and bounds due to a multitude of reasons, but two of the top reasons are (1) these methodologies are getting positive academic results and (2) students are enjoying their learning experiences.

- The increasing rise in technology use in education and learning continues to grow at a robust rate, defining it as a best practice must-have.

- The benefits of balancing movement and technology in academic environments include an increase in academic performance and achievement, enhanced brain function and memory, fueling the body and brain with chemicals and novelty for optimal learning, improved concentration while refocusing and stimulating the brain, increased motivation while differentiating, increased attendance while decreasing behavioral challenges, engaging the senses, increasing student engagement, and improving the learner as a whole.

- *ALL* stands for _academic achievement_, _learner attention and focus_, and the _learner as a whole_.

- Balancing movement and technology is imperative for enhancing learning, memory, and retention. Cognitive performance dominates schools, and movement and technology can play a significant role in helping students make the grade.

- Attention spans are shrinking; providing movement and technology in classroom environments will refocus and reenergize the brain to heighten academic performance and improve students' ability to attend to learning objectives.

- *Educating the learner as a whole* refers to caring about the mental/emotional, social, physical, and cognitive growth of each

*(Continued)*

(Continued)

child. These components should be given equal value and attention in schools.

- The ABCs of movement for ALL include _academic activities_, _brain boosters_, and _community connectors_.

- Academic activities bring the content to life and fall into three categories: active practices, active reviews, and active teachings. They are lively, stimulating, and energetic as they engage students in the learning process.

- What's good for the body is good for the brain! There are three examples of brain boosters: body basics, body blasts, and body breaks. _Body basics_ are physical activities that prime the brain for enhanced learning. _Body blasts_, also known as _fitness blasts_, are exercises that are appropriate for classroom settings. _Body breaks_ refer to taking time away from sitting to incorporate movement, which in turn gives the brain some recovery time from content overload.

- Community connectors promote cohesion in three areas: partners, teams, and classes. There is no questioning the importance of communal relationships in life or in schools; community connectors

will be explored in detail in the next chapter.

- The ABCDs of technology for ALL include _academic applications_, _boosting benefits (for ALL)_, _content consumptions_, and _differentiated deliveries_.

- Utilizing technology in the classroom assists students in gathering information for deeper understanding while providing avenues for them to apply their learning.

- Academic applications, content consumptions, and differentiated deliveries can all be used to boost benefits for ALL.

- Students have to consume some of their instruction independently, and technology is a highly desired option for gaining this knowledge.

- Technology has created new means for content delivery, as it has broadened our global reach for teachers and students alike. Technology has made the _impossible_ into the _very possible_.

- The time to redefine education is long overdue; active learning (combined with technological advancements) provides the educational edge we have been looking for.

# 8

# INTERCONNECTING COMMUNITIES

## BRAIN PRIORITY

### What Matters Most

Our brain is strongly connected to our bodies and is constantly working to prioritize matters. The brain processes sensory input into three states: survival, emotional, and executive (Bailey, n.d.). Safety and survival needs are ranked as the number-one priority to the brain—for example, if a student is tired, is hungry, or feels unsafe in the classroom, then this will be what the student's brain is focused on. The second priority to the brain is the social/emotional state of the learner. Emotional states govern our thoughts and behaviors and connect the mind and body. The last priority is the executive state. This is the state in which problem solving and learning can occur. Notice that the emotional state of our students is ranked higher than the executive state. This means that if the brain–body connection is not in a positive state for our students, then optimal learning cannot occur. The emotional state of a student drives their attention, which directly affects learning and memory. Emotions can send complex signals to the brain to move ahead with learning or not (Jensen, 2008). The emotional state influences learning through this signaling system. Thus, our emotional well-being takes precedence over all academic content for the brain. Increasing student learning can only exist in environments free from threat and/or intimidation (Sousa, 2017). Teachers and students must begin to work together to manage emotional states in order to create a learning environment that will allow for peak performance while developing the student as a whole. These brain priorities clearly support the value of a community connection in the movement and technology (MT) classroom. Both movement and technology foster a classroom environment in which students feel connected, accepted, and secure. Using movement and technology within the classroom creates opportunities for students to satisfy the brain's desire for comfort so that learning can occur.

## Essential for Peak Performance

In order for the brain and body to work together, our mental/emotional health cannot be ignored. Negative emotions in the classroom such as anxiety, stress, and exclusion control our reactions and our level of engagement in the classroom (Lawson, 2002). Emotionally stressful classrooms are counterproductive to student learning yet we rarely incorporate emotion into the curriculum. Positive relationships in the classroom are essential for increased academic achievement. These relationships include both teacher–student and student–student. A community connection in the MT classroom has many advantages:

- Builds unity and promotes closeness
- Strengthens learning
- Increases student interaction
- Develops valued relationships
- Shapes individual identities
- Encourages a team approach to improve vitality
- Inspires students to take care of one another
- Prevents students from feeling isolated or alienated
- Fosters a sense of belonging
- Provides feelings of safety and trust

The benefits of a community connection are invaluable to the learning process. When students feel their learning environment is safe, accepting, and comfortable, they can grow and perform at top levels. Using movement and technology equally in the classroom is an effective way to create positive emotions in direct conjunction with the learning process. Students will be able to connect those positive emotions to their educational tasks, resulting in an emotional state conducive to academic success. The MT classroom helps to eliminate educational anxiety and fosters encouraging and supportive interpersonal relationships.

# A SOCIETAL SCARE

Our current cultural obsession with technology and our devices has emphasized the fact that users are increasing digital communication and decreasing face-to-face interactions. Technology has become an integral part of the way that our students communicate with one another. There is a real fear that children and teens may be too immersed in this digital world and not present in the real world. In Chapter 3, we discussed the negative impact that digital communication has had on our students. Teenagers spend less than two hours a week socializing in person with friends outside of school. Children who engage with one another in real life acquire the skills needed to form positive relationships and participate effectively in social situations. It helps them read the emotional context clues of the situation and make decisions to act accordingly. It allows them to develop their skills in the art of conversation making. So, what happens to those skills when children aren't engaging with one another in real life anymore? Even when children are physically together, they are still using their devices. Przybylski and Weinstein (2012) showed results that proved that the presence of mobile devices in social settings interferes with human relationships. They found evidence that mobile devices have a negative impact on closeness, connection, and conversation quality. Another study done by Pierce (2009) examined the effects of technology on the social skills of high school students. She determined that there is a direct correlation between the amount of time spent on mobile devices and students' levels of social anxiety. The students in her study reported that they were more inclined to feel comfortable meeting new friends online rather than in person. In today's technological world, our students are faced with more and more opportunities to isolate themselves.

# THE SIGNIFICANCE OF RESTORING SKILLS

As educators, we need to seriously consider the lack of interpersonal and relational skills of our students. We play a role in shaping our future nation. It is our responsibility to develop ways to stop and shift this negative, isolating trend. We need to develop ways to use technology to interconnect students and build a sense of community. Students who build interpersonal skills such as patience, empathy, and cooperation are more successful in school and perform better academically (Nkere, 2014). How can we ensure that we are teaching our students these important communication skills when they live in a world where technology encourages them to limit their face-to-face interactions? The goal of the MT balance is to use technology to our advantage rather than our disadvantage. We need to provide activities that teach students to use technology as a means to restore their socialization skills, communication skills, and relationships with one another. We need to reverse the isolation that technology can inadvertently cause. We need to be cognizant of our teaching methodologies and constructively evaluate our classroom practices to ensure that our students are given the opportunity to grow and change in this area.

The MT community is a classroom that places value on listening and communicating. Providing movement and/or technology opportunities that allow students to connect with one another, relate to one another, and understand one another produces students that are equipped with important life skills. Students need to learn to share, wait, and respond appropriately to situations. They need to show patience with one another, fall into both leadership and followership roles, participate in productive group discussions, and respect the ideas and feelings of one another. Using a balanced MT approach to learning can provide students with unique opportunities to develop all of these skills while they are flawlessly engrained in the learning process and without taking away from instructional time. Students who restore these important interpersonal skills set themselves apart in today's world as professional and capable college- and career-ready individuals. Future employers and academic institutions place high regard on the ability to successfully interact and connect with other people.

# BUILDING POSITIVE CLASSROOM CULTURE

The MT classroom places significance on activities that allow students to express themselves freely and comfortably and to respond to others who do the same. "Kindness matters" is a famous saying that people use to encourage caring attitudes regarding a prevalent cause or circumstances of importance. It is meaningful and respectful. This mindset fits appropriately in almost all settings, especially in the MT classroom. When educators build an interconnected community within the classroom, they should consider the "keeping it kind" frame of thinking and operation. This attitude refers to the way students treat each other and communicate daily with one another in their learning community. The benefits of "keeping it kind" are overwhelming and vital to an MT classroom. Listed below are ten immeasurable advantages linked to this form of treatment and communication:

1.  Promotes calm communication
2.  Stresses safe and appropriate equipment/supply use
3.  Advocates for happiness for all
4.  Builds self-worth
5.  Teaches empathy
6.  Demonstrates that small actions have far-reaching consequences
7.  Strengthens leadership skills
8.  Spreads feelings of affection and concern
9.  Encourages positive interactions and exchanges
10. Fosters a desirable community feeling

"Keeping it kind" in an MT classroom promotes an environment that students would want to be a part of while working together as a community to uphold it. It would be a peaceful, active, respectful, and considerate school home where students could learn and grow. Teaching learners to communicate and treat each other with kindness would also raise desirable humanitarians. This is a reputable way of thinking, acting, and learning that members of society will happily welcome. Yes, learning academic content is essential—however, so is producing kind, respectful human beings that will be leading our country in the near future. Embracing a community connection in a classroom environment presents a win–win perspective for all people and/or circumstances in the present, the near future, and the distant future.

# COMMUNITY CONNECTORS

Community connectors are activities that promote an interconnected classroom community. In the MT classroom, both movement activities and technology activities can be successfully employed to build relationships among students and teachers alike. These community connectors imply an understanding that social and emotional development is an imperative part of the educational process. They are designed to help students have fun while interacting with their peers. Along the same lines, students also will need to navigate any challenges that may come about throughout the activity. As the students participate in the community connectors, they build a strong sense of community with one another and become invested in the success of the activity (and the classroom as a whole). They develop ownership over the positive classroom environment, are given several opportunities to learn through experiences with one another, and feel empowered to take control of their peer interactions. Simply put, community connectors subtly sneak teaching social skills into fun activities that the students enjoy doing! Deliberate and explicit use of community connectors in the MT classroom will naturally build an unspoken community belief system, created *for* the students and *by* the students through their shared experiences with one another.

## Movement Community Connectors

Movement community connectors are movement activities that promote cohesion in three areas: partners, teams, and classes. As previously explained, it can be difficult for teachers to dedicate time to a need other than academic standards; however, building relationships in the classroom affects students' comfort levels and learning potential. Academic community connectors are efficiently linked to the content and tend to be well-received by teachers and students alike while building communication skills and camaraderie. Brain booster and organized community connecters are physical activities that focus primarily on the relationships between students. Additionally, these two types of connectors may also provide students with a break from content as they reenergize the brain and body with increased oxygen and blood flow. Remember, the brain typically benefits from a break from content. Plus, high-intensity movements can be used to enhance learning states and cognitive functioning.

Movement community connectors are also fun and should be included in all classroom environments on a regular basis. As a result, students will know their peers' names, relationships will deepen, and interpersonal skills will improve throughout the year. This way of thinking defines the social and mental/emotional well-being of students as priorities in education and shows the value of developing the child as a whole. How students treat one another through their words, actions, and behaviors are critical aspects of our society, the classroom environment, and the learning process. Utilizing movement community connectors with partners, teams, and entire classes will promote unity and respect while social skills are strengthened and developed. These connected learning communities create opportunities for grades to climb, happiness to increase, and feelings of acceptance and interdependence to escalate. Community connecters are a prominent component of the ABCs of daily movement (defined in Chapter 9) as well as the STRIDES (**s**tructuring and managing, **t**ransforming with A.A.A., **r**efining movement and technology, **i**nterconnecting communities, **d**efining the balance, **e**mploying SMART activities, **s**upporting a united approach) philosophy.

## Cohesive Partners
## (Activities Designed for 2–3 Students)

Academic community connectors for building cohesion are included in the list below.

- **Practice passes:** While using a ball of any type, have students work with a partner to solve a problem or complete a worksheet while throwing/catching or kicking/trapping the ball as they practice the academic skill. For example, students can spell their sight words, count by twos, or discuss character details from a recent class reading.

- **Rapid review:** Place review questions facedown all around your classroom. Have students get a partner. Ask partners to mill around the classroom until the teacher says "rapid review." At this point, partners will go to the closest review question, flip it right-side up, and race to answer the question as fast as they can (verbally and with accuracy). The teacher will then instruct partners to mill around again and continue the process until teams get to all the review questions. Students may need to switch partners every few rounds.

- **Peer teaching on the move:** Match students with a partner and allow them to practice teaching an academic concept or skill to one another while utilizing kinesthetic means. For example, students can act out sight words, create a dance to remember the order of operations, or use a movement to recall the order of events in a story.

Brain booster community connectors for building cohesion are included in the following list. Allow students to encourage one another prior to, during, and after the task is completed.

- **Moving in unison:** Have partners perform an exercise or movement at the same time and speed while working cooperatively and respecting individual differences. These activities are effective when a time frame, such as 60 seconds, is placed on the challenge.

- **Moving in opposition:** Have partners perform an exercise or movement at the same time and speed while moving in opposition of one another. For example, one student will go up while the other goes down, one student jumps to the right while the other jumps to the left, or one moves forward as their partner moves backward. These activities are effective when a time frame, such as 60 seconds, is placed on the challenge.

- **Coordinated movements:** Have partners work together to perform a physical task that requires cooperation and coordination. Some examples include handclapping games and activities, partner cross-taps (partners tap their right feet and right hands, then switch and tap their left feet and left hands; continue with this pattern), or back-to-back sit down/stand up challenges.

Organized community connectors for building cohesion are listed below.

- **The stroll:** This is a partner walk-and-talk. Have students find a partner and walk around the classroom while discussing a personal topic. For example, teachers can have students talk about their weekend, a favorite vacation, or their hobbies. This activity can also be used as an opportunity for peer teaching on the move (described earlier) or as a way to practice or discuss academic content.

- **Written responses:** Have students stroll around the classroom with a small whiteboard. When the teacher says "Match," students pair up with a partner closest to them. The teacher reads or displays a question and the students quickly answer it on their whiteboard. Students switch boards to read their partner's response. Partners will answer two questions before finding a new student to pair up with. This is a silent social activity in which communication is written as opposed to verbal. Written responses are ideal for practicing or reviewing academic content. An additional consideration is to turn the written response into a race for speed and accuracy.

- **Max reps:** Have students perform a physical task with a partner to see how many repetitions they can get in a given time period; for example, in 60 seconds, find out how many catches students can make with their partner; how many times they can pass an object around each other while standing back to back; or how many times they can do a figure-eight pass through their legs, pass it to their partner, and continue before the object is dropped.

## Cohesive Teams
## (Activities Designed for Groups of 4–8)

Academic community connectors for building cohesion include the following:

- **Circle practice passes:** Have small groups pass a ball or object around a circle while practicing a given academic skill. For example, students can say an adjective (or a different part of speech), list the order of events in a story, practice rhyming words, or say words that have a specific vowel sound.

- **Line relay reviews:** Separate your class into small teams of four or five. Review content while incorporating relay races by asking students to stand in a line while passing the content backward or forward to get a team's answer. Answers can be either written or verbal. For example, have students perform an over/under line relay race while repeating the steps of the scientific method. The line will continue to move forward as the last person in line moves to the front of their team after sharing their response. The group that gets to a certain point in the classroom the fastest wins the race.

- **Active creations:** Place students in small groups and ask them to demonstrate an academic concept or skill to the entire class or another group through kinesthetic means. For example, students can physically show a multiple-step math problem, act out a story to retell key details or events, or physically demonstrate character traits of important individuals from a story.

Brain booster community connectors for building cohesion are listed here. These activities are effective when a time frame, such as 60 seconds, is placed on the challenge. A list of exercises is also available in Chapter 9.

- **Max reps:** Have students perform an exercise with a small group to see how many repetitions they can get in a given time period. For example, find out how many combined jumping jacks the group can get, how many times they can pass an object around their circle (or up and down their line), or how long they can hold a balance pose as a team.

- **Unison challenges:** Have small groups perform an exercise at the same time and speed while working cooperatively and respecting individual differences. Students should encourage one another prior to, during, and after the task is completed. All groups must move in unison and show team spirit.

- **Group holds:** Have small groups perform a balance exercise (for example, a circle of supported yoga poses, such as a tree pose) or holding movements (for example, a circle of squats in which all the students hold hands to support one another) while working cooperatively to accomplish a task. Having groups compete against one another is very motivational and can increase cohesion and energy.

Organized community connectors for building cohesion include the following:

- **Group mixers:** This is a social mill/match/discuss activity. Have students mill around the classroom until the teacher says "match." (For another version of the game, a number can be called and that will determine the size of the discussion groups.) At this point, students find a partner or small group based on the peers closest to them to discuss a personal topic. For example, have students talk about their favorite foods, their favorite season, or their likes and dislikes. After the question is answered, students begin to mill around again. After each round, students will have the opportunity to have a new discussion partner or group to collaborate with. This activity can also be used as an opportunity to form groups for active creations or peer teachings on the move (described earlier). Additionally, it is an ideal way to allow students to practice and discuss academic content with partners or small groups.

- **Written responses:** Have students mill around the classroom with a small whiteboard. When the teacher says "match" or calls a number, students form groups based on the teacher's directions. The teacher reads or displays a question, perhaps on a controversial topic, and the students respond on their whiteboards. Each student holds up their boards so the group can read the responses and make connections. This activity is also an effective way to practice and review academic content.

- **Unity contests:** This concept is similar to the unison challenges described earlier except that the contests are not necessarily related to exercise. For example, groups can build a tower out of cards, use their bodies to spell out a word, or complete a puzzle while racing against other teams. The important factors in these contests are that students are working together, sharing responsibilities, and treating one another with kindness and respect. Communication, cooperation, and teamwork are more important than speed in these activities.

## Cohesive Classes
## (Activities Designed for Large Groups of Varying Sizes)

Academic community connectors for building cohesion are listed below:

- **Musical chair practices:** Make small groups or teams of three or four. Place worksheets around the classroom on desks or workstations. Play music and allow students to walk around the classroom. Students can also skip, slide, gallop, or perform any other locomotor movement. When this music goes off, students get into their groups as fast as they can, find a worksheet, and complete Question 1 as a team. When the music comes back on, students move again (separate from their teammates). The next time the music goes off, they find their team and a new worksheet to complete Question 2 (you can also ask them to check or grade Question 1 before they complete Question 2). Continue as many times as needed.

- **Mill mixer reviews:** This is an academic mill/match/discuss activity for small groups. Have students mill around the classroom until the teacher says a number from two to four. At this point, students find a group as quickly as they can, based on the number given. The teacher will ask a question; the teams then discuss the answer. After the question is answered by the group, the teacher will check for accuracy and content understanding. Students then begin to mill around again. After each round, students will have the opportunity to form a new discussion group.

- **Whole-class teachings (everyone moves):** In these activities, the entire class (or most of the class) will be used to teach an academic concept. For example, the class may be used to show the various aspects of the solar system, the location of the states on a map, or how to plot points on a graph.

Brain booster community connectors for building cohesion include the following:

- **Cardio tag:** Have students walk around the classroom without touching any objects or people. Assign one or two students to be "It" and allow them to carry a ball (or something similar). The students who are "It" will use their ball to gently tag/freeze other students. After they tag three people, they will give the ball to someone else and they will become a player while a new person is "It." If a student is frozen, they can unfreeze themselves by performing a cardio exercise ten times. Each time they are frozen, they need to do a different cardio exercise to become unfrozen. Examples of cardio exercises can be found in Chapter 9. This game can be modified by using muscular exercises or balance/core holds.

- **Drill team:** Students will perform an exercise when music is playing. Everyone freezes as soon as the music stops. Exercises can be directed by the teacher or chosen by the students. It is acceptable to have all students perform the same or different exercises during each round. Turning the music on and off rapidly can add to the fun.

- **Dance creations:** Put students into larger groups of 8–15. Play music and allow teams to create a dance that they can teach to the rest of the class (or have a dance-off competition). It will be interesting to see the variety of dances that can be invented for the same song or beat.

Organized community connectors for building cohesion are listed below:

- **Beat the clock:** These are competitions in which classes try to complete a kinesthetic task while racing against the clock. For example, the teacher will time a class to see how fast they can pass a ball around the room. After determining the time to beat, the teacher can allow the class a few more opportunities to beat their previous time or they can compare the score to other classes throughout the day or week.

- **Beat the teacher:** In these activities, classes complete a kinesthetic task while racing against the teacher. For example, students might be asked to pass a ball around a circle two times while the teacher walks around the outside of the circle. Whoever gets back to the starting point the fastest (the ball or the teacher) wins the race.

- **No student left behind:** These kinesthetic activities require an entire class to complete a task or solve a problem; all students are included in the challenge. For example, ask all students to get from one side of the classroom to the other without touching the floor while the only objects that can be used are three poly spots, a jump rope, a scooter, and a hula hoop. If one student touches the floor, the entire challenge must be restarted. Teachers can also break a class into two larger groups and have them compete against one another.

## Tech Community Connectors

Tech community connectors are technology-based activities that improve social connections and promote cohesion in four areas: academic applications, boosting benefits, content consumptions, and differentiated deliveries. Similar to movement community connectors, we need to use technology to our advantage as opposed to watching it contribute to interpersonal decline. Using technology activities to build community relationships among students will have a positive outcome on both comfort level and academic success in the MT classroom. Tech community connectors increase face-to-face interactions in conjunction with technology usage, resulting in effective cooperative learning and successful instructional delivery. Tech community connectors expand the way students interact with each other rather than limit those interactions. Students are given the freedom to embrace the technology they know and love while applying the social skills they are developing. Tech community connectors also provide an opportunity for students to build relationships in the classroom without sacrificing academic time. In fact, tech community connectors are often academic in nature. The key to promoting cohesion is to use each activity to harness the power that cooperative learning has on social and emotional development.

Academic application community connectors for building cohesion given in the following list:

- **Shared video/audio files and documents:** Using platforms such as VoiceThread or Twiddla, have students work in pairs or trios to upload photos, audio commentary, video files, or documents about a given topic. These files allow others to comment on, make changes to, and share the work. Students must work together to ensure that all uploads are relevant to the topic and add value to the lot as a whole.

- **Video Hosting Sites:** Using platforms such as SchoolTube or YouTube, students work in pairs or trios to create and upload a mini-lesson to be shared with the class. The goal is to have them teach the content or concept to their peers through a video presentation. For example, students might be required to create a three-minute video explaining the rules for singular possessive nouns versus plural possessive nouns. Each student needs to be present in the video and play an active role in the instructional delivery.

- **Cooperative writing:** Students work in small groups or teams to collaborate and write a single document. This can be done using platforms such as Google Docs. Students work together in real time to contribute, edit, make changes, or comment on a shared and original writing assignment. Students must work together to develop and agree on the content and final product.

- **Presentations:** Using a variety of programs (such as PowerPoint, Google Slides, Prezi, or Swipe), students can collaborate in small groups or teams to create multimedia projects about a given topic. Students can combine a variety of media such as photos, music, or narration to customize their project and make it unique to the group.

- **Illustrating software:** Create a place for the class to upload photos about a given topic. Using sites such as Flickr, Google Photo, or Photobucket, students can add photos to the group assignment. For example, given the topic of butterflies, students might find and add photos of different species, images of the life cycle stages, map shots of butterfly locations, and so on.

- **Current event tweeting:** Each student must tweet about a current event. The event should include a link when possible and must include an original hashtag so both teachers and classmates can locate and track the tweets. Require students to post one original current event tweet and to comment or reply on the tweets of two other classmates.

Boosting benefits community connectors for building cohesion include the following:

- **Remediation groups:** These groups are intended to boost learner benefits by creating a homogeneous lesson that is tailored to the pacing of students who need remediation of a given topic. Using Google Classroom or social media sites, create a group of students who are working on below-level material at the same time.

- **Enrichment groups:** Similar to remediation groups, teachers may use Google Classroom or social media sites to create a group for those who are working on the same above-level material.

- **Tech talks:** Using apps such as Google Hangout or FaceTime, have students collaborate with partners or in small groups for a peer-tutoring question-and-answer session(s) about a given topic. One person in the group will be designated as the "expert" for each tech talk. The group is then given the opportunity to ask any questions they may have. For example, an excelling geometry student might be the "expert" for the tech talk on finding distances and midpoints on a coordinate plane. That expert would answer questions for the other students in the group during the conference.

- **Personalized learning experiences:** Allowing students some choice in the technology devices they may use allows for a personalized learning experience that not only boosts the comfort level of the individual student but also fosters camaraderie among students who choose the same devices. For example, when requiring students to conduct research, allow students to choose the group of devices they'd like to join. Some students may prefer to use the iPads, while others might use their smartphones or the classroom Chromebooks. Allow the students who are using the same devices to congregate together in the classroom to encourage sharing of resources, conversation, and collaboration.

- **Resolving conflict:** Conflict in the classroom (or in any group of people working together) is bound to happen. Often, conflict remains unresolved with children and teens for many reasons: fear, embarrassment, peer pressure, and so on. Using anonymous polling software to resolve conflict is a great way to open the lines of communication with the students and allow the power of anonymity to assist in conflict resolution. Apps such as Show of Hands allow students to be heard without saying a word at all.

- **Online discussion boards:** Creating an online forum for students to converse and debate has a variety of learner benefits. In addition to providing more opportunities for students to engage with each other, discussion boards require students to adhere to a code of respect and kindness in their written words. Students learn to interact with each other in a civilized and mature way and to listen, respect, and respond to the thoughts and feelings of others. It also provides a great opportunity for teachers to remind students that their written words leave a permanent footprint. Google Groups or Edmodo are two great places to start an online conversation with your students.

Content consumption community connectors for building cohesion include the following:

- **Simulations:** Simulations are experiences that allow students to engage with and solve problems that mimic real life. Using premade online simulators (refer to Chapter 7 for examples) or teacher-created experiences, students must collaborate with each other to solve a problem. For example, high school economics students can work in small groups to play the Tax Game (http://econ.glendale.edu), in which they must design their own tax system and can see the system's results. Simulations require students to engage in conversation with the others in their group and relate to the thought processes of others.

- **Video conferencing:** Allowing students to interact with people outside of the classroom to gain knowledge is a valuable tool for consuming content and building community. For example, invite a board member of a local business to Skype into your business and marketing classroom or invite a local zookeeper into your science classroom. Students are given the opportunity to engage in respectful dialogue and establish a rapport with the expert. Video conferencing is also unique in that the students can improve their communication skills by interpreting the body language and nonverbal cues of the speaker.

- **Cooperative reading:** Devices such as Kindles and iPads take reading assignments to a whole new cooperative level. Students can share the books they are reading with each other, take and share notes on the text, share sections of the book or specific passages with one another, and even leave comments throughout the text for others to see.

- **Multiplayer games:** Educators need to tap into the potential of online multiplayer games to build classroom cohesion. Interactive games such as The Sims allow students to build relationships with each other, learn about community and culture, and broaden their perspective on life issues.

- **WebQuests:** Similar to simulations, WebQuests are a great way for students to work together to dive into the content. Working in pairs or trios, students engage in a variety of task-based discoveries involving a specific topic. To complete the quest, students must navigate the tasks together, take turns, and learn to work at a pace that is comfortable for each of the partners. It allows students to consider the needs of others and discover ways to help their peers when needed.

- **Review games:** Online game builders such as Kahoot, Jeopardy, or Quizlet are great ways to get teams of students working together to review content. Interactive games require teamwork and collaboration and encourage students to support one another.

Differentiated delivery community connectors for building cohesion include the following:

- **Digital chats:** Using technology is a great way to get students talking with each other. Although the ultimate goal is to increase face-to-face conversations with students, starting at their comfort level allows students to work on the basics of discussions first: kindness, equal contribution, questioning, and clarity. Allow students the option to conduct their discussions through digital means such as e-mail, texting, or instant messaging.

- **Social media groups:** Create homogeneous social media groups. Add students of similar ability to those groups. Post challenges, discussion starters, or interesting video clips to the group and encourage students to comment and respond to the posts as part of their class participation or daily grade.

- **Student-Designed graphic organizers:** Students should work in pairs or trios to create graphic organizers for specific topics. Allow the students the freedom to choose the direction of their graphic or image. For example, students studying the history of mining in the U. S. could create a relative statistical graphic. Submissions might include a spreadsheet of the market prices of mined minerals over the last 100 years, a bar graph showing the decline of coal mining in the 20th century, or a timeline showing the demise of copper mining in Butte, MT.

- **Learning games:** Learning games and software cannot be underestimated for building class cohesion. Similar to review games, students enjoy the sense of teamwork and unity that comes from playing games together. Examples of using technology to foster cooperative game play are Pictionary on the whiteboard, online BINGO, online Hangman, and digital charades such as Heads Up.

- **Recording software:** Use recording software, such as Audacity, to record class discussions. This recording provides an opportunity for the students to play back their discussions, reflect on their dialogue, and evaluate the effectiveness of their communication.

- **Flexible grouping:** Create differentiated groups in the classroom by using flexible grouping. Using a tool such as Google Classroom, teachers can assign different tasks to different groups of students. These student groups are interchangeable at any time, which encourages students to work with a wide number of others within the class rather than remaining in the same group for extended periods of time.

An interconnected community in the MT classroom is a group of students who come together for a common purpose. The students work toward creating a learning environment that satisfies their emotional needs and respects the emotional needs of their peers. In the MT classroom, using both movement and tech community connectors fosters a classroom of kindness, respectful collaboration, and fun! Students will be excited to be a part of a classroom where they feel respected and important. Educators will be proud of a classroom that is restoring the faltering social skills of today's child. The balanced MT approach fosters an academic environment where both students and society win!

# WHAT DOES THIS MEAN TO ME?

### K–12 Teachers

1. Regularly include activities that allow students to work with a partner or partners while moving, such as think/pair/share on the move or partner–content walk and talks.

2. Implement activities that require the entire class to work together to accomplish a goal, such as a scavenger hunt or Jeopardy on the move (set up multiple Jeopardy boards around the classroom and allow students to circulate and play at each center).

### Administration

1. Lead your faculty in designing specialty events that occur throughout the year and focus on social interaction and building school morale.

2. Create routine initiatives with your faculty that build social connections, such as peer partnership programs or clubs (before, during, and after school). Encourage teachers to mesh communal activities with their academic content as standard procedure.

### Educational Leaders/Affiliates

1. Recognize and compliment schools that develop programs that create a community environment that focuses on students' social well-being and growth.

2. Develop policies that measure and place weight on emotional intelligence in conjunction with academic knowledge.

# CHAPTER SUMMARY

- The emotional state of a student drives their attention, which directly affects learning and memory. If the brain–body connection is not in a positive state for our students, then optimal learning cannot occur.

- Negative emotions in the classroom such as anxiety, stress, and exclusion control our reactions and our level of engagement in the classroom. Positive relationships in the classroom are essential for increased academic achievement.

*(Continued)*

(Continued)

- Technology has become an integral part of the way that our students communicate with one another. There is a real fear that children and teens may be too immersed in this digital world and not present in the real world.

- Students need to rebuild their interpersonal and communication skills, and educators play an important role in this. The MT classroom is a place where students learn to communicate and interact effectively with one another.

- "Keeping it kind" refers to the way students treat one another and communicate daily in the MT classroom.

- Community connectors are activities that promote an interconnected classroom community. In the MT classroom, both movement activities and technology activities can be successfully employed to build relationships between students and teachers.

- Movement community connectors are movement activities that promote cohesion in three areas: partners, teams, and classes.

- Utilizing movement community connectors with partners, teams, and entire classes will promote unity and respect while social skills are strengthened and developed.

- Tech community connectors are technology-based activities that improve social connections and promote cohesion in four areas: academic applications, boosting benefits, content consumption, and differentiated deliveries.

- Tech community connectors expand the way students interact with each other rather than limit those interactions. Students are given the freedom to embrace the technology they know and love while applying the social skills they are still developing.

# 9

# DEFINING THE BALANCE

## IMPLEMENTING THE POWER PLAY

A great deal of effort has been placed on showcasing the benefits of both movement and technology in the 21st-century classroom. There is no question that each concept plays a significant role in learning and both should be considered best practice methods for optimizing student success in the classroom and in life. The supportive research presented in Chapters 2 and 3 is encouraging and comprehensive. If these two teaching methodologies are strong in isolation, imagine how superior they are when they are united in today's classrooms. The movement and technology (MT) balance is the ultimate power play when it comes to best practice policies in the teaching and learning of students of all ages and abilities! These methods check a multitude of boxes for improving brain and body health while reaching peak academic performance. Once we realize all the benefits that movement and technology offer both students and teachers, it is a fundamental response to embrace this philosophy while moving full steam ahead to surround our lessons around the MT balance. It's intelligent yet basic, concerning topics from research to common sense to student happiness, fulfillment, and everything in between. The advantages of the MT balance are attractive to anyone who has a passion for education and a genuine concern for our younger generation both academically and personally.

As we move forward in this chapter, classroom applications and balancing approaches for utilizing movement and technology in the classroom will be shared. We will focus on the balancing act directly. We list examples on how to mesh these two methods together to provide students with the advantages of both. Yes, you can still consider your own personality, experience, and comforts; however, you must look ahead to define how your MT classroom will work best for you at this stage of your career. Remember, this is a temporary situation, because you will always be growing, learning, and expanding your capabilities with both movement and technology. Unifying certain examples and activities shared in Chapters 7 and 8 to include movement and technology is an obvious place to begin. For example, when you are utilizing movement in your classroom, ask yourself, "How can I incorporate technology?" When you are using technology, ask yourself, "How can I incorporate movement?" Sometimes there will be easy solutions that require minimal out-of-the-box thinking. Other circumstances may need some directed thinking and attention before you have an idea that inspires you. Either way, it can and will happen as you grow as a movement and technology educator (MTE). Throughout this book, you have been reminded that this process is not meant to occur overnight. Give yourself time as trial-and-error experiences help you find your way. The MT balance is meant for present-day classrooms, but it is also a future direction that we must build upon as we develop and mature our thinking and teachings.

## BALANCING APPROACHES

There are many ways to balance movement and technology in your classroom once you have made it a priority. As the MT philosophy grows in education and your classroom, best practice models will sharpen your ideas and you will uncover what works best for you. Innovative programs such as "R.O.C.K.* IT," developed by the educational consulting company ActivEDge, offer content-based MT lessons and are great resources as you are starting out. Ideally, since both strategies are so significant in today's learning, both will be incorporated into your lessons daily in some fashion. Remember, the goal is to use the MOST method: *move students often with a steady flow of technology*. This challenge is practical and obtainable, even to the novice MTE. As the MTE gains experience, the amount of movement and technology may not necessarily increase; however, more advanced types of tactics and applications may be implemented. For example, an educator who is starting to incorporate movement will often begin with simple brain breaks, while an active educator will use kinesthetic activities to meet standards while connecting the content to physical engagement. Technology usage will also expand to more developed and creative programs and websites once the MTE builds confidence and comfort with digital resources and their vast potentials. We are on the brink of defining an educational philosophy that can withstand the test of time and change. Technology is here to stay, and its use will only increase in education and society as our knowledge and evolutions continue on their path. The time to reverse our inactive society and bring the value and priority of increased movement back to the forefront in our culture is no longer up for debate. The following are four balancing approaches that can

---

*R.O.C.K. stands for Reaching Objectives and Curricula Kinesthetically.

be used to join movement and technology in your classroom while making the most of your teaching methodologies to increase learning while benefitting your students inside and outside the school environment.

## Side by Side

The side-by-side approach is easy to implement and works effectively in classrooms that have a limited number of technology devices. This balancing approach will allow some students to utilize digital means to reach goals while others are engaged in kinesthetic learning activities. At some point, students switch directions to experience the other methodology. This provides a win–win scenario in which students can be exposed to instruction and learning in two different ways. There are two types of side-by-side methods that can be used in the classroom.

- **Same standard/objective/skill:** In this instance, students are learning or practicing the same academic standard/objective/skill through different means. For example, students may be playing a review game on parts of speech on one side of the classroom while students on the other side of the room are working on the same skill kinesthetically; then they switch.

- **Different standard/objective/skill:** In this instance, students are learning or practicing a different standard/objective/skill, which may or may not always be academic. For example, kinesthetic brain breaks or class cohesion activities may be incorporated that have an indirect impact on academic learning. In this type of environment, some students will be learning or engaging actively to meet one particular goal while the other students have a different agenda and are using technology to meet their objectives. Then students switch their focus so both goals are met through different tactics.

## Split Timing

This type of approach balances the amount of time that movement and technology are used in the classroom. Some days, kinesthetic activities play a heavier role in the learning process, while on other days, objectives will be reached through digital means. Split timing can be looked at in many different ways, such as daily, weekly, or monthly. This concept will be explored in more detail as we progress through this chapter. Remember, you should ideally aim for the goal of using at least some form of movement and technology every day, even if it is only for a few minutes. For example, on days when technology is used extensively, incorporate exercise as a brain break for 60 seconds two or three times throughout the period. Or when kinesthetic activities are the primary method used for learning, use technology as a brain break.

## Differentiated Centers

Learning centers are a strong teaching technique for the distracted brain. Typically, a learning center has a limited time frame for students to accomplish a task before they move on to the next station. This is ideal for short attention spans and is an easy way to implement a variety of differentiated instructional mini-lessons that can reach students' learning preferences while also strengthening their weaknesses. When using this balancing approach, MTEs will have both technology and kinesthetic centers. Differentiated centers are also an easy way to support a blended teaching philosophy by incorporating traditional teaching stations. Similar to the side-by-side balancing approach, educators can use the center objectives as described on the previous page same standard/objective/skill and different standard/objective/skill. As students move around the classroom from center to center, they can practice or learn the same concept through a variety of instructional means or they can meet an array of objectives. Both means are very effective strategies for the 21st-century learner. These decisions are really up to the teachers' preferences, goals, and needs.

## United

This balancing approach is multifaceted; it combines movement and technology at the same time. This requires some solid planning and out-of-the-box thinking, but it is a fun method for utilizing education's power play. Movement and technology typically have opposing characteristics when it comes to education. Kinesthetic activities are designed for physical movement, while technology is typically linked to sitting. But what if teachers and students could unite technology and movement into one joined learning methodology? This is an exciting idea and we will focus on it in this chapter. This concept is also one that ignites and motivates developers for future expansions in this up-and-coming philosophy. At this stage in development, there are few programs and websites designed for this approach. However, this is short term. Once designers realize the power of uniting movement and technology, it will surely grow to be a "skies the limit" teaching and learning tactic.

## PLANNING PRIORITIES

Lesson planning is at the heart of being an effective MTE and is essential to the teaching and learning process. Developing interesting lessons takes a great deal of time and effort. However, good planning is worthless if motivating delivery procedures are not included and carried out. You will and should use all of the balancing approaches described in the previous section in your lesson planning throughout the school year. As an MTE, you will need to see what best fits your daily needs and requirements. For example, one lesson may lend itself more effectively to the side-by-side approach, while the next lesson perfectly aligns with the united method. What is key is that you place careful thought into your planning while continually monitoring your technique to ensure that your design is well-rounded and balanced. The following timelines can be used to gauge your deliveries to see if you are consistently balancing movement and technology in your planning and execution.

- **Lesson to lesson:** This type of planning refers to balancing movement and technology within each lesson. This is an ideal scenario, as students will be physically engaged through desirable kinesthetic activities; technology is used equally to appeal to this generation of learners. This type of delivery works perfectly by giving the body what it needs and the brain what it craves. Balancing movement and technology lesson to lesson can be difficult and impractical for a wide range of reasons. One of the top reasons is that some lessons simply lend themselves better to active learning *or* technology, not necessarily both. This approach works well in both elementary and secondary school settings.

- **Day to day:** When you are unable to balance each lesson with movement and technology, the next step would be to look at your day-to-day planning. For example, during the morning lessons, you might incorporate more technology-based instruction, but in the afternoon, you may engage students in a variety of kinesthetic activities. This perspective allows for an equal balance of movement and technology with each school day. This example is typically more applicable in an elementary school environment.

- **Week to week:** If you are unable to balance your classroom with movement and technology day to day, the next place to look would be at your week-to-week planning. For example, perhaps you will incorporate more technology-based lessons two days of the week while you utilize more kinesthetic activities two of the other days. Keep in mind, when using this strategy, you still want to make an effort to implement some movement and technology every day. This approach only means that there isn't equal usage of both methods *every day*; by the end of the week, you should be able to make the most of the MT balance.

- **Unit to unit:** When you are unable to balance your classroom with movement and technology week to week, the following focus will be on unit-to-unit planning. For example, over the course of a few days or weeks of a given unit, you might implement more technology-based lessons while you may utilize more kinesthetic activities the other days or weeks. Keep in mind that when using this strategy, you still want to make an effort to implement *some* movement and technology every day. This approach only means that there isn't equal usage of both methods every day or every week; by the end of the unit, you should be able to make the most of the MT balance.

- **Marking period to marking period:** When all else fails and you are unable to balance your classroom with movement and technology from unit to unit, your last option is to look at the entire marking period. For example, in some units, you can utilize more technology-based lessons, and in other units, you can incorporate more kinesthetic activities. Again, when using this strategy, you still want to make an effort to implement some movement and technology every day. This approach only means that there isn't equal usage of both methods every day, week, or unit; by the end of the marking period, you are able to make the most of the MT balance.

Creating and carrying out a well-balanced MT plan is critical for increasing learning potential. Often, teachers like to instruct on the fly, doing the things that pop into their mind. Although this skill is certainly meshed into the teaching and learning process, it is only one component of the profession. Developing a solid, clear lesson plan is a central document that provides the first step for a professional performance. A good lesson plan makes a confident teacher. Constantly updating plans and performances through consistent reflection and trial and error is a sizable factor that cannot be overlooked or devalued. At the top of the next page are some tips for the MTE to consider when planning their lessons. Use this checklist as a guide for careful and intentional planning. This checklist also serves as a means for self-reflection: Where are your MT practices currently and where would you like them to go?

## Planning Priorities ✔

Kinesthetic and technology activities are directly linked to the objectives.

Movement and technology (or both) are included in your learning activities daily when possible.

All materials needed for movement and technology are listed in your lesson plans and gathered and prepared ahead of time.

Online technology resources are screened and/or prepared ahead of time to ensure that they are working properly and the material is appropriate.

Movement and/or technology are used in the anticipatory set in order to pique student interest and increase motivation.

Movement and/or technology are used to play review games and check for understanding.

Transition time is considered and built in to allow for a seamless flow of activities (especially when transitioning from movement activities back to seats).

Movement and technology references are relevant to students; students can make personal connections to the activities.

A plan is in place for students who are having academic or behavioral difficulty with the movement and/or technology activity.

Activities are creative. Effort is made to refrain from overusing the same activities, programs, or websites, as they will lose novelty and become less effective.

A wide variety of movement and technology is implemented in an effort to reach the various learning styles and personalities of the students.

Time spent using movement and technology is maximized in every lesson.

Higher-level skills such as analysis, evaluation, and synthesis are considered and reached through movement and technology.

Outcomes are clearly defined, and there is a concrete way to evaluate the success of the lesson.

Lesson planning is done at a reasonable pace to ensure proper reflection and the ability to gauge success. Avoid overplanning or planning too far ahead.

Lesson plans are flexible. Be willing to change, as some activities may need more or less time than expected or may be well-received or disliked by students.

Planning is done through collaboration with colleagues in order to tap into each other's skills, knowledge, and experiences with MT activities.

## CLASSROOM APPLICATIONS: THE ABCDs

Although effective teachers are comprehensive in their thinking and planning, their interest is typically piqued by learning real classroom applications that work. All the other steps are important, but practical examples of how this looks and functions to improve the teaching and learning process is really what deepens an educator's capabilities. Ideally, after teachers have the opportunity to read this book, professional development trainings will follow in which they can actually experience the fun, practical, and successful benefits of these applications. View the activities described in the next section that unite movement and technology with a curious mind. Consider them as a springboard that propels your thinking into a new educational philosophy that directly aligns with today's learners. Ask yourself the following question: "Will this work in my classroom as is?" If the answer is *yes*, then add it to your list of ideas for future planning. If your answer is *no*, then ask yourself how you can modify it to make it work for you and your students. As educators, we too often see an awesome activity that someone else is using, but we don't always make the connection of how it can be tweaked to meet our needs. For example, if you are a math teacher who happens to be observing a movement activity in a language arts class (or other subject area), consider the concept of the movement activity and whether it is transferable and can work in your math class. Developing the skill of making modifications is significant to the success of an MTE. As of now, the united concepts are a unique approach to classroom methods for elevating student performance. Remember, this is temporary and will require you to look beyond the suggestions herein and possibly redesign them for your own purposes.

## Enhancing the ABCs of Movement With Technology

### The ABC Exchange

The following 30 suggestions include academic activities, brain boosters, and community connectors. Some of these ideas and activities overlap and are interchangeable because they unite movement, technology, and academics to benefit academic achievement, learner attention and focus, and the learner as a whole.

*Academic Activities* The following 20 suggestions are united academic activities; they connect movement and technology to enhance academic practices, reviews, and teachings.

Practices

1. **Tech treks:** Place a device on every desk or workstation. If you do not have a 1:1 student-to-device ratio, use as many devices as you can and place a traditional worksheet at the other workstations. Play music and allow students to walk around the classroom. Students can also skip, slide, gallop, or perform any other locomotor movement you would like. When the music goes off, students sit at the closest desk and complete a problem online or traditionally. When the music comes back on, they begin to move again. Each round will allow students the opportunity to sit at a new desk while experiencing both tech and traditional practices.

2. **Traveling turtle:** Place students into small groups of 3–5. Have students carefully and *slowly* pass the "turtle" (the tech device that will be used for practicing academic content in this activity) while music is being played. When the music stops, the student who is holding the turtle will answer the online practice question. Teachers can allow for individual or group answers.

3. **Laser tag:** Give all students a laser pointer. If you do not have one for every student, use as many as you have available. Dim the lights and flash content review questions up on the interactive whiteboard; include possible answers. Have students use their light to tag the correct answer. If not every student has a laser pointer, ask them to mill around the classroom and hand off the pointer every time they pass by a peer. When the question flashes, the person with the light uses it to tag the answer. Students without a laser can point to the answer.

4. **Mingle match:** Have students mill around the classroom while carrying the device you would like them to use to practice academic content online. On your command, instruct students to connect with the peer closest to them. Have students challenge one another to complete an online practice problem with accuracy and speed. If you do not have enough devices for everyone, students can form groups of two or three and work collaboratively or against one another.

5. **Link up:** Place a number of technology devices around the classroom (half as many devices as students; for example, 10 devices for 20 students). Ask students to mill around the room. On your command, students will go to the device they are closest to. There will be two students at each device. Have students work together to answer one to three online practice questions. Students should link up with a new partner in each round.

## Reviews

1. **Fitness flash:** Flash multiple-choice academic review questions on the interactive whiteboard. Have students perform an exercise to show their answer. For example, students can do jumping jacks for A, squats for B, air punches for C, or hold a tree pose for D.

2. **Face-Off:** Place a number of technology devices around the classroom (half as many devices as students; for example, 10 devices for 20 students). Ask students to mill around the room. On your command, have each student go to the device they are closest to. There will be two students at each device. Have students race against each other to identify the correct answer to an online review question. Students can also race against the other groups for the correct answer if it is more suitable for the online program that is being used.

3. **Tippy tap:** Place your students into small groups of 3–5 and have them sit in a circle. Ask students to pass a soft object around the circle. Display questions and possible answers on the interactive whiteboard. On your command, ask the student who has the object to speed-walk up to the board and gently tap ("tippy tap") the correct answer. Music can also be used to determine which student goes to the board.

4. **Move to respond:** Have students complete an online review question. Place answers around the classroom—some correct, some incorrect.

Have students move to the answer they came up with. Facilitate group discussions to show common mistakes. Play multiple rounds.

5. **Number swap:** Divide your class into 3–4 even groups and give each student a number (1, 2, 3, or 4). Have students walk around the classroom while constantly swapping their number with anyone they pass (hence, always changing their number). Call out a number. Any student with that number sits down at a technology device to complete an online review question while the other students continue with a new round. A different number is called each round. The game itself should be fast-paced and the amount of time given for online responses should be short.

## Teachings

1. **Be the teacher:** Using platforms such as SchoolTube or YouTube, have students create and upload a kinesthetic mini-lesson. The goal is to have them teach the content or concept to their peers through a video presentation.

2. **Learning on the move:** Encourage students to move while learning academic content through technological means. This could be as simple as having them walk around the classroom while watching an online video on a tablet.

3. **Writing on the move:** Have students type a few sentences on their devices. Then ask them to move around the classroom to music. When the music stops, ask them to sit at a new device, read the contents, and add one or two new sentences (depending on your goal or grade level). Continue until the stories are complete. Traditional writing stations can be utilized if the student-to-device ratio is not 1:1.

4. **Virtual labs:** Incorporate virtual labs that engage students kinesthetically. For example, foreign language and science labs often utilize hands-on activities to optimize student learning.

5. **Video alive:** Have students create or re-create the actions of an academic video they recently observed. They may need to watch it more than once or pause it numerous times to allow for processing/creation time.

6. **Active tracks:** Use personal activity tracking devices, such as pedometers or Nike+, to gain information for teaching academic skills, such as mean, median, mode, and range.

7. **Moving maps:** Include geographic information systems (such as Google Maps) in lessons to track routes or measure distances.

8. **Seek and find:** While teaching, allow students the opportunity to seek out the information that is being explained and take a picture or video of it to demonstrate their understanding. For example, ask students to take a picture of a solid, liquid, or gas in a lesson on states of matter.

9. **Google on the fly:** Place signs around your classroom regarding the content you are teaching (for example, key factors of a significant war).

Ask a question and allow students to Google the answer. Have students move to the sign (or factor) based on their findings. Ask students to show their Google search to a peer to prove their answer.

10. **WebQuest walks:** Place students in groups of 2–5. Ask each group to research a different section of a given topic on your WebQuest. Then instruct them to write hints about their section on notecards and spread them around the classroom facedown. Place signs around the classroom regarding the different topics that were researched. Have students walk around the classroom, pick up a notecard, and try to place it in the correct category. Continue until all notecards are in the correct place. Play multiple rounds.

*Brain Booster* The following five suggestions are united brain boosters; they connect movement and technology to enhance body basics, blasts, and breaks.

1. **Gamification:** Use gaming systems that incorporate a variety of movements, such as Xbox Kinect and Wii Motion Plus.

2. **Fitness factory:** Include short exercise videos for students to follow along with in-between lessons.

3. **Active websites:** Incorporate websites that utilize movement or physical activity into academic free time (examples include GoNoodle or Fit4Schools).

4. **Finding peace:** Use relaxation apps that include movement.

5. **Freestyle fun:** Feature dance and yoga videos for students to follow along with or learn from.

*Community Connectors* The following five suggestions are united community connectors; they connect movement and technology to build cohesive partners, teams, and classes.

## Partners, Teams, and Classes

1. **Charades apps:** Incorporate charade apps (such as Heads Up or Charades!) that inspire creative movements.

2. **Just Dance showdown:** Use the Just Dance game series or similar videos to instigate some friendly dance off competitions.

3. **Scavenger hunt:** Use a shared Google Doc to engage students in a social scavenger hunt while they race against the clock.

4. **The gift of exercise:** Allow students to challenge one another with age-appropriate exercises through class-approved social networks.

5. **Move together:** Ask students to set up exercise partners or groups through class-approved social networks. Once these exercise connections are made, have students move together for a quick break.

# Enhancing the ABCDs of Technology With Movement

## The ABCD Exchange

The following 24 suggestions include academic applications, content consumptions, and differentiated deliveries. These ideas and activities are often overlapping and interchangeable because they all unite movement, technology, and academics, which serve as brain boosters for academic achievement, learner attention and focus, and the learner as a whole (ALL).

*Academic Applications* The following eight suggestions are united academic applications.

1. **Writing performances:** Match students with a partner. While utilizing tech devices, have each student use description-writing skills to write step-by-step instructions on how to perform a physical skill or task (for example, a dance, a particular exercise, or a kinesthetic game). Have students switch devices or e-mail or post their descriptions to their partner. Then, ask students to read their partner's directions while trying to complete the physical task based on the instructions provided. Students that do not perform the skill or activity correctly will be able to help their partner realize where their writing was unclear.

2. **Kinesthetic PowerPoints:** Have students create and deliver a PowerPoint presentation on a given topic. Set guidelines on how often students should use movement or physical activity with their peers while presenting their information. This allows students to gain skills and knowledge regarding good presentation tactics while developing techniques to hold their audience's attention.

3. **#ExerciseTweets:** While having students utilize academic tweets, ask them to add a hashtag that describes the exercise or kinesthetic activity they used while tweeting (for example, #walkntweet, #bikentweet, or #situpsntweet). Request a respectable ratio between the number of tweets and exercises or encourage ongoing exercises so students get used to using movement frequently with tech communications.

4. **Podcast pop-ups:** Have students create an informative podcast to share with their peers that incorporates a balance of academic information with pop-ups of kinesthetic learning activities or physical brain breaks. In other words, students will have their peers pop up and move throughout the podcast.

5. **Virtual field trips:** While having students engage in a virtual field trip, hit the pause button and have them take a "bring it to life" break. This refers to having students kinesthetically become something they see or experience virtually. For example, you could ask students to become an animal they saw during a virtual trip to the zoo.

6. **Action assignments:** Include physical challenges, exercises, or kinesthetic activities with online homework assignments. Also incorporate them

when linking academic work to physical accomplishments to reach peak homework performance.

7. **Tablet team-builders:** Place tablets around the classroom that contain a variety of academic application practices. Have students mill around the classroom. Call out a number and have students form groups of that amount, go to a tablet, and complete the practice problem as a team. Continue for a designated time frame while constantly reforming new teams of different amounts.

8. **Multiplayer games:** Use competitive academic gaming systems that incorporate a variety of movements and require students to apply their knowledge.

*Content Consumptions* The following eight suggestions are united content consumptions.

1. **Video volleys**: Have students create an educational video on a given topic to share with their peers that incorporates a back-and-forth volley or a balance of academic information with kinesthetic learning activities or physical brain breaks. Have students show their video to their peers. Allow students the opportunity to provide feedback about both the academic content and the appropriateness/effectiveness of the active learning components.

2. **Google giggles:** While using communication platforms such as Google Hangouts, have students pass a "Google giggle" challenge while doing homework or class assignments. A *Google giggle* is a physical skill that requires coordination and has a certain degree of difficulty. For example, students can tap up and down on their head with their right hand while rubbing their stomach in a counterclockwise motion with their left hand or swing their right arm clockwise and their left arm counterclockwise while walking, all at the same time. The goal is to have students physically perform silly movements while completing their homework or assignments. Students who are interested can also upload videos of themselves performing their Google giggle challenge to share with the class.

3. **Illustration models:** Have students work with partners or in small groups. Ask students to use illustration software to take pictures while using their physical bodies and objects to demonstrate their understanding of the academic content being taught. For example, students can form different geometric shapes or the stages of the life cycle.

4. **Fitness fact tiles:** Use online question-and-answer tiles that contain both an exercise challenge and an academic question. Align the difficulty of the fitness challenge with the level of the question. For example, an easier question might require three jumping jacks and be worth three points if answered correctly; a more difficult question would have a strenuous fitness challenge and be worth more points.

5. **Moving maps and graphic organizers:** While utilizing online maps or statistical graphs that show important locations or content data, have

students use their bodies to represent the same information kinesthetically. Have students play as many roles as possible to symbolize the locations or data to enhance recall.

6. **Wiki walkabout:** Have students get into groups of two or three and create different content-based wikis per the teacher's guidelines. For example, each wiki might include one specific topic of a given unit. Then, give each group a review sheet to complete. Have groups split apart to search or do a "walkabout" for an answer(s) that can be found on the different wikis dispersed around the room. Partners/groups must meet back at the review sheet after each walkabout to answer the questions together before splitting up again to go to a new wiki. Continue until the review sheets are completed.

7. **Whiteboard relay:** Place students in small groups of 3–5. Assign each group a team fitness challenge, such as 20 jump squats. Once the team completes the challenge together, the designated team leader of the round races to the interactive whiteboard to complete an academic practice problem. Assign a new exercise challenge and designated team leader for each round of game play.

8. **Gamification:** Use gaming systems that incorporate a variety of movements that help students consume academic content.

*Differentiated Deliveries* The following eight suggestions are united differentiated deliveries.

1. **Simulation replication:** While viewing a virtual simulation, have students engage in a live, kinesthetic reproduction of what they are observing with a partner or small group. An example of where this connection can be made is science, technology, engineering, and mathematics (STEM) simulations.

2. **Imitation live:** Have students view a kinesthetic how-to video on any applicable academic content. Ask students to follow along while physically replicating the step-by-step details of the video.

3. **Learn or listen:** Set up technology stations around the classroom containing academic WebQuests. Give each student a questionnaire to learn the information that is contained on the WebQuests. Do not allow students to write on their own study guide, as they are only permitted to write (and whisper) answers on their peers' worksheets. Students circulate around the classroom either gaining knowledge from a WebQuest and giving that information to classmates or listening to a classmate answer a question for them on their questionnaire. Allow students to determine how much time they should take to study the WebQuests (learn) or mingle around for answers (listen). The goal is to help one another complete the study guides.

4. **Literacy walk:** Have students use a digital textbook or other informative resource while engaging in a literacy walk. This can occur a few different ways: Students can walk while reading, read then walk (and repeat), read

then go to a poster board to write a reflection, read and then walk while discussing with a peer, or a combination of the previous suggestions. The goal is to add movement to digital readings so that students' eyes have some no-screen time.

5. **Virtual manipulatives:** Have students engage in kinesthetic applications by themselves or with a partner while viewing virtual manipulative videos. Visuals are a powerful tool but so are fine-motor kinesthetic activities. Combining them is practical and differentiates the content delivery to reach more learners.

6. **Distance active education:** Create online instructional activities and assignments that include one or more physical activity for students to engage in. This can optimize learning, comprehension, and retention. There is a wide range of options for implementation, but active learning should always be a part of every academic delivery.

7. **Kinesthetic furniture:** Incorporate kinesthetic furniture options into your classroom, such as pedal desks, swivel stools, strider desks, or standing desks. If you do not have enough active furniture, utilize steady rotations so that each student receives a turn.

8. **Learning games:** Use gaming systems that incorporate a variety of movements that help students learn academic content.

## Pillars of Strength

Movement-based academic applications, content consumptions, and differentiated deliveries are boosting benefits that are new to the educational scene, as we are only now realizing the travesty of a generation that views learning and the world around them through screens alone. The following seven pillars of strength are essential to the growth and development of uniting movement, technology, and academics to provide students with futuristic, diverse learning opportunities:

1. **Educational leaders:** In all locations, teachers, administrators, curriculum developers, supervisors, and so on must demand the creation of movement-based technological advancements.

2. **Passionate students:** Students of all ages must reignite their passion for movement and voice their need for an MT balance in their life and in their learning.

3. **Innovative tech companies:** Tech companies all around the world must value a healthy society that defines the connection between technology and movement as a thriving force.

4. **Tech developers:** In all types of designs, tech developers must exude a desire to think outside the box to invent MT creations beyond what the mind can initially see.

5. **Stable societies:** In all cultures, stable societies must value balance, things in moderation, and well-proportioned ideals.

6. **Well-rounded politicians:** Politicians of all parties must uphold education as a high priority while supporting suitable MT funding.

7. **Concerned parents and guardians:** Parents and guardians in all types of environments must support and maintain an MT balance in the home and in community settings.

# A BRIGHT FUTURE

Educational models are altering, and the MTE is crafted to lead the way for these up-and-coming future expectations. As more and more products are designed to enhance education, new technologies are aggressively sweeping through schools and classrooms. Educators are in charge of determining the skills and types of knowledge students need in order to prosper in our technology-saturated workforce and world. History shows us that with rapid growth, similar to what technology has had over the last few years, significant philosophical shifts in education are inevitable. However, as consistently demonstrated throughout this book, technology cannot be our sole focus. It must be paired with thoughtful educational leaders, movement, interpersonal relationship skills, and deliberate programs that generate well-rounded learners and upstanding citizens. As we look ahead, there is no question that technology has a bright, indestructible future. But we must also ensure that movement, healthy living, physical activity, and kinesthetic learning follow a parallel path. We cannot raise or educate a generation that spends their entire day staring at screens. This would be irresponsible, to say the least. How MTEs structure and run their classrooms will determine the future of education. As digital resources continue to advance, it will be teachers and educational leaders who uncover and define the MT balance. Below are ten future MT possibilities in the making:

1. Kinesthetic furniture and flexible seating options will become a norm in classroom environments as a means of accommodating students who need more movement.

2. Both individual and collaborative workspaces will incorporate kinesthetic outlets to avoid prolonged sitting.

3. Movable classroom walls will be constructed to make space adaptable and suitable for movement activities.

4. Virtual and augmented reality capabilities will link movement or physical activity with academic content.

5. Flexible assignments will integrate kinesthetic projects and tasks as standard practice.

6. Adaptive learning software will include kinesthetic components.

7. Artificial intelligence will utilize movement on a regular basis for a multitude of learning purposes.

8. Game-based learning platforms will physically engage students in the learning process.

9. Immersive learning experiences will be created with complete sensory experiences that physically engage the learner.

10. Online learning opportunities will incorporate hands-on kinesthetic activities.

There is no question that technology has a bright future, but so does the MT balance; the overall health and well-being of our species depends on it. As you play your part in this development, there are four qualities you will need to exude. First and perhaps most importantly, you must have a "put students first" attitude. Educators should not simply give students what they *want*. Teachers must project the future skills, knowledge, and abilities that students will *need* to succeed. Sure, learners may want to be on screens all day, but is this really what is in their best interest? Second, be a voice that stands up for best practice models in education, those that are not consumed with technology alone. Third, create or be part of a team of like-minded educators who believe in a society and school system that embraces balance, particularly the MT balance. Speaking up for a comprehensive learning experience for the younger generation can be scary. Facing this challenge with a team effort is a stronger approach and will keep you from feeling alone in your mission. However, sometimes you may be alone, and you will have to dig deep to find your inner strength. Fourth, be ready for anything and everything. Education should always be changing and developing to keep up with the times; you will need to grow with it. The philosophy you develop today will need adjustments as learners transform and society continues to evolve. Be a part of this revolution with an open mind and a passionate heart; the future of the younger generation is counting on you.

# WHAT DOES THIS MEAN TO ME?

### K–12 Teachers

1. Decide which balancing approach and planning priority is the best place for you to focus your initial attention on.

2. Choose at least one classroom application from academic activities, brain boosters, and community connectors to try with your class. Consider both your comfort level and your students' personalities before you make your selections.

### Administration

1. Provide workshops during in-service days that allow teams and/or grade levels to collaborate on defining their MT balance.

2. Provide up-to-date resources to teachers with supportive research and classroom applications to help them discover their MT balance.

### Educational Leaders/Affiliates

1. Offer state and national seminars for the pillars of strength (described earlier) to expand and encourage this education direction.

2. Examine higher education curriculums to ensure that future teachers and administrators are prepared and well-informed regarding movement, technology, and the MT balance.

# CHAPTER SUMMARY

- There is no question that movement and technology play a significant role in learning; both should be considered best practice methods for optimizing student success in the classroom and in life.

- The MT balance is the ultimate power play when it comes to best practice policies in the teaching of students of all ages and abilities. These methods check all the boxes for improving brain and body health while reaching peak performance.

- There are four approaches that can be used for balancing movement and technology: side by side, split timing, differentiated centers, and united.

- Lesson planning is at the heart of being an effective MTE and is essential to the teaching and learning process. Good planning is worthless if motivating delivery procedures are not included and carried out.

- There are five different timelines for using the MOST method in the MT balance: lesson to lesson, day to day, week to week, unit to unit, and marking period to marking period.

- Constantly updating MT lesson plans and performances through consistent reflection and trial and error is a sizable factor that cannot be overlooked or devalued.

- Practical examples of how the MT balance looks and functions to improve the teaching and learning process is really what deepens an educator's capabilities.

- Developing the skill of making modifications to activities is significant to the success of an MTE.

- This chapter contains over 50 suggestions/activities that unite movement and technology to define the MT balance.

- The following seven pillars of strength are essential to the growth and development of uniting movement, technology, and academics to provide students with futuristic, diverse learning opportunities: educational leaders, passionate students, innovative tech companies, creative tech developers, stable societies, well-rounded politicians, and concerned parents and guardians.

- As we look ahead, there is no question that technology has a bright future. But we must also ensure that movement, healthy living, and physical activity follow a parallel path so we can generate well-rounded learners and upstanding citizens.

- To be an MT leader in the future of education, you must have a "put students first" attitude, be a voice that promotes balance, be part of a like-minded team of educators, and be ready for anything and everything—especially change.

# 10

# EMPLOYING SMART ACTIVITIES

## THE MENTAL/EMOTIONAL LEARNING STATE

Our mental health includes our emotional, psychological, and social well-being, all of which are directly and indirectly affected in educational environments. We need our emotions for thinking, problem solving, focusing, and paying attention. The most important thing to students is that their fundamental survival needs are being met. The brain prioritizes these basic requirements first. The second most important interest to the brain is the emotional state of the learner. We are neurologically wired, and in order to learn academic content optimally, the mind must be focused and the emotions must feel grounded and balanced. It is imperative for students to have a sense of emotional regulation in your classroom so they can remember, transfer, and recall information. Having the ability to learn new content effectively and connect it to prior knowledge is also affected by students' learning states. When students are in a negative state, these emotions take over and the brain's ability to function is compromised. This sensation results in a heightened stress-response state, which can hinder logical and critical thinking. Fear, anger, anxiety, sadness, or frustration can consume students' thoughts, making higher-level reasoning difficult and, in severe cases, impossible.

When a student feels stress or tension in your classroom, his or her brain will go into fight-or-flight mode. This state can be a positive experience because students are alert and attentive. This will work in favor of learning content. It can, however, be negative if the brain shuts down and cognitive processes become nonfunctioning. This occurs in learning environments where high levels of stress are frequent and excessive. Negative and positive emotions exist in everyone's life; we need both of them. There are five primary emotions: joy, sadness, fear, anger, and disgust. What students are thinking and how they are feeling while in their learning environment can have a significant impact on their learning potential. The brain has the capacity to change and rewire its pathways between neurons. This process is dependent upon your students' learning experiences. The neural synapses or connections can be modified by changing behaviors or perceptions. Therefore, the way in which students perceive your classroom will have a direct influence on their cognitive processing and output. As a teacher, you must be aware of this because the brain responds to perception, not reality. A student's learning state defines the brain's position for optimal learning.

Emotions drive our attention, concentration, and our view of our surroundings. In your classroom, students will develop core memories based on past events, current experiences, and relationships. These memories are critical to students' learning states. In the past, educators' sole focus was to teach the academic content. The rest was up to the parents and families. Minimal attention was given to how to best support a child's learning state, feelings, and emotions. Students were simply expected to sit quietly, pay attention, focus, and achieve. Now research suggests that educators need to direct their attention to students' learning states while incorporating strategies to improve core memories and feelings for enhanced academic performance. This seems to be yet another responsibility placed on the teacher and the school. It's one that cannot be overlooked. Educational leaders need quick, meaningful ways to reduce stress and have students feel good in their classrooms and schools while taking minimal time and attention away from the academic standards.

The reality is that educators directly influence students' perceptions, feelings, and thoughts about learning by the way they conduct their classrooms and school environments. When students walk into a classroom, it is important for them to feel positive about being in this space. Employing SMART activities on a regular basis is a simple, doable means for building positive core memories and calming feelings. *SMART* stands for **s**tress **m**anagement **a**nd **r**elaxation **t**echniques. Movement and technology educators (MTEs) will have the ability to maintain a low-stress learning environment that provides support and understanding. Feelings are powerful; they affect learning, relationships, and behaviors. As educators promote soothing emotions by utilizing SMART activities, students will be cognitively set for prime learning performances. These activities will benefit all learning environments and are practical for students of all ages. Mental health challenges are increasing in our younger generations. Utilizing SMART activities is a practical countermeasure.

# WHEN PRODUCTIVITY IS LOST

## Signs and Symptoms

Many educational facilities put pressure on teachers to cover their curriculum and standards by designated points in the school timeline. As a result, teachers push through their content to cover the material. This concept seems in complete opposition to what would be deemed as best practices in academic learning settings. Many school leaders refer to this concept as *academic overload*. Educators move deeply into their content at a pace that increases students' stress levels. As a result, productivity is lost. Students are not understanding nor retaining the information being taught. Teachers find themselves backtracking to reteach the material at a later date. This teaching approach works against time efficiency. Who is at fault in this instance? Surely educators do not support the goal of trying to proceed through their objectives at lightning speeds, whether or not their students are actually learning the subject matter. Yet, this has become a common practice in countless school districts. The concept of quality over quantity has taken a backseat in classrooms as academic demands continue to increase at unreasonable rates. If our goal is to improve student achievement and success, then our focus cannot be on how much content we can get through in the shortest amount of time. This way of thinking is not aligned with enhancing knowledge or building content depth and comprehension.

Polling all educators to uncover how many are currently utilizing stress management strategies in their classrooms would reveal interesting statistics. If it is not already a common practice at this stage in education, it will need to become one as we move forward. As discussed previously, managing students' emotional states is critical to students' learning potential. Sadly, we live in a culture where a lot of bad things happen day in and day out to our children and adolescents. There are tragedies all over the world and in the homes of many of the students we teach. Youngsters face intense anxieties and fears outside of school, which are terrifying and will surely affect their frame of mind in their learning environments. It is no wonder that these students may not be able to perform at top academic levels. Although teachers cannot control what happens outside of their classrooms, they can definitely influence their students' frame of mind during their learning experiences. Employing SMART activities is a teacher–student friendly approach that promotes comforting, reassuring classroom environments.

MTEs will need to identify when and how frequently SMART activities should be used. This may or may not change throughout the school year (based on unforeseeable circumstances). Ideally, these strategies should be utilized before productivity is lost, but this will not always be the case. Consider what increases your students' stress levels. Relationships are one of the top factors. How students connect with you and their classmates is significant and will affect their learning and cognitive processing. Teachers are encouraged to look for signs that students are having negative feelings or thoughts. Here are some signs to watch for:

- Clenching jaws or fists
- Gritting teeth
- Blushing or sweating
- Pronounced swallowing
- Stomach pains or bathroom issues

- Difficulty concentrating
- Trouble learning new content
- Forgetful, disorganized, and confused
- Difficulty in making decisions
- Fidgeting or nervous habits
- Increased frustration, irritability, or edginess
- Overreaction to annoyances
- Obsessive or compulsive behaviors
- Reduced work efficiency or productivity
- Lies or excuses to cover up poor work

- Rapid or mumbled speech
- Excessive defensiveness or suspiciousness
- Frequent urination
- Chest pain or rapid pulse
- Excessive anxiety or worry
- Increased anger or frustration
- Mood swings
- Problems in communication or sharing
- Social withdrawal or isolation
- Weight gain or loss
- Constant tiredness or fatigue

This is an extensive list, but what it really comes down to is this: Teachers need to know their students well enough to recognize changes and shifts in their behaviors or emotions. If we aim for peak academic performance, the emotional state must take precedence over the academic content. This isn't an opinion; it's simply how the brain prioritizes what matters most. Comprehending academic information will always be less important than the emotional well-being of the learner. Therefore, this emphasis is relevant to all teachers, and incorporating SMART activities on a regular basis will help to foster an ideal learning environment. This book is filled with strategies to help the educator accomplish this task. Implementing STRIDES (structuring and managing, transforming with A.A.A., refining movement and technology, interconnecting communities, defining the balance, employing SMART activities, supporting a united approach) creates a comprehensive, encouraging environment where everyone can flourish and grow peacefully.

## A PROACTIVE APPROACH

Whenever possible, SMART activities should be used as preventative measures. If students are stressed out in an academic setting, it may be difficult to redirect this negative state, as damage has already occurred. If MTEs teach students to self-regulate their thoughts and emotions or they have routine practices in place, there is a better chance of cultivating optimistic school environments. Too often, teachers can feel tensions building in their classrooms, but they are consumed with covering their content and continue to press forward. This is a recipe for failure because students' cognitive functioning will slow down or cease and information will be jumbled or lost. Educators will eventually end up reteaching the material or students will need to learn it on their own. It can be frightening to suggest that we stop teaching academic standards to attend to what the brain really needs—which is often anything but the subject matter we are focused on. But remember, the emotional state of the learner matters more to the brain than academic standards.

In a learning community where emotions affect intellectual achievement, movement and physical activity will enhance positive emotions. When we engage in exercise and certain physical activities, there are five brain chemicals (described below) that the body may release that affect the emotional state (Friedrich, 2016):

1. **Serotonin:** Boosts mood and spirit

2. **Norepinephrine:** Increases memory retrieval, alertness, and focus

3. **BDNF (brain-derived neurotropic factor):** Promotes new connections between nerve cells, protects your brain, improves cognitive function, and fosters long-term brain health

4. **Dopamine:** The motivation and reward brain chemical that makes you feel you can accomplish something

5. **Endorphins:** The feel-good chemicals that can help to relieve pain, anxiety, and fears

Ratey (2008) describes exercise as the body's natural Ritalin and Zoloft. Implementing active learning strategies can build an academic community in which students feel good emotionally and are connected to their peers. As a result, students will be able to create a positive emotional state, which is ideal for intellectual achievement. In this united environment, students will engage in movements that can increase brain chemicals that aid in improved cognitive functioning and productivity. A community that fosters positive relationships while providing continual opportunities for physical activity creates a strong venue for learning.

Being proactive means that educators will need to make students aware of a multitude of SMART activities. Students should also be encouraged to utilize these techniques while doing homework or during other stressful times in their lives. These skills will teach children and adolescents to monitor their state of mind while taking steps to improve their thinking and feelings. This is an invaluable life skill. The harmful effects of stress and negative thinking are detrimental to the mind and body, and there are numerous diseases and health problems linked to these mental toxins. Teaching our children to use SMART activities effectively and when necessary can provide them with lifesaving strategies to improve their mental/emotional health and well-being. To simplify this way of thinking, utilizing SMART activities is smart!

# THE BENEFITS OF SMART

Classrooms are meant to be busy environments in which students are pushed to perform at peak levels. Sometimes there will be feelings of joy and success; at other times, there will be sadness, frustration, and failure. This is acceptable because not all students will learn academic concepts with ease or with a 100% success rate. Even students who are very bright and achieve the highest scores day in and day out will feel negative thoughts and feelings in learning environments. Sometimes these particular students struggle with positive social relationships with their peers. They can lack patience and sympathy when their classmates cannot keep up with their quick-paced learning or depth of knowledge. No matter the skill level of a student, it is impossible for classrooms to operate with total positivity every day of a school year. Something is bound to happen that will cause stress, anxiety, frustration, and/or negativity.

Despite the challenges that all classroom teachers face, it is imperative to continue to strive for a comforting, positive environment in which all students can enjoy their peers and the learning process. The benefits of managing stress levels and optimistic thinking are well worth the minimal time and attention it will require. Below is a list of potential outcomes from employing SMART activities:

- **Lowers risk of illness:** Influences school attendance and stamina during learning

- **Boosts memory, focus, and brain functioning:** Essential for academic success

- **Increases willingness to tackle challenging tasks:** Important for content rigor and enrichment

- **Helps with decision making:** Aids with time management and prioritizing

- **Lowers frustration levels:** Affects positive thinking and performance

- **Benefits relationships and communication:** Enhances the emotional learning state

- **Decreases impatience, irritability, and anger:** Results in a calming environment

- **Gives greater access to intuition:** Important in making academic decisions

- **Eliminates unnecessary energy drain:** Improves attention and focus on content

- **Improves overall happiness:** Promotes a positive learning experience

These benefits can improve academic success while helping students feel supported and valued as human beings. Employing SMART activities on a regular basis focuses on students' mental/emotional health. This objective should have equal importance to content gains and achievements, especially since they work hand-in-hand. Students who feel a sense of rejection or negativity in your classroom can shut down both cognitively and personally. This will minimize learning potential, interest, and motivation. By understanding this connection, educators recognize students' mental/emotional state as more important than the content. Considering the manner in which the brain functions and operates supports this notion. As MTEs work their way through STRIDES, they are encouraged not to glaze over SMART activities. Instead, MTEs should welcome their value and make them a standard in classroom practices and procedures.

# SMART ACTIVITIES

In the pages that follow are ten applicable SMART activities for your consideration.

# Yoga

The concept of incorporating yoga into classrooms and school environments has become a well-accepted phenomenon. There are books, websites, and established companies that focus specifically on this peaceful type of exercise due to the ample benefits that result. Yoga has positive effects on the mind, body, and spirit while producing an overall sense of well-being. One physical advantage includes developing a strong, flexible body to improve balance, body awareness, coordination, posture, and alignment while strengthening the immune system. A few examples of ways in which it helps the mind include increased concentration, focus, and attention span; relief from tension, anxiety, and stress; expanded imagination and creativity, and a clarity of mind. Examples of how yoga benefits the spirit include increasing confidence and self-esteem, supporting character development and emotional intelligence, and inspiring self-respect and kindness toward others while encouraging self-expression and individuality. These potential gains make yoga an ideal example of a SMART activity. Below are five examples of yoga poses that can be used in the classroom. Consider this list as merely a starting point, as other resources concentrate solely and extensively on yoga poses and options for classroom usage. Also, it is recommended that you search for information and video demonstrations of these postures from reputable websites to obtain a visual example while hearing detailed explanations, including teaching tips. You can also purchase yoga cards at trustworthy websites, such as http://www.yoga4 classrooms.com.

- **Tree pose:** Stand with your arms at your side. Shift your weight to your left foot, place your hands on your hips, look straight ahead, lift your right leg, and place it on the inner thigh (or as high as it can go), while lifting your arms above your head. Hold, then repeat on the other side.

- **Triangle pose:** Stand with your feet wide apart and your right foot forward. Align your heels, turn your right foot out 90 degrees, and pivot the left foot inward 45 degrees. Raise your arms until they are parallel with the floor, extend your torso over your right leg, and bend at the hip. Rest your right hand on your shin or ankle (or floor) outside the right foot. Stretch your left arm to the ceiling, keeping your head neutral. Hold, then repeat on the other side.

- **Warrior 1 pose:** Stand in a high lunge pose. Bend your right knee directly above your foot. Place your hands on your hips, then square your hips and shoulders to the front wall. Open your chest, lifting your arms straight above the head, then arch your back and look gently to the ceiling. Hold, then repeat on the other side.

- **Chair pose:** Stand with your feet together. Place your hands on your hips, then bend your knees and push your buttocks out behind you (as if you were sitting in an imaginary chair with a straight back). Tighten your body and raise your hands overhead with your palms facing one another. Hold.

- **Eagle pose:** Stand with your arms and legs by your side. Balance on your right foot while bending slightly, then cross your left thigh over your right (hook your toes on your calf if possible). Fix your gaze, extend your arms, and drop your left arm over your right. Bend your elbow and wrap your arms to press your palms together (or as close as you can). Square your body. Hold, then repeat on the other side.

## Manipulatives

Utilizing manipulatives is a great way to help students relax and focus. There are many vendors that sell a wide selection of manipulatives. Some of the most common are stress balls, fidget spinners, and silly putty (or similar forms of it). Many teachers do not like to use these types of relaxation gadgets because students misuse them and they can quickly become a distraction. Although this can be true, it is not always the case. They can be extremely effective regarding their intended purpose, as long as educators maintain consistent classroom management strategies. Another learning consideration is the concept of allowing students to fidget, tap, spin, or wiggle around during times of instruction. In the past, these behaviors were deemed unacceptable and impolite. But if students aren't distracting their peers, why not allow them to use these movements as a means of calming or grounding their mindset? Often, it is the teacher who is disturbed by the motions. Students today are accustomed to a variety of things happening in their surroundings without being sidetracked or disrupted. In a sense, this is a positive skill that has been developed through our changing society. Typically, when students are squirming in their seat or creating their own version of a manipulative, they are not doing so intentionally or to be disrespectful. They simply can't help themselves. In the grand scheme of the current educational challenges, we should actually encourage movement of all types, even in this format. For many learners, this helps them become calm and focused quietly and peacefully.

## Mindfulness

Mindfulness suggests that the mind is fully attending to what's happening. It is common for our mind to take flight and drift away from the matter at hand. Often, students lose touch and entertain thoughts that are not related to the task at hand. Technological devices are often linked to this disconnect. Performing mini mindful activities helps to sharpen the skill of staying connected and attentive to the subject matter being presented. In the meantime, these conscious breaks are necessary and can refocus and reenergize the brain effectively to reach peak learning performance. Mindfulness is the basic human ability to be fully present, aware of where we are and what we are doing and not to overly react to who or what is going on around us. Being mindful is a skill that can be very difficult for most students. Attention spans are decreasing, making direct attention a problematic state. Teachers should promote two conscious mental concepts: direct attention on academic content and purposeful time spent away from instruction and subject matter. This blend of mindfulness activities can help to meet the students' needs while creating a productive, calming learning state.

It is appropriate for teachers to take a few minutes away from academic material to allow students to practice activities that improve mindfulness while reducing stress and increasing positive thinking. Students should block other thoughts during this designated time. Also, permit students to completely disengage from the lesson objectives by asking them to think about the sensations and feelings of the activity itself. Concentrating on the activity will reenergize the brain and strengthen the student's ability to be mindful with content (or without it). Mindful activities can occur during peer talks, fitness blasts, brain escapes, or any other SMART activity described herein.

## Brain Escapes

Brain escapes can be used to encourage a mindful state absent from academic content. A *brain escape* is defined as a teacher- or student-guided mental activity in which the thoughts are taken to another place or focal point. Some examples include the beach, an amusement park, on top of a mountain, or a favorite childhood memory. The places, memories, and thoughts we can go to in our mind are limitless. Encourage students to include all their senses on their brain escape. Have them visualize details of what they see, smell, feel, and/or taste. Ask them to distinguish the sounds they hear around them. Brain escapes serve as wonderful cognitive breaks that give students a short time to separate from math, science, language arts, or any other subject matter while allowing them to reduce their stress levels and think more clearly. Brain escapes should only last a few minutes, as it doesn't take long to give the brain the necessary rest it needs for recharging. Initially, educators may want to direct the brain escapes to teach students what they entail and how to include details in the vision. However, allowing students to create their own brain escapes promotes higher-level thinking and imagination, making it a worthy goal.

## Breathing Exercises

There are many educational resources that promote breathing exercises in a classroom environment. These stress-reducing techniques serve as effective brain breaks or brain boosts to relax the mind. Similar to other SMART activities, breathing exercises should last only a few minutes. Breathing exercises help to recharge and refocus the brain almost immediately upon completion. These exercises provide educators with ideal situations to confirm the importance of stress management in both life and learning. It also reassures students that their teacher is concerned about them as individuals and that cognitive achievement is not the only important goal in the classroom. These activities build students' awareness of their stressors and the means for successfully reducing them in learning and in life. This helps to educate the child as a whole while maximizing brain health and learner readiness. Here are four suggested breathing exercises to consider in an academic environment:

- **Rhythmic breathing:** Have students breathe in and out at a slow, deep rate for a specified amount of time.

- **Breathe, hold, and release:** Ask students to get in a relaxed position (eyes closed, perhaps dangling their arms at their sides or folding them in their laps), and have students take a deep breath. Hold for three seconds and release deeply and slowly.

- **Squeeze, hold, and release:** Ask students to get in a relaxed position (eyes closed, perhaps dangling their arms at their sides or folding them in their laps), and have students squeeze both fists to tighten their grip (as though they were squeezing two stress balls). Hold for three seconds and release.

- **Breathe, squeeze, hold, and release:** Ask students to get in a relaxed position (eyes closed, perhaps dangling their arms at their sides or folding them in their laps), and have students take a deep breath and hold it while squeezing both fists to tighten their grip (as though they were squeezing two stress balls) at the same time. Hold for three seconds and deeply and slowly release the breath and the squeeze.

These four breathing exercises are quick and well-received by students. They relax the body and brain for a few minutes and help to reduce anxiety. Add your own ideas or other breathing exercises to this list as your comfort level grows. Encourage students to use breathing exercises as brain breaks or to reduce stress levels at any time during the day or class period. These techniques are ideal for getting students into a calm state and can result in a second-wind mindset that prepares the learner for more academic challenges.

## Pressure Points

Another name for attending to pressure points is *acupressure*, which means to stimulate the body at certain meridians (pressure points). The goal of using acupressure is to alleviate pain, but it also helps to reduce stress, tension, and anxiety. Chronic strain can cause pain, especially in the neck and back, which can be reduced through pressure points. Encouraging students to use acupressure can have beneficial results, especially in situations where technology use is needed for extensive time frames. As a result of technology overuse (detailed in Chapter 3), headaches, neck pain, backache, and shoulder pain have become prevalent in students' lives. Headache is one of the most common discomforts that many children and adolescents suffer from at some point. They are often mild but serve as a disruption to the learning process. The most common type of headache is known as a *tension headache*, which is caused by stress, tension, fatigue, and neck pain brought on by prolonged screen time. Acupressure can be used to revive the body, minimize discomfort, and clear the mind. The following list gives ten basic pressure points that are appropriate for students to utilize when technology use is frequent. Students can hold pressure on these points for 2–3 minutes by using their index or ring finger.

- The area between the thumb and index finger
- The outer tip of the eyebrow
- One thumb-width above the midpoint of the eyebrow
- The point that lies beneath the cheekbone
- The point that lies on the outer border of the forearms, two finger-widths above the wrist
- The point that lies on the wrist in a shallow depression between the ends of the two forearm bones
- If the arm is bent at a right angle, a vertical groove will form on the front of the shoulder; this point lies at the center of this groove

- The point is located two finger-widths below the navel

- The point is located one thumb-width above the navel

- The point is located on the back, directly opposite to the navel, two finger-widths to either side

There are other pressure points that can be used to decrease discomfort so that students can focus on the academic goal as opposed to their pain. This SMART activity may be best served at the secondary level, with the exception of number one. This pressure point is used for a wide variety of ailments. Teachers are not expected to become experts on this topic. A classroom poster that provides a visual of pressure points can be an easy solution for giving students a means for managing their pain. Ideally, when teachers are incorporating STRIDES, there will be minimal to no time periods where technology is overused. However, there may be certain circumstances in which digital usage is high and applying pressure to these points can be helpful.

## Massage Therapy

This SMART activity is similar to pressure points in that educators are teaching students to manage their own areas of discomfort. *Massage therapy* in this instance refers to students using their hands, fingers, or an object (such as a stress ball) to massage muscles that are holding tension. For example, if students are sitting at their desks working on a writing assignment through traditional means or on a computer, they could use a stress ball or their fingers to massage the muscles in their neck to release tightness. This is very relaxing and can help to reduce stress and clear the mind to improve learning. The shoulders, neck, back, forehead, and temples are ideal locations for massage therapy. This SMART activity is something students can do quietly on their own, without requiring teacher guidance. Educators will only need to suggest this as an option for stress management while instructing students on what is and isn't an appropriate use of massage in a classroom setting. Similar to pressure points, this is a technique that will typically only be needed during times when technology use is frequent. When movement and technology are well balanced in the classroom, massage therapy may be a strategy that is recommended for home use rather than school, because technology use is often heavier there.

## Progressive Muscle Relaxation

Progressive muscle relaxation is a simple way for students to reduce their stress, tension, and anxiety levels in a learning environment. This strategy allows students to increase tension in designated body areas and then let it go in a controlled manner. An example would be to instruct students to tighten their fist and then release the grip, while asking them to notice the difference between tension and relaxation. It is recommended that the tensing and relaxing of the muscle groups is done in a specific order, generally beginning with the lower extremities and ending with the face or vice versa. There are scripts that educators can read or audios that can be used to take students through this process.

Once students learn this technique, they can use it at any time to reduce their anxiety in a manner that is not disruptive to their peers. Tensing and relaxing muscle groups can also be coupled with breathing exercises to get the most from the technique. Progressive muscle relaxation is an effective SMART activity that is not difficult for teachers or students to incorporate throughout their day. It can be a lengthy process that can last 10–15 minutes, but there are also examples that only last a few minutes, making this technique ideal for classroom implementation. This means for reducing stress and anxiety can be used for all grade levels, as long as students have the ability to comprehend the process and the meaning behind it.

## Affirmations and Positive Thinking

Building awareness about the thoughts and emotions that run through our minds throughout the day affects our entire outlook on life. If negative thoughts are continually present and statements of low self-worth are the norm, life will be less valued and enjoyed. This is true of our students and how they perceive a classroom environment. It is imperative that educators bring attention to students' thought processes. Teaching students to be aware of how they think about themselves and your classroom will help them to manage and control these thoughts. It is easy to get stuck on the negatives of any and all situations, just as it is easier to focus on our weaknesses as opposed to celebrating our strengths. But this type of thinking is not good for the learning process or the contentment of the student.

Teaching students to make positive, private self-affirmations on a regular basis can help to improve their self-esteem and result in positive thinking. This will have a direct impact on how they view your class and their comfort level. Educators are encouraged to give examples of positive affirmations while setting time aside to practice these skills in class. Urge students to do this often in school settings and anytime they are feeling low or at a negative place in their thoughts. Initially, this will need to be a SMART activity that is directed by the teacher. Hopefully, if practiced enough, students will begin to utilize this skill as a regular practice. Be sure students are aware of the significant role that their thoughts play on learning and their overall happiness. As you practice this technique with your students, it can also be used to uplift your own perspectives and views on your career and personal life.

## Environmental Settings

There are three controllable environmental factors that can benefit the classroom setting while reducing stress and anxiety: laughter, music, and darkening the room. Fostering a light-hearted learning space that welcomes humor and laughter will have a direct impact on students' learning potential. Students will enjoy the fun that your classroom supports and look forward to the experience. If this is not your personality by nature, allow students to create the humor as you enjoy it and accept it as an enhancer as opposed to an inhibitor. You do not want students to go overboard and turn your classroom into a circus; therefore, it is recommended that you set boundaries that allow for a proper balance. Laughter has a direct effect on a student's emotional learning state, so it should be a welcomed element in all classrooms.

Playing relaxing music or dimming the lights at certain points in the lesson can also help to relax students and produce a calming space. It is important to not overuse these tactics because they do not work for all learners. For example, some students might prefer brighter work places or no music (despite the type of music being played). In these cases, it is recommended that teachers look for a combination that seems to fit the needs of their students. It may even be possible in some classrooms to dim certain sections of the room while keeping other areas brighter and allowing students to choose where they'd like to work. If this isn't an option, look for places in the lesson where bright lights aren't needed or certain moments throughout the period where you can switch things up. Also, consider a wide range of music to play along with when it will enrich the learning and relax the students. Environmental settings are SMART tactics that can truly affect the emotional learning state of your students; be sure to include these in your planning and setup.

## Movement and Peer Relations

Two bonus SMART activities that have a profound effect on students' emotional learning states are movement and peer relations. These tactics are so critical that an entire chapter is devoted to one of them. Movement is explored throughout the book while teachers are encouraged to incorporate daily activities to benefit the learning process and increase student success. Peer relations and the concept of building learning communities are examined in Chapter 8. As previously mentioned, communication and comfort levels between peers is the second priority to the brain—more significant than the academic content that the educator is trying to teach. Implementing movement and peer relation activities are two SMART strategies that deliver the ultimate advantages for creating ideal emotional learning states, making them invaluable in all classrooms.

## SMART Activities: A Necessity

The twelve SMART activities described in this section provide clear teaching moments in which students can learn to decrease their stress levels, increase their positive thinking, and maintain desired emotional learning states. Students will learn to disconnect from content and then come back to it refocused and ready to attend to the upcoming academic goals. Learners will eventually manage their tensions after practicing strategies through teacher-directed sessions. SMART activities give our children and adolescents instrumental life skills that can be developed throughout their learning experiences. These techniques will provide opportunities for students to strengthen the ability of reengaging as well as clear their minds for a fresh cognitive start. Once these skills are learned, students will be able to take them outside of school settings to influence every aspect of their life and well-being. SMART activities are vital for all teachers in all classrooms to employ in order to improve academic achievement and educate the learner as a whole. They are necessary in order to achieve academic peak performance.

# IMPLEMENTATION CONSIDERATIONS

MTEs have four choices when deciding how to employ SMART activities in their classroom. Each method has its advantages, and it may be feasible to use all options throughout the school year. In each situation, students should be educated on the connection between learning and the emotional state. Understanding the importance of managing emotions, feelings, and thoughts is a critical skill for all students to acquire. Options are described as follows:

- **Routine based:** This refers to the concept of developing routines and practices in which students are instructed by the teacher to engage in SMART activities. This can occur daily, weekly, multiple times a day, every morning, after lunch, or at any other time. In this option, educators identify prime circumstances where stress levels tend to be elevated or negativity seems to escalate. SMART activities are then used to promote a calming state and positive thinking. Teachers can choose the SMART activity that is being used or they can establish creative practices to allow students to make the choice. Routine-based practices are especially effective at the beginning of the school year, when students are still learning classroom procedures and how to optimize their learning.

- **Situational:** This option signifies opportune times when SMART activities can be best utilized, for example, before a test, prior to learning new content, or after attending to specific content for a lengthy time. Employing SMART activities when situations are stressful or undesirable can help students perform better and think clearer. SMART activities do not need to be considered an established classroom routine but instead can be utilized only when needed or recommended by the teacher or students.

- **Student directed:** This method for employing SMART activities is guided by the teacher but managed by the student. Educators will give instructions and demonstrations on applicable activities so that students can learn to regulate their own emotional states for optimal learning. Initially, teachers may need to implement these activities so that students can become more familiar and comfortable with them. Eventually, the goal will be for students to utilize SMART activities when they feel they are in need of them. This option is directly in line with the previous notion of teaching students to build their self-awareness. If our learners can sense when they need to apply a SMART activity, then they can attend to this need and take action to reframe their own emotional state.

- **Combination:** Making this selection allows the educator to use all three choices as they see fit. The age and maturity level of the students, along with the time in the school year, may determine which method is more appropriate and beneficial for managing students' emotional states. As suggested in the opening paragraph, all options have their benefits, and circumstances may arise in which a variety of approaches may be suitable.

It is important to take the time to establish a goal(s) for employing SMART activities in your classroom. Please define your intentions and complete the questions that follow.

## SMART Goal

- List one specific, attainable, practical goal.
- What will you use to measure the level of success?
- What will you need to do or get to accomplish this goal?
- Is it a short- or long-term goal and when will you reach it?

## Questions

- Do you use stress management techniques in your own life? List examples.
- Can you see their value in your life? What about in education and in the learning process?
- Do you see high stress levels and/or negative thinking with your students regularly?
- List two or three of your favorite SMART activities from the choices provided.
- How often do you plan on using them?
- Will they be teacher directed, situational, student directed, or use a combination approach?
- Can you add any of your own ideas to the list provided?

## WHAT DOES THIS MEAN TO ME?

### K–12 Teachers

1. Discuss the importance of learning states with your students and lead them through one or two of the SMART activities described in this chapter.
2. Decide which method(s) you will utilize to employ SMART activities in your classroom.

### Administration

1. Create school-based programs that allow students to discuss and manage their mental/emotional well-being.
2. Provide professional development trainings that show teachers how to implement strategies to manage learners' feelings, emotions, and perceptions within the school culture.

*(Continued)*

(Continued)

**Educational Leaders/Affiliates**

1. Initiate open discussions on mental health, acceptance, support, and understanding.

2. Present and provide information on how and why the mental/emotional well-being of students affects their state of mind and learning potential. Encourage educators to make this a priority.

# CHAPTER SUMMARY

- It is imperative for students to have a sense of emotional regulation in your classroom so they can remember, transfer, and recall information. Having the ability to learn new information effectively and connect it to prior knowledge is also affected by students' emotional learning states.

- Emotions drive our attention, concentration, and how we view our surroundings. In your classroom, students will develop core memories based on past events, current experiences, and relationships. These memories are critical to students' learning states.

- Employing SMART activities on a regular basis is a simple, doable means for building positive core memories and calming feelings. *SMART* stands for **s**tress **m**anagement **a**nd **r**elaxation **t**echniques.

- Academic overload occurs when teachers move deeply into their content at a pace that increases students' stress levels to the point where productivity is lost. If we aim for optimal academic performance, the emotional state must take precedence over the academic content.

- SMART activities should be used as a proactive approach for maintaining positive learning states because of the following benefits: lowered risk of illness; increased memory, focus, and brain functioning; increased willingness to tackle challenging tasks; better decision making; lowered frustration levels; better relationships and communication; decreased impatience, irritability, and anger; greater access to intuition; elimination of unnecessary energy drain; and a positive learning experience.

- SMART activities include yoga, manipulatives, mindfulness, brain escapes, breathing exercises, pressure points, massage therapy, progressive muscle relaxation, affirmations and positive thinking, environmental settings, movement, and peer relations.

- Educators have four choices for deciding how to employ SMART activities in their classroom: routine based, situational, student directed, or a combination.

- It is important for teachers to take the time to establish a goal(s) for employing SMART activities in their classroom.

# 11

# SUPPORTING A
# UNITED APPROACH

## AN EDUCATIONAL PIONEER

### The Power of Influence

Throughout this book, we've introduced you to a new and exciting concept in education: becoming a movement and technology educator (MTE). Your commitment to changing the direction of education for the 21st-century learner is not one to be taken lightly. Extraordinary change requires extraordinary people, and MTEs—without a doubt—are educational pioneers! Your passion for change, your willingness to try something new, and your sincere care for the well-being of your students is what drives you to embrace this innovative teaching methodology. That mindset needs to extend outside your classroom walls to create a united approach of teaching and learning! As an educational pioneer, you are in the unique position to influence and connect others to this method, both inside and outside of school. Educational leaders hold a significant amount of influence and power among colleagues, students, administrators, parents, and community professionals. Sharing what you have learned on your journey of combining movement and technology allows people of all backgrounds to connect with each other and come together to support an educational philosophy that facilitates not only increased academic success, but a shift in physical and social/emotional well-being for our future generations. MTEs are not meant to stand alone: No one person can make the necessary shift in education without the support of those around them. This is where the power of influence becomes an extremely important and effective tool for increasing the movement and technology (MT) balance in schools throughout the United States and perhaps the world! You never know who is watching you, and your example can encourage and motivate the people around you, from students (who are our future teachers!) to colleagues to complete strangers. Let's explore the three directions that your power of influence can take you.

## Leading Up

All too often in the educational world, teachers feel frustrated by academic policy and decision making that is done by officials who aren't actually in the classroom. Being down in the trenches, actually observing and experiencing the changes that our students have faced over the years, provides educators with a level of expertise that is highly valuable to the school organization. MTEs have a level of education and experience that can effectively influence their superiors and provide them with the insight they need to get on board with this new and innovative teaching methodology. The idea is to help our school administrators, superintendents, and school boards see and understand why balancing movement and technology in the classroom is an important way to reach our current learners. Gaining the support of your superiors is going to aid you in achieving your personal classroom MT goals and will ultimately create a trickle-down effect as those administrators in turn influence their peers, their own superiors, and their subordinates.

Influencing your superior is sometimes referred to as *leading up*. It is an active process in which you ultimately have to allow your confidence to be your guide as you put yourself out there with your administration and stretch your comfort level. Armed with research from this book, as well as your personal successes in implementing an MT classroom thus far, you can shift your focus to the greater good: creating real and positive change in education for the 21st century. Without a doubt, this can be an intimidating charge. It is important that you prepare yourself mentally and actively search for opportunities to lead up with your administration. Start by developing personal relationships with the superiors you want to influence. Learn about who they are as administrators and try to anticipate where their reservations will be. Be prepared with your knowledge and research, and let the amazing job you've been doing as an MTE lead your approach. More importantly, believe that your voice is heard, be ready to have honest conversations, and be willing to take a risk! Here are some simple ideas to use as a jumping-off point for leading up:

- Invite your administrator to your classroom to observe your balanced MT lessons.

- Share your recent successes with your administration through e-mail, at faculty meetings, or during evaluation meetings.

- Write a letter to the principal detailing the research behind a balanced MT classroom.

- Write a letter to the school board and/or superintendent detailing your new initiatives in the classroom.

- Present a videotaped MT lesson to the board at their monthly meeting.

- Arrange face-to-face meetings with your administrators to share your successes with them.

- Apply for a grant to fund your initiatives so your superiors can recognize your effort.

- Create and send a short PowerPoint presentation to your principal(s) about the benefits of an MT classroom. Encourage them to share it at the next faculty meeting.

## Leading Down

*Leading down* is exactly what it sounds like: looking for leadership opportunities with those who are below you in the chain of command. In this case, leading down is directly influencing our students to become part of the positive change that occurs both inside and outside of the MT classroom. They will be the teachers, politicians, board members, parents, and community members who will ultimately advocate for permanent change (or not) within our schools. We have written the chapters in this book with our students in mind, wanting what's best for them academically, physically, mentally, and socially/emotionally. It only makes sense that we would also encourage them to come alongside us, advocating for a school experience that is tailored to meet their needs, and becoming an active part of the success of the MT classroom. As educators, we are always influencing our students in some way. Becoming an MTE is going to change the classroom experience for your students forever. We are strengthening their problem-solving skills, improving their peer-to-peer relationships and interpersonal skills, increasing their overall sense of well-being, and teaching them to maintain a healthy lifestyle (all while meeting rigorous curriculum standards). Why not teach students to be lifelong learners and active and engaged members of their own environment? When students feel passionate about something, they can be vigorous—and quite effective—agents for change! Here are some simple ideas for getting your students involved in advocating for change:

- Encourage students to talk it up with anyone who will listen (peers in other schools, family members, coaches, etc.). Even students as young as kindergarten age can share what they love about the MT classroom!

- Ask for student volunteers to film video testimonials.

- Arrange a student meeting with administration to explain why an MT classroom is important to them.

- Inspire students to attend and speak up at board meetings about their positive experiences.

- Include students in the MT planning: Ask students for their opinion, have them generate their own ideas for movement and technology, and allow for a level of ownership over the classroom activities whenever possible.

- Send students into the community. Create a project in which students pick a community organization to reach out to and share the good things that are happening in their educational experience.

- Require students to balance movement and technology on their own whenever they complete a task, project, or homework assignment.

- Set a good example: Show your students that when it comes to balancing movement and technology, it's *do as I do* not *do as I say*.

## Leading Across

*Leading across* (sometimes called *leading sideways*) is the ability to influence your peers, colleagues, or teams of people who have equal authority as you. In the school setting, your peers are not limited to your fellow teachers. Consider that leading across can also include your influence on paraprofessionals, guidance counselors, secretarial staff, custodial staff, nursing staff, individuals from outside agencies (for example, therapeutic staff support or behavioral health specialists), and the parents and guardians of your students. While this is not an all-inclusive list, it is meant to give you a glimpse of how broad leading across can be. As an educational pioneer, you receive the respect and admiration of your peers. It is that respect that creates the unique power of influence you have in these situations. While you may certainly be taking the lead when it comes to becoming an MTE, involving your peers in the process is not only good for the initiative; it's good for the overall health of your school, as it allows everyone the opportunity to take a role in creating positive change and increasing students' success. If we want permanent change in our schools, we can't stand alone. Encouraging your peers to join you in this crusade results in strength in numbers, an obvious advantage for you when it comes to leading up. Your influence among your peers can create a comfortable and safe outlet for gathering multiple sources of ideas, facilitating collaboration among other potential MTEs, and increasing the buzz in the community. Combining your expertise and drive with your ability to mobilize others to get on board will initiate the momentum needed in our schools for real change to begin. Here are some simple ideas for motivating your peers to support this innovative way of teaching and learning:

- Make noise! Allow your colleagues to see and hear what's going on in your classroom.

- Offer to be a mentor. Share what you've learned about becoming an MTE and help others as they encounter the same obstacles that you have.

- Challenge your peers to track the technological usage versus physical movement of their children or themselves for one week. It will be eye opening!

- Start a YouTube channel and post videos of your successful integrated lessons. Encourage parents and colleagues to subscribe.

- Organize a presentation on movement and technology for Back to School night or Meet the Teacher night.

- Create a brief pamphlet on the research that supports the need for change in the classroom.

- Create your lesson plans using Google Docs and share them with your teaching team. Ask for their input or suggestions on designing MT lessons.

- Organize a think tank/work session/fishbowl exercise to encourage others to try balancing movement and technology.

- Create a Facebook group as a place to collaborate and share ideas and invite parents, colleagues, and friends to join.

## Leading by Example

Effective leaders always lead by example. When you lead by example, you become an inspiration to others. As an MTE, your positive example will influence administrators, teachers, and students alike as well as create notoriety outside of the school setting. All hands are needed on deck if we want to make this vision a reality. We need to change the mindset of a lot of people, including both the supporters and the naysayers. To do this, some important qualities are needed to effectively lead by example: honesty, transparency, confidence, and professionalism. Honesty *is* always the best policy, and transparency is key to being a leader. Colleagues will find that they can rely on your experiences to shape their own attempts at becoming an MTE because you have always been honest and transparent about what has been successful, what has failed, and what has failed at first and then been successful. Confidence is also required to effectively lead by example. You've been armed with the research that backs your choice to make this positive change in your classroom. Without confidence, true leadership cannot exist! Being professional requires more than acting mature and being well kept. A true professional is a listener, a leader, and a delegator. Demonstrate your leadership by modeling what you've learned but never be afraid of delegating tasks for others to try. True professionalism is not only the ability to share what you know, but the courage to admit what others may know better.

Notice we didn't include the word *expertise* in our list. *You do not have to be an expert in integrating movement and technology into the classroom in order to lead by example.* While the other qualities listed can make or break you as a leader, being considered an expert isn't absolutely necessary. In fact, it is often the ability to fail with grace (and being honest and transparent about those failures) that earns the most respect from others. When you publicly fail, you are allowing those you lead to accept and embrace their own failures. It solidifies the idea that failure is a natural part of any process and is necessary to facilitate growth and change. Messing up means we have to clean up. Every mistake requires problem solving and solution-oriented planning in order to overcome the mistake, developing key leadership skills. The persistence to work through obstacles and challenges is not only admirable but offers a high level of personal and professional growth and encourages healthy self-reflection. It is safe to say that our failures actually *contribute* to becoming an expert rather than hinder those efforts.

# A COMPREHENSIVE ACTION PLAN

## Goal Driven

One of the biggest problems in executing any great idea is failure to follow through. In order to facilitate real change in the 21st-century classroom, strategic planning and implementation will be necessary. As an MTE, you will need to develop an action plan that has meaningful intention. An action plan will assist you in turning visions, hopes, and dreams into tangible results. As an educational pioneer, your action plan will define the mission and objectives for creating and sustaining an MT environment. But it will also serve as an opportunity for you to bring people together to collaborate and build a consensus for why this change is pertinent for the school as a whole. Developing an action plan can foster a place in which a group of educators reflects on past educational practice, evaluates what has and hasn't worked, and unites together to move forward on building a better future for our students. Action plans should include both long- and short-term goals with detailed, step-by-step plans that yield immediate responses and a way of measuring progress along the way. Setting goals is a fundamental part of making dreams a reality. A goal-driven action plan would include the following:

- An overall goal

- Several smaller goals that support the broader goal

- The specific anticipated results for each goal

- A concise timeline for the goals to be completed

- A clear way to measure the progress or success of each goal

Both short- and long-term goals should be included in your MTE plan and considered critical to this progressive purpose. One of the first questions an MTE should consider when formulating goals is "Why do I want to create a classroom environment that balances movement and technology?" Was it your overall concern for the health and wellness of our future generation? Perhaps it was the astonishing statistics from Chapters 2 and 3 that really inspired you to become a part of this new idea. Whatever your reasons, use them to inspire your goals. Include both the needs of the students and your own needs as an educator. Develop goals that support quick action in the classroom with long-range thinking and a perspective of unlimited possibilities. Figure 11.1 shows us an example of an action plan for the MTE. Keep in mind that this example is merely that: a sample to use as a springboard for launching your own ideas. Your action plan may be similar or completely different in style, goals, and overall objectives.

##  Prepare for Resistance

Resistance is the normal human reaction to change. People often resist change out of fear: fear of losing control or not being able to adapt to the new normal. Considering that education and instructional delivery strategies have remained relatively the same for decades, it only makes sense that there will be some resistance to this innovative way of looking at the classroom experience. Although best practice for teachers is to commit to lifelong learning, it is easy (and common) to get into a rut and become creatures of habit. Lessons that have worked in the past build credibility and are repeated. We are deeply emotional and passionate about the field we've dedicated our lives to, and it is exactly that emotion that prevents us from embracing change, no matter how logical it may be. The MTE knows better, though. You know that today's student has different needs, interacts with a different world, and has been shown to be physiologically different than any student who

| **FIGURE 11.1** ■ **Sample Action Plan** | | | | |
|---|---|---|---|---|
| **Overall Goal** *Long-Term Goal* | **Supporting Goals** *Short-Term Goal(s)* | **Timeline** *When will it be done?* | **Strategy** *How will I do it?* | **Results** *How can I measure success?* |
| To get my students moving more during research assignments | Students will move through stations during our recurring current events lessons. | End of 2nd marking period | • Place technology at stations around the room. <br>• Raise desk height for writing while standing. <br>• Add flexible seating. <br>• Explicitly teach the technology rotation model. | • Stations will be visible and clearly marked. <br>• Students will be explicitly taught how to use the stations. <br>• Lesson plans will include details for rotation and movement combined with technology objectives. |
| To convince my teaching team to try an MT approach with research assignments | 1. Invite teachers to observe my current events lesson. <br>2. Teachers will increase the rate of technology to movement in their classroom to 1:1. | End of 3rd marking period | 1.1 Ask administration to get coverage for observations. <br>1.2 Present mock lesson at spring in-service day. <br>2.1 Meet with a team to plan for brainstorming session. <br>2.2 Create and share a Google Doc lesson plan as a sample of a balanced technology and movement lesson. | 1.1 Observations will occur. <br>1.2 Post-observation feedback will be gathered. <br>2.1 Teachers will calculate and report the minutes spent on both movement and technology during their recurring current events lessons. |

graduated in the 20th century. It is our responsibility to these students to ensure that our teaching methodologies roll with the changes, too.

Be aware that when you offer a new approach to teaching and learning, educators may feel defensive, intimidated, or even standoffish. Be ready to encourage them and validate and identify with their feelings, but insist that they listen with an open mind before jumping to any conclusions. One final thing to consider is that the resistance you may face may not come from the teachers and other professionals you are trying to influence; it may come from the students themselves. Although we know that students need to move more, and we know that technology usage needs to be embraced yet balanced, the MT classroom looks different than other classrooms. Students are used to sitting at their desks, but now we are going to make them move. Students are used to communicating digitally, but now we are going to ask them to collaborate in multiple ways. Students are used to fading into the background while using their devices, but now we are bringing the devices to the forefront and actively using them with purpose. It will be important to validate our students' feelings, assure them that all will be okay, and involve them in the process. Ask them for their input and feedback. In the end, though, we know that this is what's best for them, so be ready to hold students accountable. The students need to understand that you run an MT classroom and that all activities, both movement and technology based, are not optional.

## Dealing With Doubt

As an educational pioneer who is leading by example, your confidence is one of your key qualities. You are a distinguished teacher who serves as a role model for your students and peers alike. Hang on to that confidence tightly; unfortunately, you may encounter those who doubt not only the effectiveness of this forward-thinking teaching method but also your rationale for embracing it in the first place. According to entrepreneur and best-selling author Kevin Daum (2013), there are five great ways to deal with the doubters:

1. **Redirect them:** Point them in the direction of their own situation or activities.

2. **Give them credence:** Give them credit for pointing out potential flaws in your plan and offer to take the advice under consideration.

3. **Answer their objections:** Be ready to show them facts and support your argument with knowledge.

4. **Recruit them:** Ask them to share their knowledge with you and join in your mission.

5. **Eliminate them:** It's okay to let them go!

Point the doubters in the direction of their own classroom. Consider if what they are saying has any merit, and if so, heed their advice (or discard it if it's without merit!). Hold fast to what we know about the brain–body connection. Be prepared to share the statistics and research behind why you've committed to this endeavor. If you value their opinion, ask them to join you in becoming an MTE. Mostly, though, keep sharing your success! No argument produces stronger results than one with evidence. When doubters see and hear about the changes you're experiencing, the increased success of your students, the passion that has been ignited, and the love of learning that your students feel, they will not be able to argue. It is important to surround yourself with those who support you; don't take to heart all the negativity. You only have to justify your philosophy to yourself, and the only ones you owe anything to are your students. They are, after all, the whole reason we are here.

## Celebrate Small Victories

Small victories are the measurable progress points you make throughout your action plan. We've already talked about ensuring that your plan has measurable goals. Breaking down any task into manageable chunks is a key detail in strategic planning. The road to a united approach to teaching and learning can be a long one and can overwhelm even the most veteran teacher. Breaking our overall goals into smaller, measurable, short-term goals can make this daunting task feel a little smaller. And despite those best-laid plans, unexpected circumstances or challenges can always arise to deter us from our course. The little wins make us feel happy and help us keep our eye on the prize despite the curve balls being thrown at us (and in education, that feels like it happens a lot, right?). Taking time to celebrate the things that are going well and the goals we've met build our confidence levels and motivate us to keep going with the action plan. Remembered to pencil body breaks into your lesson plans? Planned a community connector and incorporated teams using iPads? Tossed your study guide and planned an active review game instead? These are all great wins that deserve recognition! Treat yourself to a little something from the faculty lounge vending machine, brag to your coworkers at lunch, or drop an e-mail to your principal to share the good news. With each little win, you are getting closer to your overall goal, so go ahead and celebrate those small victories!

# REACHING THE HOME

## Involving Parents and Families

It is much easier for teachers and administrators to control what happens throughout the school day compared to what happens in the home environment. Yet, building and maintaining a school–home connection is significant in optimizing student success. Research consistently shows that parent involvement improves overall student achievement. With this in mind, passionate MTEs take on the responsibility of informing families of the purpose and extreme benefits of **m**oving students **o**ften with a **s**teady flow of **t**echnology (MOST) throughout the academic day. Having supportive families is important to your process and is worth the extra effort it may take. Many educators don't engage with parents and families because they think they can't. They worry that parents aren't interested in what's happening or don't want to be involved. The truth is, most parents don't know *how* to be involved in the classroom experience. There are a variety of circumstances that can lead to this feeling. Working multiple jobs, a negative experience with schooling, a language barrier, medical or mental health issues, and finances (causing lack of transportation or technology in the home) can all negatively affect a parent's ability to engage in their child's education. It is extremely important that MTEs break through these potential barriers. Teachers and parents alike want to improve the school experience for students and ensure that they are engaged in a supportive and caring learning environment.

The best way to begin involving parents and families is to open the lines of communication. We want to talk with parents about what is happening in the classroom and we want to get them talking about the MT balance at home. Ideally, it would be nice to invite family members into the school to provide information and show examples of activities that will be used in the MT classroom. Face-to-face conversations and presentations are the best way to convey your enthusiasm and passion for the well-being of your students. You can also share the information during Meet the Teacher night, open house, or parent–teacher conferences held at the school. Developing a website, informational brochures, or newsletters are other effective ways to communicate your goals and objectives to the home. E-mails or mobile communication apps (such as auto callers like Parent Link or SMS apps like Remind) can provide an accessible and efficient way to reach multiple families at once. There are a variety of ways to effectively open the lines of communication and be sure that your objectives and goals are being heard. Let's not forget, though, that listening is another important aspect of communication. MTEs need to listen to the concerns of the families. Communicating with parents helps us truly get to know our students. Learning about their home lives helps us understand their background, the skills they come to school with (or lack), and how their home life affects and shapes their education. As we move toward building an innovative classroom for the 21st century, this background knowledge is essential.

##  Getting Buy-In

Convincing others that change is necessary can be a daunting task. As a leader in education, you'll quickly find that you need to have parents and families buy in to your vision for the MT classroom. Even with the best-laid action plan and the greatest intentions, pioneering change and creating a united approach to education can only be done with the support of everyone affected; this includes the students and their families. Consider this:

> Ongoing research shows that family engagement in schools improves student achievement, reduces absenteeism and restores parents' confidence in their children's education. Students with involved parents or other caregivers earn higher grades and test scores, have better social skills and show improved behavior. (Garcia & Thornton, 2015)

The benefits of family engagement on student achievement are exactly the same outcomes we are looking for in an MT classroom. When parents truly believe in what we are doing in the classroom, they are more likely to offer assistance to the classroom teacher, challenge their child to persevere, and contribute to their child's overall achievement. Parents and families who buy into the MT philosophy will also assist you in extending your influential reach. Businesses often know that one of the most powerful marketing tactics is word of mouth. MTEs must embrace this strategy as well! What better way to facilitate the change we so desire in schools than to have our very own students and their families spreading the word about the amazing things that are going on in the classroom! Here are some ways to foster parent and family buy-in and get people talking about what's happening in your classroom:

- **Get the information out there:** Parents can't be excited about something they know nothing about. You will need to develop a way (or better yet, several ways) to let parents know about your MT classroom. Be sure to include specific details about what it is and how it differs from most traditional educational settings.

- **Explain the *why*:** Telling parents why you have embarked on this journey will be crucial to getting buy-in. Parents need to know the astonishing statistics outlined in Chapters 2 and 3, the declining overall academic achievement of our students, and the threat that our sedentary lifestyle places on their children's future. In fact, you may want to consider leading your informational delivery with the *why* for a more significant impact!

- **Explain the *why* some more!** For most of us, committing to becoming an MTE was an emotional decision, one driven by our passionate response to what we presently see happening and our predicted future. We need to tap into that same emotional response for parents, and this will come from repeatedly stating why this change is needed in our schools.

- **Ask for input:** Allowing parents to offer suggestions, give feedback or constructive criticism, and ask questions helps them feel like they are contributors to your idea rather than merely receptors. Asking for input communicates to parents that you value them as a partner in this endeavor.

- **Arm yourself:** Be ready for battle with stories of change and success. Every new idea will have its critics, but they can't argue with proven results. You'll need to share the big ways that you've seen positive change for your students.

- **Wear your emotions:** Allowing parents to see your enthusiasm, your passion, and your heart helps them identify your intentions. When parents believe that you truly have their child's best interests at heart, they will always be on your side. Let them see why this is important to you and how much you truly care for your students and their future.

##  Strengthening the Home–School Connection

In order for real change to occur for our nation's future, we need to bridge the gap of recognizing the importance of balanced movement and technology at school *and* at home. This is a strong message to support. Many parents are aware of and concerned about the sedentary lifestyle of their children. How many times have you heard a parent or grandparent say, "When we got home from school, we were outside until the sun went down, not like kids these days"? This common statement is meant to imply that today's child isn't only sitting still all day at school, but they are coming home and sitting still. While there are exceptions (after-school activities and sports, for example), what percentage of the at-home hours are today's youth spending being active? Parents are frustrated with technology addiction, lack of motivation, unhealthy eating and exercise habits, and general lazy attitudes. When we communicate the importance of the MT classroom and show parents that we are actively pursuing ways to even the score among screen time, sit time, and movement, we are encouraging them that they can also try to find more balance with this at home. Strengthening the home–school connection plays a huge role in shaping healthier habits for students using technology both inside and outside of school. That being said, many parents may not know where to begin. They will need to rely on your expertise and creativity to guide them along the way. Remember that parents may be intimidated by movement or technology, as you once were. Some simple suggestions that are a great place for parents to start with their children might be to include allowing movement or standing during tech time, encouraging pacing or walking up and down the steps while talking on the phone, playing active video games (including those with motion-sensing devices, such as the Xbox Kinect) or using apps that are active (such as a charades app), setting a timer for intervals of screen time and stretch breaks, making kids earn their screen time through an equivalent number of active minutes, or carving out specific technology-free family time that is nonnegotiable. Parents who are receptive and value teacher input will be grateful for your concern and interest in their child. Building an MT classroom creates a wonderful opportunity to connect with parents about something new and exciting that will benefit the whole child and redirect their potential future wellness.

# REACHING THE COMMUNITY

##  Communicating the *Why*

Creating a partnership between the school and the community enables the students to thrive in an atmosphere that supports and promotes their overall success and well-being. As an educational pioneer, we must bring together diverse organizations that all have one thing in common: being stakeholders in the education of the children in a given community. By extending the opportunity for community organizations to contribute to the health and wellness of our youth, they are directly pouring their resources back into the same youth that frequent their businesses or partake in their services. Working together with the community to embrace an MT philosophy will have a positive impact on both the academic success and healthy lifestyles of our students. Schools (or more specifically, teachers) cannot change the future alone. It requires a shared sense of responsibility and accountability for the overall wellness of our nation. This can only be expressed through continual communication of why we need to implement MT classrooms across the nation. It is our responsibility as MTEs to open the eyes of the community to an ongoing crisis in and out of our schools. Leveraging the services that the community has to offer will improve the effectiveness of the MT classroom, support the efforts of the parents at home, and contribute to the betterment of society as a whole.

##  Creating Partnerships

Strong community partnerships are essential in creating a 21st-century educational experience that goes way beyond college and career readiness. Community partnerships should enhance the school experience and support the needs of the students. We need to strategically work together to achieve physical, social, and mental/emotional wellness for the next generation.

In all fairness, creating a successful community–school partnership is not easy. In fact, it can be a time-consuming and challenging journey to embark on. In order to make the best use of your time and effort, attempting to create a community partnership needs to be a well-thought-out process with willing participants on both sides. We encourage you to take advantage of the connections you've made while leading up and across, as having a large source of other professionals who can add their expertise and assistance will certainly come in handy. You will be at an advantage when you have a broad range of individuals with varying experiences and perspectives to draw from for input and advice. These teams will positively impact your ability to manage the organizational workload, obtain or disperse resources, and follow through with ideas without becoming overwhelmed or frustrated. Here are some simple ideas for creating community partnership events that positively impact the MT classroom. Use them to inspire your own ideas or let them motivate you to reach out to the organizations in your community.

- Partner with the local library to obtain funding for kinesthetic furniture for use in their computer rooms. Promote the use of the library to your students.

- Invite affiliates from local hospitals or clinics to become regular guests and active participants in your MT classroom. As they build relationships with the students, they can influence them to make healthy lifestyle choices.

- Work with a local park to offer summer activity programs that get kids outside and offer to promote them within the school.

- Partner with law enforcement to hold workshops on cyberbullying, conflict resolution, and interpersonal skills—these are all important skills in the MT classroom.

- Have students join efforts with a neighborhood-beautifying group. Encourage students to form a team using social media and networking. Then get outside and get moving!

- Partner with a local gym to offer student incentives: Students can earn gym time through participation in educational activities at school. Students can also earn rewards at school for time spent at the gym.

# FINAL THOUGHTS: A MOTIVATIONAL MAGNET

## Fun for All

Throughout the course of the book, we've discussed the ways that balancing technology and movement in the classroom creates a stimulating learning environment that increases academic success and improves overall health and wellness. One thing that should not be overlooked is the measure of fun that the MT classroom brings. Having fun is a motivational magnet. It has a positive effect on how ready we are to learn and how much we retain. Winston Churchill once said, "I'm always ready to learn, although I do not always like being taught." How many adults and children can identify with this? It sadly seems that we have come to a point in education where the word *fun* is not a consideration. We are focused on such words as *rigor*, *standards*, *achievement*, *proficiency*, *testing*, and *attentiveness*. What about bringing some enjoyment to what we are learning? Why is there an incorrect association that having fun means being off-task? How many of our students are ready to learn but do not like being taught? The MT classroom embraces a united approach in which both movement and technology combine to entice the brain and body to come together for learning. Content is strategically woven in and around the two, creating an environment where the work is so fun that the students forget that they are learning. Having fun in the classroom has a positive impact on learning, retention and recall, and willingness to try new things. Students grow outside their comfort zone, interact more personally with one another, and become active and willing participants in the learning process. As we think back to our own school experiences, what wouldn't we give to have been in a classroom like that!

## Individual Abilities and Interests

As educators, we know that a one-size-fits-all approach to education doesn't work. That's why *differentiation* is and has been such a buzz word for many years. Each student has a way of learning that is personalized and effective, and it's our responsibility to tap into that for each and every student. The MT classroom fully supports education that is tailored to individual abilities and interests. We need to shake things up a little bit in education, thinking outside the box to provide our students with various types of instructional delivery to meet their varying needs. Using movement in the classroom helps students focus better, process information more deeply, and recall more clearly. It reduces behavioral challenges and increases student participation and engagement. It creates a novelty that is attractive to the brain. It considers the students' attention spans, interests, and the needs of the body. Using technology in the classroom engages students on a level that they are comfortable with by bringing devices that are ingrained in their lifestyles into the classroom. Technology allows for easily collaborating with others. It brings an entire world of information to the students' fingertips. It piques their interests in assignments because it is comfortable and familiar to them. Both movement and technology, either individually or in combination with one another, can act as a catalyst to developing each student's unique learning style. The MT classroom combines all of those benefits into one truly original and innovative experience for the 21st-century learner because it allows students to find and rely on their own individual strengths as they combat and grow through their weaknesses. It provides a teaching methodology that caters to differentiation by allowing students to work at various paces and on various assignments at any given time. Teachers can move students through progressively challenging tasks at a pace that is tailored to the students' needs and is delivered in a style that is tailored to students' interests. This approach to learning unites teachers and students by creating a classroom partnership that everyone enjoys.

## Increasing Students' Love for Learning

In the end, all educators, whether MTEs or not, want to inspire a true love of learning in their students. The real goal in education is to create true learners: students who embrace challenges, persevere through setbacks, think critically about problems, and collaborate with others to find solutions. We want students to *want* to learn. We want students to *love* to learn. We want students who are *ready and willing* to learn. In the world of continuously changing educational initiatives, our best allies are the students themselves. What better way to foster that than through an instructional delivery that intentionally exposes the idea that learning can be engaging and fun? We're not trying to hide our curriculum behind the screens or in the movements. We're allowing students to see that the brain and body are connected and that using the methods that satisfy those needs creates the ideal learning environment. We're showing students that we care enough about their entire well-being to think beyond paper and pencil, beyond desks and chairs. We're encouraging them to find happiness in school and allowing *their* physical needs and *their* personal interests to play a role in designing *their* educational experience. The MT classroom provides a way for students to do things differently, to try something in a new way, and to develop a love for the process. We're keeping the students at the heart of our instruction, which is how it always should be.

# WHAT DOES THIS MEAN TO ME?

### K–12 Teachers

1. Provide parents, guardians, and family members with information about the MT balance and why it is a primary focus in your classroom. Include the pros of kinesthetic learning, the concerns of too much technology, and the benefits of combining these two concepts to improve learning while educating the child as a whole.

2. Talk with colleagues and administrators about the importance of the MT balance along with the changes you are making or have made in your classroom and perhaps in your own personal life as well.

### Administration

1. Work with your faculty to hold a community event that shares information on the significance of the MT balance and the ways to increase movement in the home and community.

2. Commend and acknowledge teachers in your school that are leaders in implementing a successful, workable balance between movement and technology. Invite them to share their experiences with their peers.

### Educational Leaders/Affiliates

1. Design a course of action that strengthens the school–home–community connection so that changes can be comprehensive and cultural as opposed to solely educational.

2. Increase awareness through more research and through discussions regarding the problems related to excessive technology use in schools, homes, and communities. Support and praise learning institutes that develop balanced programs, especially ones that include an all-inclusive, united approach.

# CHAPTER SUMMARY

- As an educational pioneer, you hold a significant amount of influence and power among colleagues, students, administrators, parents, and community professionals. This power of influence is an effective tool for increasing the MT balance in schools throughout the United States.

- Using your influence to lead up, down, and across will help gain the support of the school and surrounding community and will help them understand why balancing movement and technology in the classroom is an important way to reach our current learners.

- Combining your expertise and drive with your ability to mobilize others to get on board will initiate the momentum needed in our schools for real change to begin.

- Honesty and transparency, confidence, and professionalism are the important qualities needed to effectively lead by example. Additionally, you do not have to be an expert in integrating movement and technology into the classroom in order to lead by example.

- In order to facilitate real change in the 21st-century classroom, strategic planning and implementation will be necessary. As an MTE, you will need to develop an action plan that has meaningful intentions.

- Action plans should include an overall goal, several smaller goals that support the broader goal, the specific anticipated results for each goal, a concise timeline for the goals to be completed, and a clear way to measure the progress or success of each goal.

- As you work through your action plan and influence the educational community around you, prepare to manage the initial resistance that may be shown by colleagues, parents, and students alike.

- Be sure to celebrate the small successes along the journey through your action plan. They will motivate you to keep going and will help the process seem less daunting.

- Parent involvement improves overall student achievement. It is extremely important that MTEs open the lines of communication with parents to ensure that we provide a supportive and caring learning environment for our students.

- Creating a partnership between the school and the community enables students to thrive in an atmosphere that supports and promotes their overall success and well-being. Strong community partnerships enhance the school experience and support the needs of the students.

- Balancing technology and movement in the classroom creates a fun and stimulating learning environment that increases academic success and improves student motivation.

- MTEs provide a teaching methodology that easily differentiates and caters to students' individual abilities and interests.

- A united approach inspires a true love of learning in our students and keeps their best interests at the heart of our instructional delivery.

# REFERENCES AND RESOURCES

ACHPER National. (2011). *Sitness vs. fitness*. Retrieved from http://achper.org.au

Adams, J. U. (2013, October 21). Physical activity may help kids do better in school, studies say. *The Washington Post*. Retrieved from https://www.washingtonpost.com/national/health-science/physical-activity-may-help-kids-do-better-in-school-studies-say/2013/10/21/e7f86306-2b87-11e3-97a3-ff2758228523_story.html

Ahamed, Y., Macdonald, H., Reed, K., Naylor, P. J., Liu-Ambrose, T., & McKay, H. (2007). School-based physical activity does not compromise children's academic performance. *Medicine and Science in Sports and Exercise*, *39*(2), 371–376.

Alsop, R. (2014, July 17). Instant gratification & its dark side. *Bucknell University*. Retrieved from https://www.bucknell.edu/about-bucknell/communications/bucknell-magazine/recent-issues/summer-2014/instant-gratification-and-its-dark-side

American Academy of Pediatrics. (2011). Combining physical activity with classroom lessons results in improved test scores. *Science Daily*. Retrieved from https://sciencedaily.com/release/2011/05/110501183653.htm

American Optometric Association (AOA). (2015, July 28). The 21st century child: Increased technology use may lead to future eye health and vision issues. *American Optometric Association*. Retrieved from https://www.aoa.org/newsroom/the-21st-century-child-increased-technology-use-may-lead-to-future-eye-health-and-vision-issues

Anderson, M., Perrin, A., & Jiang, J. (2018, March 5). 11% of Americans don't use the Internet. Who are they? *Pew Research Center*. Retrieved from http://www.pewresearch.org/fact-tank/2018/03/05/some-americans-dont-use-the-internet-who-are-they/

Bailey, B. (n.d.). The conscious discipline brain state model. *Conscious Discipline*. Retrieved from https://consciousdiscipline.com/methodology/brain-state-model/

Barker, B. (2018, July 20). Too much screen time hurting kids' eyes. *Record-Courier*. Retrieved from http://www.record-courier.com/news/20180720/too-much-screen-time-hurting-kids-eyes

Bartholomew, J. B., & Jowers, E. M. (2011). Physically active academic lessons in elementary children. *Preventative Medicine*, *52*(Supplement 1), S51–S54.

Basch, C. E. (2010). Healthier students are better learners: A missing link in efforts to close achievement gaps. *Journal of School Health*, *81*(10). Retrieved from https://onlinelibrary.wiley.com/doi/epdf/10.1111/j.1746-1561.2011.00632.x

Baxter, S. D., Royer, J. A., Hardin, J. W., Guinn, C. H., & Devlin, C. M. (2011). The relationship of school absenteeism with body mass index, academic achievement, and socioeconomic status among fourth grade children. *Journal of School Health*, *81*(7), 417–423.

Beck, M. M., Lind, R. R., Geertsen, S. S., Ritz, C., Lundbye-Jensen, J., & Wienecke J. (2016). Motor-enriched learning activities can improve mathematical performance in preadolescent children. *Frontiers in Human Neuroscience*, *10*, 645. doi: 10.3389/fnhum.2016.00645

Benden, M. E., Blake, J. J., Wendel, M. L., & Huber Jr., J. C. (2011). The impact of stand-biased desks in classrooms on calorie expenditure in children. *America Journal of Public Health*, *101*(8), 1433–1436.

Best, J. R. (2010). Effects of physical activity on children's executive function: Contributions of experimental research on aerobic exercise. *Developmental Review: DR*, *30*(4), 331–551.

Biddle, S. J., & Asare, M. (2011). Physical activity and mental health in children and adolescents: A review of reviews. *British Journal of Sports Medicine*, *45*(11), 886–895.

Blakemore, C. L. (2003). Movement is essential to learning. *Journal of Physical Education Recreation and Dance*, *74*(9), 22–28.

Blaydes Madigan, J. (1999). *Thinking on your feet*. Murphy, TX: Action Based Learning.

Blaydes Madigan, J. (2009). *Building better brains through movement.* Murphy, TX: Action Based Learning.

Blaydes Madigan, J., & Hess, C. (2004). *Action based learning lab manual.* Murphy, TX: Action Based Learning.

Blom, L. C., Alvarez, J., Zhang, L., & Kolbo, J. (2011). Association between health-related physical fitness, academic achievement and selected academic behaviors of elementary and middle school students in the state of Mississippi. *ICHPER-SD Journal of Research, 6*(1), 28–34.

Brage, S., Ekelund, U., Haapala, E. A., Laaka, T., Lintu, N., Poikkeus, A., & Wesgate, K. (2016). Physical activity and sedentary time in relation to academic achievement in children. *Journal of Science and Medicine in Sport.* Retrieved from http://dx.doi.org/10.1016/j.jsams.2016.11.003

Braniff, C. (2011). Perceptions of an active classroom: Exploration of movement and collaboration with fourth grade students. *Networks, 13*(1). Retrieved from http://journals.sfu.ca/uwmadison/index.php/networks/article/viewFile/282/461

Budde, H., Voelcker-Rehage, C., Pietrabyk Kendziorra, S., Ribeiro, P, & Tidow, G. (2008). Acute coordinative exercise improves attentional performance across the human lifespan. *Neuroscience Letters, 441*(2), 219–223.

Burden, P. (2006). *Classroom management: Creating a successful K–12 learning community.* Hoboken, NJ: John Wiley & Sons.

Burkhalter, T. M., & Hillman, C. H. (2011). A narrative review of physical activity, nutrition and obesity to cognition and scholastic performance across the human lifespan. *Advances in Nutrition, 2*(2), S201–S2016.

Caine, R., Caine, G., McClintic, C., & Klimek, K. (2009). *The 12 brain/mind learning principles in action: Developing executive functions of the human brain.* Thousand Oaks, CA: Corwin.

Campbell, L., Campbell, B., & Dickson, D. (2004). *Teaching and learning through multiple intelligences.* New York, NY: Pearson.

Castelli, D. M., Glowacki, E., Barcelona, J. M., Calvert, H. G., & Hwang, J. (2015). *Active education: Growing evidence on physical activity and academic performance.* San Diego, CA: Active Living Research. Retrieved from http://www.activelivingresearch.org

Castelli, D. M., Hillman, C. H., Buck, S. M., & Erwin, H. (2007). Physical fitness and academic achievement in 3rd and 5th grade students. *Sports Exercise Psychology, 29*(2), 239–252.

Castelli, D. M., Hillman, C. H., Hirsch, J., Hirsch, A., & Drollette, E. (2011). Fit kids: Time in target heart zone and cognitive performance. *Preventative Medicine, 52*, 55–59.

Centers for Disease Control and Prevention. (2018, June 5). Hearing loss in children. *Centers for Disease Control and Prevention.* Retrieved from http://www.cdc.gov/ncbddd/hearingloss/index.html

Chaddock, L., Erickson, K. I., Prakash, R. S., Kim, J. S., Voss, M. W., VanPatter, M., Pontifex, M. B., . . . & Hillman, C. H. (2010a). A neuroimaging investigation of the association between aerobic fitness, hippocampal volume, and memory performance in preadolescent children. *Brain Research, 1358*, 172–183.

Chaddock, L., Erickson, K. I., Prakash, R. S., VanPatter, M., Voss, M. W., Pontifex, M. B., Raine, L. B., . . . & Kramer, A. F. (2010b). Basal ganglia volume is associated with aerobic fitness in preadolescent children. *Developmental Neuroscience, 32*(3), 249–256.

Chaddock, L., Erickson, K. I., Prakash, R. S., Voss, M. W., VanPatter, M., Pontifex, M. B., Hillman, C. H., & Kramer, A. F. (2012). A functional MRI investigation of the association between childhood aerobic fitness and neurocognitive control. *Biological Psychology, 89*(1), 260–268.

Chaddock, L., Hillman, C. H., Buck, S. M., & Cohen, N. J. (2011). Aerobic fitness and executive control of relational memory in preadolescent children. *Medicine and Science in Sport and Exercise, 43*(2), 344.

Chaddock, L., Kramer, A. F., Hillman, C. H., & Pontifex, M. B. (2011). A review of the relation of aerobic fitness and physical activity to brain structure and function in children. *Journal of the International Neuropsychological Society, 17*(6), 975–985.

Chaddock-Heyman, L., Erickson, K. I., Holtrop, J. L., Voss, M. W., Pontifex, M. B., Raine, L. B., Hillman, C. H., & Kramer, A. F. (2014). Aerobic fitness is associated with greater white matter integrity in children. *Frontiers in Human Neuroscience, 8*, 584.10.3389/fnhum.2014.00584

Chaddock-Heyman, L., Erickson, K. I., Kienzler, C., King, M., Pontifex, M. B., Raine, L. B., Hillman, C. H., & Kramer, A. F. (2015). The role of aerobic fitness in cortical thickness and mathematics achievement in preadolescent children. https://doi.org/10.1371/journal.pone.0134115

Chang, Y. K., & Etnier, J. L. (2009). Effects of an acute bout of localized resistance exercise on cognitive performance in middle-aged adults: A randomized controlled trial study. *Psychology of Sport and Exercise, 10*(1), 19–24.

Cheung, A., & Slavin, R. (2012, May 21). How features of educational technology applications affect student reading outcomes: A meta-analysis. *ScienceDirect*. Retrieved from https://www.sciencedirect.com/science/article/pii/S1747938X12000401

Cheung, A., & Slavin, R. (2013, January 18). The effectiveness of educational technology applications for enhancing mathematics achievement in K–12 classrooms: A meta-analysis. *ScienceDirect*. Retrieved from https://www.sciencedirect.com/science/article/pii/S1747938X13000031

Chih, C. H., & Chen, J. F. (2011). The relationship between physical education performance, fitness tests, and academic achievement in elementary school. *International Journal of Sport and Society, 2*(1), 65–73.

Childhood Obesity Foundation. (2015). What are the complications of childhood obesity? *Childhood Obesity Foundation*. Retrieved from http://childhoodobesityfoundation.ca/what-is-childhood-obesity/complications-childhood-obesity/

Coe, D. P., Pivarnik, J. M., Womack, C. J., Reeves, M. J., & Malina, R. M. (2012). Health-related fitness and academic achievement in middle school students. *The Journal of Sports Medicine and Physical Fitness, 52*(6), 654–660.

Cohen, H. (2017, November 16). How we consume content now (and what it means for your marketing). [Infographic]. *Heidi Cohen actionable marketing guide*. Retrieved from https://heidicohen.com/infographic-how-we-consume-content-now-what-it-means-for-your-marketing/

Committee on Physical Activity and Physical Education in the School Environment: Food and Nutrition Board; Institute of Medicine. (2013, October 30). Educating the student body: Taking physical activity and physical education to school. *Washington (DC): National Academy Press*. (H. W. Kohl III & H. D. Cook, Eds.). Retrieved from https://www.ncbi.nlm.nih.gov/books/NBK201497/

D'Agostino, E. M. (2016). *The effects of health-related fitness on school attendance in New York City 6th–8th grade youth*. CUNY Academic Works. Retrieved from http://academicworks.cuny.edu/gc_etds/1561

Daum, K. (2013, August 23). 5 ways to overcome the naysayers. *Inc.com*. Retrieved from https://www.inc.com/kevin-daum/5-ways-to-overcome-the-naysayers.html

Davis, C. L., Tomporowski, P. D., McDowell, J. E., Austin, B. P., Miller, P. H., Yanasak, N. E., Allison, J. D., & Naglieri, J. A. (2011). Exercise improves executive function and achievement and alters brain activation in overweight children: A randomized, controlled trial. *Health Psychology, 30*(1), 91–98.

Donnelly, J. E., & Lambourne, K. (2011). Classroom-based physical activity, cognition, and academic achievement. *Preventative Medicine, 52*(1), S36–S42.

Donnelly, J. E., Greene, J. L., Gibson, C. A., Smith, B. K., Washburn, R. A., Sullivan, D. K., DuBose, K., . . . & Ryan, J. J. (2009). Physical activity across the curriculum (PAAC): A randomized controlled trial to promote physical activity and diminish overweight and obesity in elementary school children. *Preventive Medicine, 49*(4), 336–341.

Dunkley, V. L. (2012, July 23). Electronic screen syndrome: An unrecognized disorder? *Psychology Today*. Retrieved from https://www.psychologytoday.com/us/blog/mental-wealth/201207/electronic-screen-syndrome-unrecognized-disorder

EdTech Staff. (2017, February 1). More than 50 percent of teachers report 1:1 computing. *EdTech*. Retrieved from https://edtechmagazine.com/k12/article/2017/02/more-50-percent-teachers-report-11-computing

Edwards, J. U., Mauch, L., & Winkleman, M. R. (2011). Relationship of nutrition and physical activity behaviors and fitness measures to academic performance for sixth graders in a Midwest city school district. *Journal of School Health, 81*, 65–73.

Ehmke, R. (2018, August 6). How using social media affects teenagers. *Child Mind Institute*. Retrieved from https://childmind.org/article/how-using-social-media-affects-teenagers/

Ellemberg, D., & St-Louis-Deschenes, M. (2010). The effect of acute physical exercise on cognitive function during development. *Psychology of Sport and Exercise, 11*(2), 122–126.

Erickson, K. I., Voss, M. W., Prakash, R. S., Basak, C., Szabo, A., Chaddock, L., Kim, J. S., . . . & White, S. M. (2011). Exercise training increases the hippocampus and improves memory. *Proceedings of the National Academy of Sciences of the United States of America, 108*(7), 3017–3022.

Eveland-Sayers, B. M., Farley, R. S., Fuller, D. K., Morgan, D. W., & Caputo, J. L. (2009). Physical fitness and academic achievement in elementary school children. *Journal of Physical Activity and Health*, *6*(1), 99.

Fedewa, A. L., & Ahn, S. (2011). The effects of physical activity and physical fitness on children's achievement and cognitive outcomes: A meta-analysis. *Research Quarterly for Exercise and Sport*, *82*(3), 521–535.

Fine, D. (2014). *Beyond texting: The fine art of face-to-face communication for teenagers*. Greenwood Village, CO: Canon.

Fine, D. (2017, December 7). 8 steps to teaching teens how to make conversation. *Huffpost*. Retrieved from https://www.huffingtonpost.com/debra-fine/8-steps-to-teaching-teens_b_5233380.html

Firth, J., Richards, J., Rosenbaum, S., Schuch, F. B., Sui, X., Stubbs, B., & Ward, P. B. (2016). Are lower levels of cardiorespiratory fitness associated with incident depression? A systematic review of prospective cohort studies. *Preventative Medicine*, *93*, 159–164.

Friedrich, C. (2016, May 15). 5 brain-boosting chemicals released during exercise. *Cathe*. Retrieved from https://cathe.com/5-brain-boosting-chemicals-released-during-exercise/

Gable, S., Krull, J. L., & Chang, Y. (2012). Boys and girls weight status and math performance from kindergarten entry through fifth grade: A mediated analysis. *Child Development*, *83*(5), 1822–1839.

Gaille, B. (2017, May 20). 17 average attention span statistics and trends. *Brandon Gaille*. Retrieved from https://brandongaille.com/average-attention-span-statistics-and-trends/

Garcia, L., & Thornton, O. (2015, April 29). The enduring importance of parental involvement. *NEAToday*. Retrieved from http://neatoday.org/2014/11/18/the-enduring-importance-of-parental-involvement-2/

Gardner, H. (1983). *Frames of mind*. New York, NY: Basic Books.

Gavin, M. L. (2015). Why exercise is wise. *TeensHealth*. Retrieved from http://kidshealth.org/en/teens/exercise-wise.html?ref=search

Gazzaley, A., & Rosen, L. (2016). *The distracted mind: Ancient brains in a high-tech world*. Cambridge, MA: MIT Press.

Godlewski, N. (2016, July 12). Teens say they're ditching texting for Snapchat because it's more casual. *Business Insider*. Retrieved from https://www.businessinsider.com/teens-message-in-snapchat-2016-7

Grieco, L. A., Jowers, E. M., & Bartholomew, J. B. (2009). Physically active academic lessons and time on task: The moderating effect of body mass index. *Medicine and Science in Sports and Exercise*, *41*(10), 1921–1926.

Hamilton, M. (2008). Too little exercise and too much sitting: Inactivity physiology and the need for new recommendations on sedentary behavior. *Current Cardiovascular Risk Report*, *2*(4), 292–298.

HealthCorps. (2016, May 19). Is your teen suffering with neck pain? *HealthCorps*. Retrieved from https://www.healthcorps.org/teen-suffering-neck-pain/

Hillman, C. H., Buck, S. M., Themanson, J. T., Pontifex, M. B., & Castelli, D. M. (2009). Aerobic fitness and cognitive development: Event-related brain potential and task performance indices of executive control in preadolescent children. *Developmental Psychology*, *45*, 114–129.

Hillman, C. H., Erickson, K. I., & Kramer, A. F. (2008). Be smart, exercise your heart: Exercise effects on brain and cognition. *National Review Neuroscience*, *9*(1), 58–65.

Hillman, C. H., Pontifex, M. B., Raine, L. B., Castelli, D. M., Hall, E. E., & Kramer, A. F. (2009). The effect of acute treadmill walking on cognitive control and academic achievement in preadolescent children. *Neuroscience*, *159*(3), 1044–1054

Howard, J. (2016). Americans devote more than 10 hours a day to screen time, and growing. *CNN*. Retrieved from https://www.cnn.com/2016/06/30/health/americans-screen-time-nielsen/

Hsin, W. J., & Cigas, J. (2013). Short videos improve student learning in online education. *Journal of Computing Sciences in Colleges*, *28*, 253–259.

Hurley, K. (2018, February 13). Social media and teens: How does social media affect mental health? *Psycom*. Retrieved from https://www.psycom.net/social-media-teen-mental-health

Is social networking changing childhood? (2009, August 10). *Common Sense Media*. Retrieved from https://www.commonsensemedia.org/about-us/news/press-releases/is-social-networking-changing-childhood

Jane. (2013). 6 core human needs by Anthony Robbins. *Habits for Wellbeing.* Retrieved from https://www.habitsforwellbeing.com/6-core-human-needs-by-anthony-robbins/

Jensen, E. (2000). *Learning with the body in mind.* San Diego, CA: The Brain Store.

Jensen, E. (2008). *Brain-based learning: The new paradigm of teaching.* Thousand Oaks, CA: Corwin.

Jolly, J. (2018, April 3). Tech neck, texting thumb: Our bad tech habits leave us in pain. Here's how to feel better. *USA Today.* Retrieved from https://www.usatoday.com/story/tech/columnist/2018/04/03/tech-neck-texting-thumb-top-bad-tech-habits-and-how-fix-them/443637002/

Kelly, R. (2018, January 11). 7 ed tech trends to watch in 2018. *Campus Technology.* Retrieved from https://campustechnology.com/Articles/2018/01/11/7-Ed-Tech-Trends-to-Watch-in-2018.aspx?Page=3

Kibbe, D. E., Hackett, J., Hurley, M., McFarland, A., Schubert, K. G., Schultz, A., & Harris, S. (2011). Ten years of TAKE 10: Integrating physical activity with academic concepts in elementary school classrooms. *Preventive Medicine, 52*(Supplement), S43–S50.

Kluger, J. (2012). We never talk anymore: The problem with text messaging. *Time.* Retrieved from http://techland.time.com/2012/08/16/we-never-talk-anymore-the-problem-with-text-messaging/

Konigs, M., Oosterlaan, J., Scherder, E., & Verbeurgh, L. (2014). Physical exercise and executive functions in preadolescent children, adolescents, and young adults: A meta-analysis review. *British Journal of Sports Medicine, 48*(12), 973–979.

Kuczala, M., & Lengel, T. (2018). *Ready, set, go: The kinesthetic classroom 2.0.* Thousand Oaks, CA: Corwin.

Landmark Report: U.S. teens use an average of nine hours of media per day, tweens use six. (2015, November 3). *Common Sense Media.* Retrieved from https://www.commonsensemedia.org/about-us/news/press-releases/landmark-report-us-teens-use-an-average-of-nine-hours-of-media-per-day

Lawson, C. (2002). The connections between emotions and learning. *The Center for Development & Learning.* Retrieved from http://www.cdl.org/articles/the-connections-between-emotions-and-learning/

Lengel, T., & Kuczala, M. (2010). *The kinesthetic classroom: Teaching and learning through movement.* Thousand Oaks, CA: Corwin.

Lenhart, A. (2007, June 27). Cyberbullying. *Pew Research Center.* Retrieved from http://www.pewinternet.org/2007/06/27/cyberbullying/

Lenhart, A., Ling, R., Campbell, S., & Purcell, K. (2010, April 20). Teens and mobile phones. *Pew Research Center.* Retrieved from http://www.pewinternet.org/2010/04/20/teens-and-mobile-phones/

London, R. A., & Castrechini, S. (2011). A longitudinal examination of the link between youth physical fitness and academic achievement. *Journal of School Health, 81*(7), 400–408.

Medina, J. (2008). *Brain Rules.* Seattle, WA: Pear Press.

Mercola, J. (2012, September 28). Physical fitness in childhood linked to higher reading and math scores. *Mercola.* Retrieved from https://fitness.mercola.com/sites/fitness/archive/2012/09/28/physical-activity-improves-academic-performance.aspx

Misra, S., Cheng, L., Genevie, J., & Yuan, M. (2014). The iPhone effect: The quality of in-person social interactions in the presence of mobile device. *Environment & Behavior,* 1–24.

Mitchell, M. (2009). *Physical activity may strengthen children's ability to pay attention.* University of Illinois at Urbana-Champaign: New Bureau.

Moize, J., & Hess, C. (2017). *ABL primary lab manual* (2nd ed., Vol 1). Huger, SC: Kidsfit.

Mullender-Wijnsma, M. J., Hartman, E., de Greeff, J. W., Bosker, R. J., Doolaard, S., & Visscher, C. (2015). Moderate-to-vigorous physically active academic lessons and academic engagement in children with and without a social disadvantage: A within subject experimental design. *BMC Public Health, 15*(404). 10.1186/s12889-015-1745-y

Mullender-Wijnsma, M. J., Hartman, E., de Greeff, J. W., Doolaard, S., Bosker, R. J., & Visscher, C. (2016). Physically active math and language lessons improve academic achievement: A cluster randomized controlled trial. *Pediatrics, 137,* e20152743. doi: 10.1542/peds.2015-2743.

National Geographic. (2018, April 25). Tech's impact on young brains: America inside out with Katie Couric. *YouTube* [video]. Retrieved from http://www.youtube.com/watch?v=cK6p8VyyvCs

Nielsen. (2017, February 28). Mobile kids: The parent, the child and the smartphone. *The Nielsen Company.*

Retrieved from https://www.nielsen.com/us/en/insights/news/2017/mobile-kids--the-parent-the-child-and-the-smartphone.html

Nkere, N. (2014, January 5). Guiding principles. *Brain Based Learning*. Retrieved from http://www.brainbasedlearning.net/guiding-principles-for-brain-based-education/

Oberparleiter, L. (2004). Brain-based teaching and learning. *Department of Education, Gratz College. Graduate Course Training Manual.* Randolph, NJ: Center for Lifelong Learning.

Oberparleiter, L. (2011). *The role of emotion and reflection in student achievement.* Bloomington, IN: AuthorHouse.

Owen, N., Healy, G. N., Matthews, C. E., & Dunstan D. W. (2010). Too much sitting: The population health science of sedentary behavior. *Exercise and Sport Science Reviews, 38*(3), 105–113.

Packer, L. (2015, August 10). Hearing loss among kids and teens. *Healthy Hearing.* Retrieved from https://www.healthyhearing.com/report/52500-Hearing-loss-among-kids-and-teens

Pesce, C., Crova, C., Cereatti, L, Casella, R., & Bellucci, M. (2009). Physical activity and mental performance in preadolescents: Effects of acute exercise on free-recall memory. *Mental Health and Physical Activity, 2*(1), 16–22.

Pica, R. (2006). *A running start: How play, physical activity, and free time create a successful child.* New York, NY: Marlowe and Company.

Pierce, T. (2009, July 11). Social anxiety and technology: Face-to-face communication versus technological communication among teens. *Computers in Human Behavior.* Retrieved from https://www.sciencedirect.com/science/article/pii/S0747563209000971

Piliouras, T., Yu, R., Villanueva, K., Chen, Y., Robillard, H., Berson, M.,. . . & Attre, M. (2014). *A deeper understanding of technology is needed for workforce readiness—Playing games, texting, and tweets aren't enough to make students tech-savvy.* Retrieved from http://www.asee.org/documents/conferences/annual/2016/Zone1-Best-Paper.pdf

Pontifex, M. B., Saliba, B. J., Raine, L. B., Picchietti, D. L., & Hillman, C. H. (2013). Exercise improves behavioral, neurophysiologic, and scholastic performance in children with ADHD. *Journal of Pediatrics, 162,* 543–551.

Przybylski, A. K., & Weinstein, N. (2012). Can you connect with me now? How the presence of mobile communication technology influences face-to-face conversation quality. *Journal of Social and Personal Relationships,* 1–10.

Putnam, S. C. (2003, February). Attention deficit: Medical or environmental disorder? *Principal Leadership, 3*(6), 59–61.

Radiological Society of North America. (2016, November 30). Aerobic exercise preserves brain volume and improves cognitive function. *ScienceDaily.* Retrieved from http://www.sciencedaily.com/releases/2016/11/161130130916.htm

Rasberry, C. N., Lee, S. M., Robin, L., Laris, B. A., Russell, L. A., Coyle, K. K., & Nihiser, A. J. (2011). The association between school-based physical activity, including physical education, and academic performance: A systematic review of the literature. *Preventative Medicine, 52*(Supplement 1), S10–S20.

Ratey, J. (2008). *SPARK: The revolutionary new science of exercise and the brain.* New York, NY: Bantam Books.

Reed, J. A., Einstein, G., Hahn, E., Hooker, S. P., Gross, V. P., & Kravitz, J. (2010). Examining the impact of integrating physical activity on fluid intelligence and academic performance in an elementary school setting: A preliminary investigation. *Journal of Physical Activity and Health, 7*(3), 343–351.

Richtel, M. (2010, August 24). Digital devices deprive brain of needed downtime. *The New York Times.* Retrieved from https://www.nytimes.com/2010/08/25/technology/25brain.html

Rideout, V. (2011). *Zero to eight: Children's media use in America.* San Francisco, CA: *Common Sense Media.* Retrieved from https://www.commonsensemedia.org/research/zero-to-eight-childrens-media-use-in-america

Robinson, T., Banda, J., Hale, L., Shirong Lu, A., Fleming-Milici, F., Calvert, S., & Wartella, E. (2017, November). Screen media exposure and obesity in children and adolescents. *Pediatrics, 140*(Supplement 2). Retrieved from http://pediatrics.aappublications.org/content/140/Supplement_2/S97.long

Rosen, L. (2012). *iDisorder: Understanding our obsession with technology and overcoming its hold on us.* New York, NY: Palgrave Macmillan.

Singh, A., Uijtdeweilligen, L., Twisk, J. W. R, van Mechelen, W., & Chinapaw. M. J. M. (2012). Physical activity and performance in school: A systematic review of the literature including a methodological quality assessment. *Archives of Pediatrics and Adolescent Medicine, 166*(1), 49–55.

Sinicropi, S. (2016, September 9). 5 simple steps to prevent tech neck. *Spine-health.* Retrieved from https://www.spine-health.com/blog/5-simple-steps-prevent-tech-neck

Smith, P. J., Blumenthal, J. A., Hoffman, B. M., Cooper, H., Strauman, T. A., Welsh-Bohmer, K., Browndyke, J. N., & Sherwood, A. (2010). Aerobic exercise and neuro-cognitive performance: A meta-analytic review of randomized controlled trials. *Psychosomatic Medicine, 72*(3), 239–252.

Sousa, D. (2017). *How the brain learns.* Thousand Oaks, CA: Corwin.

Stagman, S., & Cooper, J. L. (2010, April). Children's mental health: What every policymaker should know. *National Center for Children in Poverty.* Retrieved from http://www.nccp.org/publications/pdf/text_929.pdf

Starr, L. (2003). Technology in the classroom: How teachers view technology. *Education World.* Retrieved fromhttps://www.educationworld.com/a_tech/tech/tech180.shtml

Tan, B. W. Z., Pooley, J. A., & Speelman C. P. (2016). A meta-analytic review of the efficacy of physical exercise interventions on cognition in individuals with autism spectrum disorder and ADHD. *Journal of Autism and Developmental Disorders, 46*(9), 3126–3143.

Tandon, P. S., Zhou, C., Lozano, P., & Christakis, D. A. (2011). Preschoolers' total daily screen time at home and by type of child care. *Journal of Pediatrics, 158*, 297–300.

Thomas, A. G., Dennis, A., Bandettini, P. A., & Johansen-Berg, H. (2012). The effects of aerobic activity on brain structure. *Frontiers in Psychology, 3*, 1–9.

Thompson, R. (2017, April 20). How modern technology is damaging our hearing. *Healthy Hearing.* Retrieved from https://www.healthyhearing.com/report/52747-How-modern-technology-is-damaging-our-hearing

Tomporowski, P. D., Davis, C. L., Lambourne, K., Gregoski, M., & Tkacz, J. (2008). Task switching in overweight children: Effects of acute exercise and age. *Sports Exercise Psychology, 30*, 497–511.

Tomporowski, P. D., Davis, C. L., Miller, P. H., & Naglieri, J. A. (2008). Exercise and children's intelligence, cognition, and academic achievement. *Educational Psychology Review, 20*, 111–131.

Tomporowski, P. D., Lambourne, K., & Okumura, M. S. (2011). Physical activity interventions and children's mental function: An introduction and overview. *Preventative Medicine, 52*(Supplement 1), S3–S9.

Tomporowski, P. D., McCullick, B., Pendleton, D. M., & Pesce, C. (2015). Exercise and children's cognition: The role of exercise characteristics and a place for metacognition. *Journal of Sport and Health Medicine, 4*(1), 47–55. https://doi.org/10.1016/j.jshs.2014.09.003

Trost, S. G., & van der Mars, H. (2009). Why we should not cut P.E. *Educational Leadership, 67*(4), 60–65.

Trudeau, F., & Shepard, R. J. (2008). Physical education, school physical activity, sports and academic performance. *International Journal of Behavioral Nutrition and Physical Activity, 5*, 10.

Trudeau, F., & Shephard, R. J. (2010). Relationships of physical activity to brain health and the academic performance of schoolchildren. *American Journal of Lifestyle Medicine, 4*, 138–150.

Twenge, J. (2017, November 19). Perspective: Teenage depression and suicide are way up—and so is smartphone use. *Washington Post.* Retrieved from https://www.washingtonpost.com/national/health-science/teenage-depression-and-suicide-are-way-up--and-so-is-smartphone-use/2017/11/17/624641ea-ca13-11e7-8321-481fd63f174d_story.html

Twenge, J. M. (2018, January 6). Why Teens Aren't Partying Anymore. *Wired.* Retrieved from https://www.wired.com/story/why-teens-arent-partying-anymore/

U.S. Department of Health & Human Services. (2017, January 26). Facts & statistics. *President's Council on Sports, Fitness & Nutrition.* Retrieved from https://www.hhs.gov/fitness/resource-center/facts-and-statistics/index.html

U.S. Department of Health and Human Services, Centers for Disease Control and Prevention, National Center for Chronic Disease Prevention and Health Promotion, & Division of Adolescent and School Health. (2010, July). *The association between school-based physical activity, including physical education, and academic performance.* Retrieved from https://www.cdc.gov/healthyyouth/health_and_academics/pdf/pa-pe_paper.pdf

Van Dusen, D. P., Kelder, S. H., Kohl III, H. W., Ranjit, N., & Perry, C. L. Associations of physical fitness and academic performance among schoolchildren. *Journal of School Health*, *81*(12), 733–740.

Welk, G. J., Jackson, A. W., Morrow, J., James, R., Haskell, W. H., Meredith, M. D., & Cooper, K. H. (2010). The association of health-related fitness with indicators of academic performance in Texas Schools. *Research Quarterly for Exercise and Sport*, *81*(Supplement 2), S16–S23.

Weng, C-B., Qian, R-B., Fu, X-M., Lin, B., Han, X-P., Niu, C-S., & Wang, Y-H. (2013, August). Gray matter and white matter abnormalities in online game addiction. *European Journal of Radiology*, *82*(8), 1308–1312. doi: 10.1016/j.ejrad.2013.01.031.

Widenhorn-Muller, K., Hille, K., Klenke, J., & Weiland, U. (2008). Influence of having breakfast on cognitive performance and mood in 13- to 20-year-old high school students: Results of a crossover trial. *Pediatric*, *122*(2), 279–284.

Wiley-Blackwell. (2009, January). Physically fit kids do better in school. *ScienceDaily*. Retrieved from http://www.sciencedaily.com/releases/2009/01/090128113246.htm

Winterfeld, A. (2007). PE makes a comeback. *State Legislatures Magazine*, *33*(10), 36–37.

Wittberg, R., Cottrell, L. A., Davis, C. L., & Northrup, K. L. (2010). Aerobic fitness thresholds associated with fifth grade academic achievement. *American Journal of Health Education*, *41*(5), 284–291.

Womack, C. J., Reeves, M. J., & Malina, R. M. (2012). Health-related fitness and academic achievement in middle school students. *Journal of Sports Medicine and Physical Fitness*, *52*(6), 654–660.

Wootan, F. C., & Mulligan, C. H. (2007). *Not in my classroom: A teacher's guide to effective classroom management*. Avon, MA: Adams Media.

Wooten Green, A. (2016). Physical education and recess improve behavior, test scores. *Carolina Parent*. Retrieved from http://www.carolinaparent.com/Physical-Education-and-Recess-Improve-Behavior-Test-Scores/

# INDEX

A SAGE Publishing Company

Helping educators make the greatest impact

**CORWIN HAS ONE MISSION:** to enhance education through intentional professional learning.

We build long-term relationships with our authors, educators, clients, and associations who partner with us to develop and continuously improve the best evidence-based practices that establish and support lifelong learning.

# Solutions *YOU WANT* | Experts *YOU TRUST* | Results *YOU NEED*

**EVENTS**  >>> **INSTITUTES**

Corwin Institutes provide large regional events where educators collaborate with peers and learn from industry experts. Prepare to be recharged and motivated!

**corwin.com/institutes**

**ON-SITE PD**  >>> **ON-SITE PROFESSIONAL LEARNING**

Corwin on-site PD is delivered through high-energy keynotes, practical workshops, and custom coaching services designed to support knowledge development and implementation.

**corwin.com/pd**

>>> **PROFESSIONAL DEVELOPMENT RESOURCE CENTER**

The PD Resource Center provides school and district PD facilitators with the tools and resources needed to deliver effective PD.

**corwin.com/pdrc**

**ONLINE**  >>> **ADVANCE**

Designed for K–12 teachers, Advance offers a range of online learning options that can qualify for graduate-level credit and apply toward license renewal.

**corwin.com/advance**

**Contact a PD Advisor at (800) 831-6640 or visit www.corwin.com for more information**